Real-Time Systems Education

Real-Time Systems Education

Edited by

Janusz Zalewski
Department of Electrical and Computer Engineering
University of Central Florida

Sponsored by

Embry-Riddle Aeronautical University

In cooperation with

IEEE Computer Society Technical Committee
on Real-Time Systems (TCRTS)

IEEE Computer Society Technical Committee
on Complexity in Computing (TCCC)

IEEE Computer Society Press
Los Alamitos, California

Washington • Brussels • Tokyo

IEEE Computer Society Press
10662 Los Vaqueros Circle
P.O. Box 3014
Los Alamitos, CA 90720-1264

IEEE Computer Society Press Order Number PR07649
IEEE Order Plan Catalog Number 96TB100060
Library of Congress Number 96-77020
ISBN 0-8186-7649-3
Microfiche ISBN 0-8186-7651-5

Additional copies may be ordered from:

IEEE Computer Society Press	IEEE Service Center	IEEE Computer Society	IEEE Computer Society
Customer Service Center	445 Hoes Lane	13, Avenue de l'Aquilon	Ooshima Building
10662 Los Vaqueros Circle	P.O. Box 1331	B-1200 Brussels	2-19-1 Minami-Aoyama
P.O. Box 3014	Piscataway, NJ 08855-1331	BELGIUM	Minato-ku, Tokyo 107
Los Alamitos, CA 90720-1314	Tel: +1-908-981-1393	Tel: +32-2-770-2198	JAPAN
Tel: +1-714-821-8380	Fax: +1-908-981-9667	Fax: +32-2-770-8505	Tel: +81-3-3408-3118
Fax: +1-714-821-4641	misc.custserv@computer.org	euro.ofc@computr.org	Fax: +81-3-3408-3553
Email: cs.books@computer.org			tokyo.ofc@computer.org

Editorial production by Penny Storms
Cover by Alex Torres
Printed in the United States of America by KNI, Inc.

 The Institute of Electrical and Electronics Engineers, Inc.

Contents

Chapter 4: Teaching Formal Methods for Real-Time Systems

Chapter 5: Real-Time Systems in Systems and Control Engineering

Real-Time Systems Education: An Introduction

Janusz Zalewski

Dept. of Electrical & Computer Engineering
University of Central Florida
Orlando, FL 32816-2450, USA
+1 (407)823-6171
jza@ece.engr.ucf.edu

Abstract

This introduction presents an historical perspective on teaching real-time systems courses – first, in the 1980's and then in the 1990's. Next, it discusses individual contributions to this volume that have been grouped into five categories: individual courses on real-time systems, real-time curricula, teaching real-time systems at Embry-Riddle, applying formal methods in teaching real-time systems, and real-time systems in systems engineering and control engineering curricula.

1. Prolog

Educators interested in teaching real-time systems courses have been meeting informally at birds-of-a-feather sessions and other, more formal, gatherings at various conferences for the last couple of years. Following are a few notable examples:

- NATO Advanced Study Institute, Sint Maarten, Dutch Antilles, October 1992;
- IEEE Real-Time Systems Symposium, Phoenix, Arizona, December 1992;
- Ada Software Engineering Education and Training Symposium, Monterey, California, January 1993;
- SIGCSE Technical Symposium, Indianapolis, Indiana, February 1993;
- SEI Conference on Software Engineering Education, San Antonio, Texas, January 1994;
- IEEE Workshop on Real-Time Operating Systems and Software, Seattle, Washington, May 1994.

At all of those meetings, various issues were informally discussed by a handful of people, but neither individual contributions nor minutes of these sessions were published, except [1]. The major outcome of these meetings resulted in the realization that coordinated activities would provide significant benefits to the entire real-time systems community. In this context, therefore, this current collection of articles is an artifact that is long overdue.

2. Historical Perspective

Activities related to real-time systems education started in the 1980's [2–16], once people realized the importance of proper education of engineers on the cutting edge of developing hardware and software for critical applications. Up until the 1990's, however, very little had been accomplished in the area of curriculum development for real-time systems courses in the US. The literature overview by the author reveals that at that time, the US [4, 5, 9, 11, 12, 15] was approximately 2-3 years behind Europe, where interesting developments were taking place in Germany [6, 7], Switzerland [8], and the UK [14, 16]. This observation is also true when comparing the US with Canada [3, 10] and South Africa [2, 13] during the same period.

With the advent of the 1990's, however, everything began to change in the US. Big projects were launched – such as the Superconducting Super Collider and the Space Station – along with similar nuclear, aerospace, and other applications. Project managers and developers soon began to realize that the most challenging problems in such critical applications are always "real-time related" and that rigorous development methods can only be applied successfully by a well-educated workforce.

The net effect of such rapid technological progress, and the new challenges it presented, resulted in increased pressure on **educators** to keep pace with technology and enhance their curricula. Therefore, recent developments in real-time systems education cover its all important aspects, such as high-level development methodologies [18, 20], projects, prototyping and commercial tools [17, 21, 22, 34], real-time languages and operating systems [28, 33, 35], hardware architectures [26, 27, 29, 30, 31, 32], laboratories [23, 24, 25], and comprehensive curriculum design [19].

As various aspects of real-time systems curriculum were being developed, a need arose to exchange all kinds of information, on syllabi, textbooks, tools, projects, laboratories, etc. Some aspects of these developments were noticed by the IEEE Technical Committee on Real-Time Systems, which made its ftp site available at `ftp-cs.bu.edu/IEEE-RTTC/public` to collect pertinent information on education, and additionally asked me to become a liaison with the diverse community of real-time systems educators. As a result of this effort, this book is a formal compilation of some of the important developments and subsequent activities reported.

3. Contents of Book

This book is based on the papers presented at the Real-Time Systems Education Workshop, held at Embry-Riddle Aeronautical University, in Daytona Beach, Florida, on April 20, 1996. All presented papers have been refereed and other papers that were submitted (but could not be presented) underwent the same refereeing process, once the authors accepted an invitation to contribute to this volume.

The structure of the book reflects the-state-of-the-art in real-time systems education. The material is organized in a way as to give a comprehensive view of the most significant – as well as the most recent – activities in this field. In five parts, it covers individual courses, complete curricula, an example of one curriculum at my former parent institution, an important part of the formal background for educating real-time engineers, and external ties placed in the broader context of two related disciplines.

Teaching concurrency is, in many curricula, an important prerequisite before teaching real-time systems. However, the desired focus of this book, combined with a lack of space, prevented us from including articles on this subject, so respective literature list has been added [36–48]. The literature on a related subject, teaching parallel and distributed computing, can be found in a separate publication[49].

Chapter 1 of the book presents two papers on individual courses and three papers on courses that have been enhanced by the use of effective tools in a classroom environment. What is interesting about the first two papers, by Shaw and Gomaa, is that they both present complete courses based on these authors' textbooks. This gives the reader an opportunity to look at the instructional material contained in the paper and apply it in class using the textbook (Shaw's book has yet to be published, however).

Papers by Jacker, Schwarz and colleagues, and Shepard and colleagues, discuss the contents of respective courses along with the authors' experiences in using professional tools: a real-time operating system and hardware (Jacker); a homemade tool for real-time graphical programming (Schwarz); and an object-oriented design tool (Shepard). What makes these three papers particularly valuable is that they talk about not only the real advantages of teaching students how to use these tools in solving real-time problems, but also about the difficulties and dangers of using such tools in a classroom setting.

Complete real-time systems curricula are discussed in four papers chosen for Chapter 2. My paper with Halang, provides a template for designing such a curriculum. Sandén, on the other hand, presents his own views and experiences with courses focusing on real-time systems nested in a broader software engineering curriculum. The next two papers, by Piatkowski and colleagues, and by Mejia and Ferro, discuss two approaches to designing the curriculum. It is instructive to see that they differ – not because one has been developed to serve a technologically advanced country and the other a developing country – but because they were designed for computer engineering and computer science programs, respectively.

Chapter 3, including the description of educational activities in real-time systems at Embry-Riddle, can be thought of as an extension of Chapter 2 since it describes the details of one particular implementation of a real-time systems curriculum.

Obviously, it has become more and more important to apply rigorous and systematic methods of real-time software development. In this context then, it is imperative that real-time engineers are well-educated in formal mathematical techniques. Chapter 4 covers these issues in three papers dealing with a combination of Z and Fusion (France and Bruel), Z and RTL (Hilburn), and Petri nets (Mikolajczak). Since it is not only unclear how to apply formal methods in practice but also how to teach this subject, a selection of literature resources on teaching formal methods in general is included [50–59], and may prove useful to some readers in considering various approaches to teaching their own courses.

Finally, Chapter 5 allows us to look at real-time systems education from the broader perspective. It includes two papers related to systems engineering and two related to control engineering. Systems engineering education is a very broad subject and can be traced back to at least the early discussions initiated by Andrew P. Sage [60], who would be pleased that two papers from his current School of Information Technology and Engineering at George Mason University are included in the first two chapters of this book, although the most recent publications present many new ideas [61]. The first systems related paper, by Krysander and Törne, falls into this category and presents one noteworthy approach to including embedded real-time systems into a broader systems engineering curriculum. In the second paper, Marlowe, Stoyenko, and colleagues, diverge from this view of systems education and deal with it on the systems programming level, challenging a more established view of computer science as a discipline comprised of mathematics, engineering, and science components.

The second part of Chapter 5 covers real-time issues in control engineering education. The value of looking into control engineering approaches to real-time systems education cannot be overestimated since practically all real-time systems met in practice are control systems (based on the feedback principle, the essence of control engineering and automation). Both papers, by Hanzálek, and by Pous and colleagues, deal with organizing laboratories – a critical element in the preparation of real-time engineers to enter the job market. Since the control engineering community has a lot more to share than has been included in this book, an ample literature list focusing on laboratories, is included in references [62–84].

4. Summary

Although several educators currently involved in interesting research on teaching real-time systems and curriculum development were unable to come to the workshop or contribute to this volume, the presented collection of papers is believed to be a fairly thorough representation of this field. This is true in several respects:

- a complete cross section of the subject has been covered (individual courses, entire curricula, underlying basics, and broader context);
- the crucial issue of laboratories is discussed in five papers and both computer science and computer engineering points of view have been articulated;
- the relationship with interdisciplinary areas, such as systems engineering and control engineering, has been stressed;
- contributions from as many as eight countries are included, which means good coverage of a variety of geographical areas.

One important issue has to be mentioned for future consideration – including knowledge on digital signal processing (DSP) into real-time systems courses. This area has grown dramatically during the last decade and most of the newly designed real-time applications include signal processors. This fact has been recognized by the DSP community, which has begun to design their own real-time courses [87]. To give the reader a broader perspective, selected references to other articles on DSP education have also been included [85–92].

Finally, if something appears to be missing in this book, you can look at the web pages of three IEEE Technical Committees (Real-Time Systems, Complexity in Computing, and Engineering of Computer Based Systems, respectively), that are deeply involved in related educational activities, at the following Universal Resource Locators:

`http://cs-www.bu.edu/pub/ieee-rts/`

`http://www.cl.cam.ac.uk/IEEE-TSC-ECCS/`

`http://www.ece.arizona.edu/department/ecbs`

Acknowledgements

The following individuals served on the program committee of the workshop and participated in the refereeing process:

- Ted Baker,
  Florida State University
- Doris Carver,
  Louisiana State University
- Juan de la Puente,
  Universidad Politecnica de Madrid
- Richard Eckhouse,
  University of Massachusetts at Boston
- Don Gillies,
  University of British Columbia
- Janusz Górski,
  Franco-Polish School of I&T Technologies
- Wolfgang Halang,
  FernUniversität Hagen
- Phil Laplante,
  New Jersey Institute of Technology

- Nancy Mead,
  Software Engineering Institute

- Leo Motus,
  Tallinn Technical University

- Thomas Piatkowski,
  Western Michigan University

- Ian Pyle,
  University of Wales at Aberystwyth

- Michael Rodd,
  University of Wales at Swansea

- Krzysztof Sacha,
  Warsaw University of Technology

- Bo Sandén,
  George Mason University

- Jean-Jacques Schwarz,
  Institut National des Sciences Appliquées de Lyon

- Terry Shepard,
  Royal Military College of Canada

- John Stankovic,
  University of Massachusetts at Amherst

- Jan van Katwijk,
  Delft University of Technology

Support of the IEEE Technical Committee on Real-Time Systems, chaired by Al Mok, University of Texas at Austin, and the support of the IEEE Technical Committee on Complexity in Computing, chaired by Alex Stoyenko, New Jersey Institute of Technology, is greatly appreciated. Furthermore, the support of the IEEE Computer Society Education Board, chaired by Doris Carver, as well as the unofficial support provided by John Werth, University of Texas at Austin, Chairman of the ACM Board on Education, is also gratefully acknowledged.

In addition, thanks are due to the Department of Computer Science of Embry-Riddle Aeronautical University, chaired by Iraj Hirmanpour, for their financial support, and to the Organizing Committee members, Tom Hilburn and Andrew Kornecki (both of whom are from Embry-Riddle), for their involvement and assistance in making the workshop both a reality and a success.

Finally, I would like to thank IEEE CS Press editorial staff for helping me to organize this introduction.

References

[1] L. Budin, M. Colnaric, J. Skubich, J. Zalewski, Minutes of the Birds-of-a-Feather Session on "Real-Time Systems Education", Proc. NATO Advanced Study Institute "Real-Time Computing", W. Halang, A. Stoyenko, eds., Springer-Verlag, Berlin, 1995, pp. 750-754

Real-Time Systems (before 1990)

[2] H.S. Bradlow, An Undergraduate Course in Real-Time Computer Systems, Int. J. Electrical Engineering Education, Vol. 19, 1982, pp. 367-377

[3] R.J.A. Buhr, Lessons from Practical Experience Teaching Hands-on Real-Time Embedded System Programming with Ada, Ada Letters, Vol. 5, No. 2, September/October 1985, pp. 210-216

[4] F. DiCesare, S.M. Bunten, P.M. DeRusso, Microcomputers for Data Acquisition, Control, and Automation - A Laboratory Course for Preengineering Students, IEEE Trans. Education, Vol. 28, No. 2, May 1985, pp. 69-75

[5] B. Furht, P.S. Liu, An Advanced Laboratory for Microprocessor Interfacing and Communication, IEEE Trans. Education, Vol. 32, No. 2, May 1989, pp. 124-128

[6] W.A. Halang, Education of Real-Time Systems Engineers, Microprocessing and Microprogramming, Vol. 25, No. 1-5, 1989, pp. 71-75

[7] W.A. Halang, A Curriculum for Real-Time Computer and Control Systems Engineering, IEEE Trans. on Education. Vol. 33, No. 2, May 1990, pp. 171-178

[8] C. Jean, A. Strohmeier, An Experience in Teaching OOD for Ada Software. Software Engineering Notes, Vol. 15, No. 5, October 1990, pp. 44-49

[9] J.R. Lambert, Instrumentation Lab Upgrade with the NSF/ILI Grant, Advances in Instrumentation and Control, Vol. 45, Proc. ISA '90 Int'l Conf. and Exhibit, New Orleans, La., October 14-18, 1990, pp. 2119-2129

[10] G. Lapalme, P. Chartray, An Educational System for the Study of Tasking in Ada, IEEE Trans. Education, Vol. 30, No. 3, August 1987, pp. 185-191

[11] J.W. McCormick, Using a Model Railroad to Teach Digital Process Control, SIGCSE Bulletin, Vol. 20, No. 1, March 1988, pp. 304-308

[12] J.D. Schoeffler, Real-Time Programming and Its Support Environment, IEEE Trans. Education, Vol. 32, No. 3, August 1989, pp. 377-181

[13] B.G. Sherlock, H.S. Bradlow, Undergraduate Teaching of Real-Time Computer Control Using a Multiuser Process Interface, IEEE Trans. Education, Vol. 28, No. 3, August 1985, pp. 164-168

[14] R.E. Seviora, A Real-Time Project for Software Engineering Course, Proc. 2nd Int'l Conf. Software Engineering for Real-Time Systems, IEE Conf. Publication 309, IEE, London, 1989, pp. 65-69

[15] S.J. Szablya, J.K. Jachinowski, R.A. Baker, An Undegraduate Power Laboratory Using Microcomputer Based Instrumentation, IEEE Trans. Power Apparatus and Systems, Vol. 104, No. 12, December 1985, pp. 3314-3319

[16] R.N. Zobel, Real-Time Systems Education in Computer Science at Manchester University, Microprocessing and Microprogramming, Vol. 24, 1988, pp. 835-840

Real-Time Systems (after 1990)

[17] R.A. Brown, A Software Testbed for Advanced Projects in Real-Time and Distributed Computing, SIGCSE Bulletin, Vol. 25, No. 1, March 1993, pp. 247-250

[18] C. Goodman Marchewka, Teaching Software Engineering for Real-Time Design, Proc. 5th SEI Conference on Software Engineering Education, J.E. Tomayko, ed., Springer-Verlag, Berlin, 1991, pp. 235-344

[19] W.A. Halang, Recommendations for a Real-Time Systems Curriculum, Real-Time Systems Engineering and Applications, M. Schiebe, S. Pferrer, eds., Kluwer Academic Publishers, Boston, Mass., 1992, pp. 419-434

[20] C.L. Hoover, The Role of Software Engineer in Real-Time Software Development: An Introductory Course, Proc. 8th SEI Conf. Software Engineering Education, R.L. Ibrahim, ed., Springer-Verlag, Berlin, 1995, pp. 167-186

[21] Luqi et al., Prototyping Hard Real-Time Ada Systems in a Classroom Environment, Proc. 7th Ann. Ada Software Engineering Education and Training (ASEET) Symp., Monterey, Calif., January 12-14, 1993, pp. 103-117

[22] Luqi, M. Shing, Teaching Hard Real-Time Software Development via Prototyping, Proc. ACM/IEEE Workshop Software Engineering Education, Sorrento, Italy, May 21, 1994, pp. 199-211

[23] J.W. McCormick, Using a Model Railroad to Teach Ada and Software Engineering, Proc. TRI-Ada '91, San Jose, Calif., October 21-25, 1991, ACM, New York, 1991, pp. 511-514

[24] J.W. McCormick, A Laboratory for Teaching the Development of Real-Time Software Systems, SIGCSE Bulletin, Vol. 23, No. 1, March 1991, pp. 260-264

[25] J.W. McCormick, A Model Railroad for Ada and Software Engineering, Communications of the ACM, Vol. 35, No. 11, November 1992, pp. 68-70

[26] P.H. Meckl, R. Shoureshi, Real-Time Microprocessor Control Laboratory, Proc. 12th Triennial World Congress of IFAC, Sydney, Australia, July 18-23, 1993, Vol. 5, Pergamon, Oxford, 1993, pp. 761-764

[27] H. Pollard et al., A New Computer System for Education, Computers in Electrical Engineering, Vol. 17, No. 4, 1991, pp. 261-266

[28] T.W. Schultz, Peripheral Hardware and a Hands-on Multitasking Lab, IEEE Micro, Vol. 11, No. 1, February 1991, pp. 30-33 and 80-82

[29] R. Shoureshi, A Course on Microprocessor-Based Control Systems, IEEE Control Systems, Vol. 11, No. 3, June 1992, pp. 39-42

[30] R. Shoureshi, P.H. Meckl, Control Education in the Era of Microprocessors, Proc. American Control Conf., Chicago, Ill., June 24-26, 1992, pp. 455-459

[31] R. Shoureshi, P.H. Meckl, Microprocessors in Control Education, Proc. American Control Conf., Baltimore, MD, June 1994, pp. 374-377

[32] F. Vallejo, M. Gonzalez Harbour, J.A. Gregorio, A Laboratory for Microprocessor Teaching at Different Levels, IEEE Trans. Education, Vol. 35, No. 3, August 1992, pp. 199-203

[33] J. Zalewski, A Real-Time Systems Course Based on Ada, Proc. 7th Ann. Ada Software Engineering Education and Training (ASEET) Symp., Monterey, Calif., January 12-14, 1993, pp. 25-49

[34] J. Zalewski, Cohesive Use of Commercial Tools in a Classroom, Proc. 7th SEI Conf. Software Engineering Education, J.L. Diaz-Herrera, ed., Springer-Verlag, Berlin, 1994, pp. 65-75

[35] J. Zalewski, What Every Engineer Needs to Know about Rate-Monotonic Scheduling: A Tutorial, Real-Time Magazine (Brussels), Issue 1/95, 1st Quarter 1995, pp. 6-24

Concurrency

[36] M. Ben-Ari, Using Inheritance to Implement Concurrency, SIGCSE Bulletin, Vol. 28, No. 1, March 1996, pp. 180-184

[37] T.S. Berk, A Simple Student Environment for Lightweight Process Concurrent Programming under SunOS, SIGCSE Bulletin, Vol. 28, No. 1, March 1996, pp. 165-169

[38] M.B. Feldman, The Portable Dining Philosophers: A Movable Feast of Concurrency and Software Engineering, SIGCSE Bulletin, Vol. 24, No. 1, March 1992, pp. 276-280

[39] M.B. Feldman, A. V. Lopez, M. Perez, Small-Ada: Personal Courseware for Studying Concurrent Programming, SIGCSE Bulletin, Vol. 22, No. 1, March 1990, pp. 206-211

[40] S.J. Hartley, Experience with the Language SR in an Undergraduate Operating Systems Course, SIGCSE Bulletin, Vol. 24, No. 1, March 1992, pp. 176-180

[41] C. Higgenbotham, R. Morelli, A System for Teaching Concurrent Programming, SIGCSE Bulletin, Vol. 23, No. 1, March 1991, pp. 309-316

[42] R.C. Hilzer, Jr., Concurrency with Semaphores, SIGCSE Bulletin, Vol. 24, No. 3, September 1992, pp. 45-50

[43] D. Jackson, A Mini-Course on Concurrency, SIGCSE Bulletin, Vol. 23, No. 1, March 1991, pp. 92-96

[44] C. McDonald, Teaching Concurrency with Joyce and Linda, SIGCSE Bulletin, Vol. 24, No. 1, March 1992, pp. 46-52

[45] R.A. Olson, C.M. McNamee, Tools for Teaching CCRs, Monitors, and CSP Concurrent Programming Concepts, SIGCSE Bulletin, Vol. 27, No. 2, June 1995, pp. 31-40

[46] J.L. Silver, Concurrent Programming in an Upper-Level Operating Systems Course, SIGCSE Bulletin, Vol. 21, No. 1, February 1989, pp. 217-221

[47] M.A. de Tomas, L. Gomez, A. Perez, Vestal: A Tool for Teaching Concurrency in Ada, Proc. TRI-Ada '91, San Jose, Calif., October 21-25, 1991, ACM, New York, 1991, pp. 498-506

[48] D.P. Yeager, Teaching Concurrency in the Programming Languages Course, SIGCSE Bulletin, Vol. 23, No. 1, March 1991, pp. 155-159

[49] M. Paprzycki, R. Wasniowski, J. Zalewski, Parallel and Distributed Computing Education: A Software Engineering Approach, Proc. 8th SEI Conf. Software Engineering Education, R.L. Ibrahim, ed., Springer-Verlag, Berlin, 1995, pp. 187-204

Formal Methods

[50] M.W. Au, C.H. Lee, Integrating Use of VDM and Z. Software Engineering Education, B.Z. Barta, S.L. Hung, K.R. Cox, eds., Elsevier Science, Amsterdam, 1993, pp. 119-128

[51] N. Dean, M.G. Hinchey, Introducing Formal Methods through Role-Playing, SIGCSE Bulletin, Vol. 27, No. 1, March 1995, pp. 302-306

[52] A. Fekete, Reasoning about Programs: Integrating Verification and Analysis of Algorithms into the Introductory Programming Course, SIGCSE Bulletin, Vol. 25, No. 1, March 1993, pp. 198-202

[53] K-.K. Lau, V.J. Bush, P.J. Jinks, Towards an Introductory Formal Programming Course, SIGCSE Bulletin, Vol. 26, No. 1, March 1994, pp. 121-125

[54] I. Morrey et al., Use of a Specification Construction and Animation Tool to Teach Formal Methods, Proc. COMPSAC'93, Phoenix, Ariz., November 1-5, 1993, pp. 327-333

[55] T.V. Palmer, J.C. Pleasant, Attitudes Toward the Teaching of Formal Methods of Software Development in the Undergraduate Computer Science Curriculum: A Survey, SIGCSE Bulletin, Vol. 27, No. 3, September 1995, pp. 53-59

[56] R.M. Snyder, Teaching Program Correctness to Beginners, J. of Computing in Small Colleges, Vol. 9, No. 2, November 1993, pp. 127-134

[57] A.E.K. Sobel, Experience Integrating a Formal Method into a Software Engineering Course, SIGCSE Bulletin, Vol. 28, No. 1, March 1996, pp. 271-274

[58] T.H. Tse, Formal or Informal, Practical or Impractical: Towards Integrating Formal Methods with Informal Practices in Software Engineering Education. Software Engineering Education, B.Z. Barta, S.L. Hung, K.R. Cox, eds., Elsevier Science, Amsterdam, 1993, pp. 189-197

[59] J.S. Warford, An Experience Teaching Formal Methods in Discrete Mathematics, SIGCSE Bulletin, Vol. 27, No. 3, September 1995, pp. 60-64

Systems Engineering

[60] A.P. Sage, Editorial: Desiderata for Systems Engineering Education, IEEE Trans. Systems, Man, and Cybernetics, Vol. 10, No. 12, December 1980, pp. 777-780

[61] M. Eslami, Improving Engineering Education into the Next Century, IEEE Control Systems, Vol. 16, No. 2, April 1996, pp. 96-102

Control Engineering

[62] K.J. Aström, M. Lundh, Lund Control Program Combines Theory with Hands-on Experience, IEEE Control Systems, Vol. 12, No. 3, June 1992, pp. 22-30

[63] J.E. Beaini et al., Integrated Electromechanical Controls Laboratory Using Programmable Logic Controllers, Proc. American Control Conf., San Francisco, Calif., June 1993, pp. 2036-2039

[64] P. Dorato, A Survey of Control Systems Education in the United States, IEEE Trans. Education, Vol. 33, No. 3, August 1990, pp. 306-310

[65] K.T. Erickson, Experiments for an Undergraduate Automation Laboratory, Proc. American Control Conf., San Francisco, Calif., June 1993, pp. 2032-2035

[66] A. Feliachi, Control Systems Curriculum National Survey, Proc. American Control Conf., Boston, Mass., June 1991, pp. 298-303

[67] A. Feliachi, Control Systems Curriculum National Survey, IEEE Trans Education, Vol. 37, No. 3, August 1994, pp. 257-263

[68] K. Furuta et al., A New Inverted Pendulum Apparatus for Education, Proc. IFAC Conf. Advances in Control Educaation, Boston, Mass., June 24-25, 1991

[69] W. Grega, A. Maciejczyk, Digital Control of a Tank System, IEEE Trans. Education, Vol. 37, No. 3, August 1994, pp. 271-276

[70] G.M. Huang, L. Fu, J. Fleming, The Development of An Undergraduate Laboratory for Control Systems Design, Proc. American Control Conf., San Francisco, Calif., June 1993, pp. 2018-2022

[71] A. Jana, S.S. Chehl, Developing Instrumentation Laboratory with Real-Time Control Component, Proc. American Control Conf., San Francisco, Calif., June 2-4, 1993, pp. 2046-2049

[72] N.A. Kheir et al., Control Systems Engineering Education, Automatica, Vol. 32, No. 2, February 1996, pp. 147-166

[73] H. Klee, J. Dumas, Theory, Simulation, Experimentation: An Integrated Approach to Teaching Digital Control Systems, IEEE Trans. Education, Vol. 37, No. 1, February 1994, pp. 57-62

[74] D.E. Lyon, P.H. Meckl, O.D.I. Nwokah, Senior Control Systems Laboratoru at Purdue University, IEEE Trans. Education, Vol. 37, No. 1, February 1994, pp. 71-76

[75] M. Masten, Challenges for Control Systems Educators, Proc. American Control Conf., Boston, Mass., 1991, pp. 304-305

[76] P.D. Oliver, L. Boyce, Networked Digital Control and Data Acquisition for an Undergraduate Controls and Robotics Laboratory: A Progress Report, Proc. American Control Conf., San Francisco, Calif., June 1993, pp. 2028-2031

[77] U. Ozguner, Three-Course Control Laboratory Sequence, IEEE Control Systems, Vol. 8, No. 3, June 1989, pp. 14-18

[78] R.R. Rhinehart, An Integrated Process Control Laboratory, Proc. American Control Conf., Baltimore, MD, June 1994, pp. 378-382

[79] J. Vagners, Control Systems Laboratory Development, Proc. American Control Conf., San Francisco, Calif., June 1993, pp. 2023-2027

[80] P.E. Wellstead, Teaching Control with Laboratory Scale Models, IEEE Trans. Education, Vol. 33, No. 3, August 1990, p. 285-290

[81] S. Yurkovich, The Instructional Control Laboratories in Electrical Engineering at The Ohio State University, Proc. American Control Conf., San Francisco, Calif., June 1993, pp. 2014-2017

[82] S. Yurkovich, Advances in Control Education, IEEE Control Systems, Vol. 12, No. 3, June 1992, pp. 18-21

[83] J.J. Zhu, Control Education: A World Showcase, IEEE Control Systems, Vol. 16, No. 2, April 1996, pp. 8-10

[84] A. Zilouchian, Development of a Real-Time Digital Computer Control Laboratory, Proc. American Control Conf., Chicago, Ill., June 24-26, 1992, pp. 473-474

Digital Signal Processors

[85] T. Bose, A Digital Signal Processing Laboratory for Undergraduates, IEEE Trans. on Education, Vol. 37, No. 3, August 1994, pp. 243-246

[86] R. Chassaing, A Senior Project Course in Digital Signal Processing with the TMS320, IEEE Trans. Education, Vol. 32, No. 2, May 1989, pp. 139-145

[87] S.M. Kuo, G.D. Miller, An Innovative Course Emphasizing Real-Time Digital Signal Processing Applications, IEEE Trans. Education, Vol. 39, No. 2, May 1996, pp. 109-113

[88] V.K. Ingle, J.G. Proakis, A DSP Course Based on Lecture/Lab Integration, IEEE Signal Processing Magazine, October 1992, pp. 25-29

[89] J.D. Mellot, F.J. Taylor, Signal Processing's Education Survey Results, IEEE Signal Processing Magazine, October 1992, pp. 16-19

[90] M. Nahvi, Design-Oriented DSP Courseware: Hardware, Software, and Simulation, IEEE Signal Processing Magazine, October 1992, pp. 30-35

[91] F.J. Taylor, J.D. Mellot, SPECtra: A Signal Processing Engineering Curriculum, IEEE Trans. Education, Vol. 39, No. 2, May 1996, pp. 180-185

[92] M.D. Zoltowski, J.P. Allebach, C.A. Bouman, Digital Signal Processing with Applications: A New and Successful Approach to Undergraduate DSP Education, IEEE Trans. Education, Vol. 39, No. 2, May 1996, pp. 120-126

Chapter 1
Individual Courses
and Tools

A Course in Real-Time Software Principles (with Practice)

Alan Shaw
Department of Computer Science and Engineering
University of Washington
Box 352350, Seattle, WA 98195-2350
shaw@cs.washington.edu

Abstract

Some details of a concepts course in real-time software, the accompanying text book, and projects are presented. The material is divided into four main areas: software architectures, specification methods, timing analysis and clocks, and language and operating system mechanisms.

1. Introduction

During the last 10 years, we have been developing and teaching courses in real-time systems, primarily to university students but also to working engineers. The university version is a regular one-term course for computer science and engineering majors at the senior and graduate student levels. It has been a regular course offering at the University of Washington, and has also been taught at the University of Paris VI, the University of California at Santa Cruz, and Ecole Nationale Superieure Des Telecommunications (Paris). Short intensive industrial classes, without homeworks and projects, have also been given on NTU by satellite television, at the Summer Institute in Computer Science at the University of California at Santa Cruz, and on-site. The prerequisites are courses in operating systems, machine organization and assembly language, data structures, and programming, or the equivalent.

In the same spirit as established systems classes, e.g., operating systems, that are a part of most CSE programs, ours is a concepts course with exercises, an exam, and a project. The course is part of our offerings in computer systems and software engineering. It could also be a component of a general systems engineering curriculum, or it could be part of a specialized program in, for example, control systems or embedded systems. The next section discusses our rationale for the course and some issues. The main part of the paper presents our definition of the "principles", how these are organized into a coherent whole, the course materials, and examples of accompanying projects.

2. Issues and Rationale

It could be argued that most of the topics in a real-time software course should be, or are, covered in standard existing courses. For example, specification methods as part of a software engineering course, scheduling in operating systems, clock synchronization in distributed computing, deterministic timing analysis in performance analysis, and Ada in a programming languages course. However, quite often an important real-time topic is either not treated in one of these classes or it is not covered in sufficient breadth or depth; it is also the case that real-time is usually considered just one application of many. The reality, however, is that the field contains an interesting, challenging, and coherent set of engineering and scientific ideas, applications are numerous, ubiquitous, and non-trivial, and there is a growing demand for people trained in the area. Among other things, the field is concerned with one of the most basic questions of computing theory and practice: the timing behavior of computations.

Another approach to presenting a systems topic, especially a relatively new one, is through case studies. We rejected a case study approach in favor of one based on principles for the same reasons that we prefer a "principles" approach to most fields of study: namely, case studies are less efficient because many unecessary details have to be learned, and a concepts course forces the student (and teacher) to understand the underlying principles that apply to many applications and situations. We should emphasize here that our philosophy is that concepts must be accompanied by many examples explaining and justifying their use. At the other extreme, a course restricted solely to the theory of real-time systems might not be appropriate either unless there also existed some practical or applied offering.

3. Course Contents

Until recently, our materials consisted of a large and changing set of papers from the literature, with an occasional handout. However, the topics, i.e., the concepts presented, and the organization have remained surprisingly constant. These now appear in our first draft of a text book on real-time software. The Appendix contains the Table of Contents of the book which is also the course topics outline. The book and course lectures are divided into five parts with the following general topics and goals:

- The introduction defines some basic terms, gives examples of real-time systems and applications, discusses some issues concerning predictable hardware platforms, provides an historical perspective of the field, and introduces real-time software engineering.
- The second part is concerned with the organization and components of real-time software. The standard model of periodic and sporadic processes is presented. We then describe and analyse various architectures for implementing and controlling these process objects, including the cyclic executive and general operating systems structures.
- The next part covers informal and formal methods for specifying requirements and designs, including timing behaviors. Imperative state-based techniques, such as statecharts and communicating real-time state machines (CRSMs), are emphasized. Some attention is also given to more declarative notations, such as tabular methods, extended regular expressions, and assertional logics, especially real-time logic.
- Part four is a large section devoted to timing analysis and clocks. Under this heading, we first discuss the major ideas in deterministic scheduling theory and show how they can be used in practice. Next presented are methods for measuring and predicting the timing behavior of programs, for example, worst case execution times. The last part studies the general problem of keeping time on computers and maintaining desirable properties of computer clocks, such as monotonicity and synchronization.
- Software systems mechanisms are treated in the last section. The three main topics here are real-time programming languages, operating systems, and fault tolerance. After discussing some general requirements for real-time programming languages, the features of several seminal languages, such as Ada, are described. Under operating systems, we again give a general discussion of desirable features, accompanied by research and commercial examples. Recovery blocks and n-version programming are presented as two principal approaches to software fault tolerance.

There are a number of topics that we don't treat in the course (and book), mainly because of time constraints, that other educators might reasonably wish to include. Examples are (more) real-time communications, real-time data bases, Petri nets, and techniques for important softer real-time applications, such as multimedia processing.

Paper homeworks are fairly straightforward exercises in analysis and synthesis. Typical design and implementation projects are as follows:

- use our CRSM tools to construct and simulate some toy but non-trivial application such as a simple air traffic monitoring system;
- expand, or develop an application on, our home-built real-time operating system kernel (Examples have been a network controller, a real-time file system, and distributed clock synchronization.);
- compare experimentally several processor scheduling algorithms;
- build a clock, timer, or calendar package;
- simulate an elaborate multi-function digital watch.

We have also occasionally had paper projects that involved reading and evaluating some papers in the literature, for example:

- compare several real-time object-oriented operating systems;
- evaluate the suitability of Z as a real-time specification language;
- examine some timed temporal logics.

4. Conclusions

The material is technically diverse, for example, including state machines, logic, concurrent programming, and scheduling algorithms. We were concerned that this diversity would result in too difficult or too shallow an offering, or one that could not be integrated into a coherent whole. This has not been the case, partly because *time* provided a unifying theme. Our experience is that the course provides the right academic background for either real-time research or practice, within the context of a standard CSE program. More generally, we believe that such a course should be part of the normal computer science or computer engineering curriculum.

Appendix

Courses on Software Design Methods
for Concurrent and Real-Time Systems

Hassan Gomaa
Department of Information & Software Systems Engineering
George Mason University
Fairfax, Virginia 22030-4444
hgomaa@isse.gmu.edu

Abstract

This paper describes two graduate courses based around the author's book "Software Design Methods for Concurrent and Real-Time Systems". The first is a course on Software Design and the second is a Software Project Lab course. Both courses are part of the Master of Science degree in Software Systems Engineering at George Mason University.

1. Introduction

The Master of Science program in Software Systems Engineering was established at George Mason University in the fall of 1989 [1]. This was a year after the introduction of the Graduate Certificate program in Software Systems Engineering, which is a software engineering specialization taken by Masters students in related disciplines, such as Computer Science, Information Systems, or Systems Engineering.

The Masters and Certificate programs are housed in the Department of Information and Software Systems Engineering (ISSE) in the School of Information Technology and Engineering at George Mason University. Many of the software engineering courses are cross-listed with the Computer Science Department, which assists in teaching the courses.

To qualify for the Masters degree in Software Systems Engineering, students must complete 30 semester hours of graduate work. Students have a choice of a professional track, consisting of six core courses and four electives, and a research track, consisting of six core courses, two electives, and a six hour Masters thesis. The core courses are:

Software Construction
Software Requirements and Prototyping
Software Design

Formal Methods and Models
Software Project Management
Software Project Lab

Students may choose either software engineering electives or electives from related disciplines. Software engineering electives include Software Engineering Economics, Software Testing and Quality Assurance, Object Oriented Software Development, User Interface Development, Advance Software Requirements, Advanced Software Design Methods, Special Topics in Software Engineering, and Directed Readings in Software Engineering.

Graduate students in other degree programs who are also enrolled in the Certificate Program take five software engineering courses: Software Construction, Software Requirements and Prototyping, Software Design, and two other software engineering courses.

The teaching faculty consists of four full time professors in the ISSE department and one professor who has a joint appointment with the CS and ISSE departments, assisted by 1 or 2 research assistant professors (funded primarily by research contracts) and a few adjunct professors. In addition to the core courses, there are usually two or three electives taught each semester.

Student enrollment in the two programs has grown rapidly. Approximately 60 students graduate from the Masters program each year. As is typical of George Mason graduate programs, the majority of our students are part-time students who work primarily for federal government agencies and high technology companies located in the Metropolitan Washington area, which includes Northern Virginia where George Mason is located. In spite of the fact that many of them have full-time jobs, we are constantly impressed by their hard work, dedication and enthusiasm.

2. Software Design Course

When the MS Program in Software Systems Engineering first started, there was one course on Software Requirements, Prototyping and Design. However, it was soon found that there was insufficient time to do justice to both requirements and design in one course, and so the course was subsequently split into the two courses now being offered: Software Requirements and Prototyping, and Software Design. Each of these courses has a substantial group project component.

The Software Design course covers concepts and methods for the architectural design of software systems of sufficient size and complexity to require the effort of several people for many months. Fundamental design concepts are introduced. Several design methods are presented and compared, with examples of their use. Emphasis is on the design of concurrent and real-time systems. The course is based around the author's book "Software Design Methods for Concurrent and Real-Time Systems" [6].

The methods presented are Real-time Structured Analysis and Design [7,16,10,17], DARTS (Design Approach for Real-Time Systems) [3], Jackson System Development (JSD) [8,13], Parnas' Naval Research Lab/Software Cost Reduction Method [11,12], and Object-Oriented Design [2]. The course also covers two related object-oriented methods in more detail -- ADARTS (SM) (Ada-based Design Approach for Real-Time Systems) [5,6] and CODARTS (COncurrent Design Approach for Real-Time Systems) [6], which build on the earlier methods. The methods are compared by applying them to two common problems, an automobile cruise control problem and an automated teller machine problem. Students undertake a term project working in small groups addressing the design of a relatively complex software system using the CODARTS method. Past projects have included an automated gas station system and an automated supermarket checkout system.

To teach the course according to the book, it would be necessary to teach the above five methods, compare them, and then present the ADARTS and CODARTS methods. Unfortunately, this would introduce CODARTS too late for the students to use it on the term project. Instead, the presentation of CODARTS is interleaved with the presentation of the other methods. This can be accomodated by the fact that CODARTS builds on other methods, and in particular different phases of CODARTS build on different methods. Thus

the Task structuring phase of CODARTS builds on the DARTS and JSD methods, while the Information Hiding Module Structuring Phase of CODARTS builds on Parnas' Naval Research Lab/Software Cost Reduction Method and Object-Oriented Design. The detailed syllabus for the Software Design course showing this interleaving is given in Appendix A.

3. The CODARTS Design method

3.1 Introduction

The section of the course that covers CODARTS closely follows part 3 of the book, which describes the ADARTS and CODARTS methods. Whereas ADARTS is Ada oriented, CODARTS is language independent. However, the two methods have several steps in common. ADARTS and CODARTS attempt to build on the strengths of the NRL, OOD, JSD, and DARTS methods by emphasizing both information hiding module and task structuring. Key features of both ADARTS and CODARTS are the principles for decomposing a real-time system into concurrent tasks and information hiding modules. To achieve the goal of developing maintainable and reusable software components, the two methods incorporate a combination of the NRL module structuring criteria and the OOD object structuring criteria. To achieve the goal of structuring a system into concurrent tasks, they use a set of task structuring criteria that are a refinement of those originally developed for the DARTS design method.

Using the NRL method, it is often a large step from the black box Requirements Specification to the module hierarchy, and because of this it is sometimes difficult to identify all the modules in the system. Instead, ADARTS starts with a behavioral model developed using Real-Time Structured Analysis (RTSA). CODARTS provides an alternative approach to Real-Time Structured Analysis for analyzing and modeling the system, namely Concurrent Object-Based Real-Time Analysis (COBRA).

Both the task structuring criteria and the module structuring criteria are applied to the objects and/or functions of the behavioral model, which are represented by data and control transformations on the data flow / control flow diagrams. When performing task and module structuring, the behavioral model is viewed from two perspectives, the dynamic and static structuring views. The dynamic view is provided by the concurrent tasks, which are determined using the task structuring criteria. The static view is provided by the information hiding modules, which are determined using the module structuring criteria. Guidelines are then provided for integrating the task and module views.

The task structuring criteria are applied first followed by the module structuring criteria, although it is intended that applying the two sets of criteria should be an iterative exercise. The reason for applying the task structuring criteria first is to allow an early performance analysis of the concurrent tasking design to be made, an important consideration in real-time systems.

3.2 Steps in Using ADARTS and CODARTS

(1) Develop Environmental and Behavioral Model of System.

ADARTS uses RTSA for analyzing and modeling the problem domain, while CODARTS uses the COBRA method. COBRA provides an alternative decomposition strategy to RTSA for concurrent and real-time systems. It provides guidelines for developing the environmental model based on the system context diagram. It provides structuring criteria for decomposing a system into subsystems, which may potentially be distributed. It also provides criteria for determining the objects and functions within a subsystem. Finally, it provides a behavioral approach for determining how the objects and functions within a subsystem interact with each other using event sequencing scenarios.

(2) Structure the system into distributed subsystems.

This is an optional step taken for distributed concurrent and distributed real-time applications. Thus CODARTS/DA provides criteria for structuring a system into subsystems that can execute on geographically distributed nodes and communicate over a network by means of messages. CODARTS/DA builds on and substantially refines and extends the ideas from DARTS/DA [4].

(3) Structure the system (or subsystem) into concurrent tasks.

The concurrent tasks in the system (or subsystem of a distributed application) are determined by applying the task structuring criteria. The inter-task communication and synchronization interfaces are defined. Task

structuring is applied to the whole system in the case of a non-distributed design. In the case of a distributed design, where the subsystems have already been defined, task structuring is applied to each subsystem. The performance of the concurrent tasking design is analyzed.

(4) Structure the system (or subsystem) into information hiding modules.

The information hiding modules in the system (or subsystem of a distributed application) are determined by applying the information hiding module structuring criteria. A module aggregation hierarchy is created in which the information hiding modules are categorized.

(5) Integrate the task and module views.

Tasks, determined using the task structuring criteria of Step 3, and information hiding modules, determined using the module structuring criteria of Step 4, are now integrated to produce a software architecture.

(6) Develop an Ada-based architectural design.

This step is used in ADARTS to address the Ada specific aspects of the design. In this step, Ada support tasks are added and Ada task interfaces are defined. Additional tasks are usually required in an Ada application to address loosely coupled inter-task communication and synchronization of access to shared data.

(7) Define component interface specifications for tasks and modules. These represent the externally visible view of each component.

(8) Develop the software incrementally.

3.3 Performance Analysis of ADARTS and CODARTS Designs

The quantitative analysis of a software design is useful to allow the early detection of any potential performance problems. This analysis is for the software design conceptually executing on a given hardware configuration with a given external workload applied to it. Early detection of potential performance problems allows alternative software designs and hardware configurations to be investigated. Performance analysis of software designs is particularly important for real-time systems. The approach used by ADARTS and CODARTS is based on Rate Monotonic

Analysis, which is a real-time scheduling theory developed at SEI [14,15]. It addresses the issues of priority-based scheduling of concurrent tasks with hard deadlines. The theory addresses how to determine whether a group of tasks, whose individual CPU utilization is known, will meet their deadlines. The theory assumes a dynamic priority preemption scheduling algorithm.

4. Software Project Lab Course

The Software Project Lab course represents the culmination of the Masters program in Software Systems Engineering, where students, working in teams, apply the project management and technical skills they have acquired to the development of a software system. The project lab is intended to simulate industrial conditions [9].

In the Software Project Lab course, the students work in groups to develop a software system, addressing both the technical and project management aspects of the software life cycle. Usually the artifact developed progresses from software requirements analysis through system test. Past projects have included an automated gas station system and a flexible manufacturing system.

The project components of the requirements and design courses together with the project lab occasionally allow a group of students to elaborate one and the same project over two or more semesters. We cannot systematically rely on multi-term projects, however, since most students are part-time and do not progress together as one class through a sequence of courses.

The project lab has made it necessary for us to introduce a common program design language. We have selected Ada, which has proven to be a good choice particularly in a geographical area where many students have a background in systems development for government and defense.

The scope of the project lab varies by instructor. When I teach it, students use the CODARTS method, which they have usually experienced in SWSE 621, to develop the system. In developing a real-time system, a subset of the group develops an environment simulator to simulate the sensors and actuators that interface to the system.

The instructor plays multiple roles in the project lab, including software vice president, user, software quality reviewer, and software development method consultant. The students also play multiple roles during the project

and the roles can change in different phases. Roles include Project Leader, Chief Software Analyst, Software Architect, Chief Programmer, Test Team Leader.

The students are given an informal problem description at the start of the semester, as well as a project assignment (see Appendix B). They form into teams. We have experimented with teams of size 4 through 20. For the automated gas station project, teams of five are assigned. For the Flexible Manufacturing System, which is a larger system, the group size is 8-10. A group of 20 is divided up into four teams of five, with each team developing a relatively independent subsystem. With this approach, the instructor plays a more active role making sure that each group's subsystem is consistent with the others.

5. Conclusions

This paper has described two graduate courses based around the author's book "Software Design Methods for Concurrent and Real-Time Systems". The first is a course on Software Design and the second is a Software Project Lab course. Both courses are part of the Master of Science degree in Software Systems Engineering at George Mason University. Experience with teaching the courses has shown that it is necessary to teach a software design method in considerable detail for students to be able to apply it on real-world projects.

References

[1] P. Ammann, H. Gomaa, J. Offutt, D. Rine, B. Sanden, "A Five Year Perspective on Software Engineering Graduate Programs at George Mason University", Proc. SEI Software Engineering Education Conference, San Antonio, January 1994, Springer-Verlag, New York, 1994.

[2] G. Booch, "Object-Oriented Design with Applications", Benjamin Cummings, Redwood City, Calif., 1991.

[3] H. Gomaa, "A Software Design Method for Real-Time Systems", Communications ACM, September, 1984.

[4] H. Gomaa, "A Software Design Method for Distributed Real-Time Applications", Journal of Systems and Software, February 1989.

[5] H. Gomaa, "Structuring Criteria for Real-Time System Design", Proc. 11th International Conference on Software Engineering, May 1989, IEEE Computer Society Press, 1989.

[6] H. Gomaa, "Software Design Methods for Concurrent and Real-Time Systems", Addison-Wesley, Reading, Mass., 1993.

[7] D. Hatley and I. Pirbhai, "Strategies for Real-Time System Specification", Dorset House, New York, 1988.

[8] M.A. Jackson, "System Development, Prentice Hall, Englewood Cliffs, NJ, 1983.

[9] W.M. McKeeman, "Experience with a Software Engineering Project Course", Proc SEI Conference on Software Engineering Education, N. Gibbs and R. Fairley, Eds., Springer-Verlag, New York, 1987.

[10] M. Page-Jones, "The Practical Guide to Structured Systems Design", 2nd Edition, Prentice Hall, Englewood Cliffs, NJ, 1988.

[11] D.L. Parnas, "On the Criteria to be Used In Decomposing Systems into Modules", Communications ACM, December 1972.

[12] D.L. Parnas, P. Clements and D. Weiss, "The Modular Structure of Complex Systems", Proc. Seventh International Conference on Software Engineering, March 1984, IEEE Computer Society Press, 1984.

[13] B. Sanden, "Software Systems Construction", Prentice Hall, Englewood Cliffs, NJ, 1994.

[14] L. Sha and J.B. Goodenough, "Real-Time Scheduling Theory and Ada." IEEE Computer, Vol. 23, No. 4, April 1990.

[15] M. Klein et. al., "A Practioner's Handbook for Real-Time Analysis - Guide to Rate Monotonic Analysis for Real-Time Systems", Kluwer Academic Publishers, Boston, Mass., 1993.

[16] P. Ward, "The Transformational Schema: An Extension of the Data Flow Diagram to Represent Control and Timing", IEEE Transactions on Software Engineering, February 1986.

[17] E. Yourdon & L. Constantine, "Structured Design", Prentice Hall, Englewood Cliffs, NJ, 1978.

ADARTS(SM) is the registered servicemark of the Software Productivity Consortium Limited Partnership.

Appendix A

Syllabus for Software Design Course

Course Description:

This is a course in concepts and methods for the architectural design of software systems of sufficient size and complexity to require the effort of several people for many months. Fundamental design concepts and design notations are introduced. Several design methods are presented and compared, with examples of their use. Students will undertake a term project working in small groups addressing the design of a relatively complex software system.

Course Text:

H. Gomaa, "Software Design Methods for Concurrent and Real-Time Systems", Addison-Wesley, Reading, Mass., 1993.

Course Content and Readings:

Introduction: Overview of Software Design, Software Design Process, Software Design Concepts, Overview of Software Design Methods.

Readings: Gomaa, Chapters 2, 3.1, 3.4, 3.5, 3.6, 4.

Structured Analysis and Design - Structured Analysis: Functional decomposition, information modeling - entity relationship diagrams, mapping information model to relational data base; Real-Time Structured Analysis. Structured Design - module coupling and cohesion criteria; Design strategies: Transform Analysis, Transaction Analysis.

Readings: Gomaa, Chapter 5

DARTS - Design Approach for Real-Time Systems; Deficiencies of Structured Analysis and Design; concurrent task design, task interface design.

Readings: Gomaa, Chapter 6

Introduction to ADARTS (Ada based Design Approach for Real-Time Systems) and CODARTS (Concurrent Design Approach for Real-Time Systems).

Readings: Gomaa, Chapter 12

Analysis and Modeling for Concurrent and Real-Time Systems - Environmental model, system decomposition into subsystems, structuring criteria for objects and functions, behavioral analysis.

Readings: Gomaa, Chapter 13, 22.1

Distributed application design - Environments for concurrent and distributed processing. Decomposition into distributed subsystems. Message communication in distributed applications. Client / server applications.

Readings: Gomaa, Chapter 3.1 - 3.3, 20.5

ADARTS and CODARTS: Concurrent Task Structuring; Task Interfaces - message communication, event synchronization, information hiding modules.

Readings: Gomaa, Chapters 14, 22.2.

Naval Research Laboratory Software Cost Reduction Method. Concepts: information hiding, abstract interfaces. Module structuring - module hierarchy.

Readings: Gomaa, Chapter 8

Object Oriented Design. Concepts: information hiding objects, classes, inheritance. Object structuring.

Readings: Gomaa, Chapter 9

ADARTS and CODARTS: information hiding module structuring criteria; integrating task structuring and information hiding module structuring criteria; Ada specific considerations.

Readings: Gomaa, Chapters 15, 22.3, 16, 22.4, 17, 22.5.

Jackson System Development and Entity Life Modeling- Concepts; Modelling Phase; Network Phase; Implementation Phase. JSD extensions: Entity Life Modeling.

Readings: Gomaa, Chapter 7, Sanden Chapters 7, 8.

Review: Comparison of Software Design Methods.

Readings: Gomaa, Chapter 10.

Appendix B

Project Assignment for Software Project Lab Course

You have been requested by the Unusually Flexible Organization (UFO) to develop a System Specification and an Architectural Design Specification for the software system to be used in a distributed real-time Flexible Manufacturing System (FMS) application. An informal problem definition for the system is described in a separate document.

The following deliverables are required:

(1) A System Specification developed using COBRA (Concurrent Object-based Real-Time Analysis). Use scenarios to develop the System Specification. The System Specification should include:

a) Description of the scenarios that fully define the system. Describe each scenario first as a black box scenario, then in terms of the objects impacted by it.

b) System Context Diagram showing how the system interfaces to the external environment.

c) An entity-relationship diagram showing the entities, the attributes of the entities and the relationships between the entities.

d) State Transition Diagram(s) showing the different states of the state dependent objects.

e) Hierarchical set of data flow / control flow diagrams.

f) A Data Dictionary.

g) Mini-specifications briefly describing each leaf level object and/or function. These should describe what the object or function does in Precise or Structured English, not how. In particular there is no need to use detailed Pseudo-code, since these are meant to be understood by a user.

(2) An Architectural Design Specification. The design should include:

a) A Distributed System Architecture document developed using CODARTS/DA, the Concurrent Design Approach for Real-Time Systems / extensions for Distributed Applications. This should describe how the FMS system is decomposed into subsystems and the message interfaces between the subsystems. It should also explain how the subsystems were determined.

b) A Subsystem Architecture document for each subsystem, developed using CODARTS, containing:

i) An overview description of the software architecture, including the criteria used for task and information hiding module structuring.

ii) A Task Architecture diagram showing the concurrent tasks in the subsystem and the interfaces between them.

iii) A Software Architecture diagram showing how the tasks and modules in the subsystem relate to each other.

iv) Task behavior specifications for the concurrent tasks in the subsystem, showing how each task responds to the inputs it receives.

v) Information hiding module specifications for the information hiding modules in the subsystem.

c) Use the scenarios created for the System Specification as a basis for developing event sequence diagrams based on the software architecture diagrams.

(3) Detailed Design Specifications for the concurrent tasks in Program Description Language (PDL).

(4) A detailed test specification. This should describe integration and system test cases based on the scenarios developed above.

(5) A working system, written in the language of your choice, using environment simulators to simulate the external entities that the system interfaces with. The code should be fully documented and tested using the test cases developed in (4).

Each deliverable can include updates to earlier deliverables to ensure overall consistency.

From a project management perspective, the following plans should be developed and maintained throughout the project:

(1) A work breakdown structure (WBS) describing the project activities.

(2) A project schedule.

(3) A software development plan, including plans for the incremental development of the software showing the planned system subsets.

(4) A software test plan, including plans for environment simulation software and incremental testing of the system.

Real-Time Instructional Technology: Experiences with Multi-User Real-Time Systems

Kenneth H. Jacker
Computer Science Department
Appalachian State University
Boone, NC 28608 USA
khj@cs.appstate.edu

Abstract

We begin by discussing the configuration of our initial PC-based environment. Then, details of the new system bought with funds supplied by the National Science Foundation (NSF) and Appalachian State University are examined. Once the elements of the two systems have been presented, a discussion follows detailing the advantages of the multi-user, network-accessible system over the stand-alone personal computer. After reviewing the prerequisites for our Real-Time Systems course, a description of typical lab assignments is given. Finally, difficulties encountered in teaching an applied, systems-oriented, undergraduate real-time systems course are presented.

1 Introduction

Our senior *Real-Time Systems* course (CS4620) introduces the basic principles of applied real-time computation. Topics covered in the lectures include: analysis and design of real-time systems, finite state machines (FSMs) and state transition diagrams, hardware and software interrupts, event-driven systems, digital input/output and interfacing, analog and digital filters, digital-to-analog and analog-to-digital conversion hardware, sampling theory, spectral analysis, and real-time languages and operating systems. These concepts are applied through weekly three-hour labs and programming assignments.

For the first few course offerings, students implemented various data acquisition, data reduction, data analysis, and data visualization applications using a dedicated personal computer (PC). Accessing analog and digital boards in an attached system expansion box, students coded solutions to various real-time problems using an interpreted programming language.

Wishing to significantly "raise the level" of the course, we submitted a proposal to the NSF Instrumentation and Laboratory Improvement (ILI) organizational unit. The proposal successfully argued that the existing hardware and software environment severely restricted the course curriculum.

In particular, the following limiting aspects of the PC system were identified:

- single-user
- non-networked
- non-standard, non-distributed computer graphics
- unfamiliar software development environment
- lack of compatibility with free software available over the Internet.

Today, personal computers are the platform of choice for *users* of real-time systems. These users include, among others, chemists, biologists, process control engineers, and electronic musicians. The advanced students in our *Real-Time Systems* course, however, require a different type of hardware and software system – one that is more accessible, familiar, and robust.

Iconic, data-flow oriented real-time systems such as LabVIEW from National Instruments Corporation[12] are quite common today. But who designs and implements such real-time environments? Connecting a "low pass filter" icon to a "power spectrum" icon is one thing; creating the functions that implement those icons is another. Training students to create such easy-to-use environments requires a more sophisticated and technical system than that provided by various "turn-key" microcomputer-based, single-user machines.

2 Initial Single-User System

2.1 Hardware

The first few course offerings of CS4620 used a stand-alone, single-user IBM PC/AT running the Disk Operating System. For that time period, the system was considered high performance with its 286 processor, floating-point co-processor, maximum primary memory, and high-resolution graphics.

In addition to the PC, additional specialized real-time hardware was obtained from Keithley Instruments, Inc. Thanks to available used demonstration equipment, we were able to buy a "Series 500 Measurement & Control System" at a significantly reduced price. This system includes an external, low-noise chassis with a precision power supply; "slots" for up to ten plug-in hardware modules; and a cable connecting the chassis to an interface board in the personal computer.

In order to support both digital and analog lab assignments, we bought hardware modules to provide software-configurable analog and digital input and output. The multi-channel AIM1 and AOM1 provide slow speed conversion of 12-bit digital samples. and the DIM1 and DOM1 boards contain sixteen TTL-compatible, bi-directional digital ports.

2.2 Software

The software used on the initial system was ASYST[10], a "A Scientific System" designed by Adaptable Laboratory Software and distributed by Macmillan Software Company. ASYST is an interpreted language with a strong similarity to Forth [2]. The awkwardness of its reverse Polish notation is offset by the quick development time provided. Unlike the more traditional edit-compile-link-test cycle, Forth-like languages allow rapid prototyping and debugging.

The ASYST package provides the original Forth programming language along with extensions such as array data types, a spreadsheet-like data editor, and interactive graphics capabilities. Optional data acquisition and data analysis modules were also purchased. These modules contain a large number of different functions that operate on sampled data – from the determination of local maxima and minima to the computation of power spectra using an optimized fast Fourier transform (FFT).

Though we no longer incorporate this single-user system in the primary teaching environment, it is still used to provide experience in collecting data from a remote "concentrator" via a simple RS-232 data link.

3 New Multi-User Real-Time System

The new real-time system was purchased from Concurrent Computer Corporation. After discussing various configurations with the company, we decided to buy a Scientific Laboratory System (SLS) Model 6450. The rack-mounted machine arrived early in the Spring semester, 1991.

3.1 Hardware

Though the system supports two central processing units (CPUs), we could only afford the single CPU model due to financial limitations. The single Motorola 68030/68882 processor was available in two different models – the SLS6350 and the SLS6450. The only difference between the two is in their CPU clock speeds (25MHz and 33MHz). We choose the more expensive SLS6450 in order to provide the fastest possible data conversion and data reduction rates. The processor is mounted on a single motherboard with a 64KB cache memory and 16MB of primary memory (expandable up to 120MB).

Knowing that the system would not be used for general purpose computing, we bought limited secondary storage. A single 663MB Winchester hard drive provides sufficient storage for the restricted set of users. The machine also has a cartridge tape drive for backups and a floppy drive for low-level booting and system software updates. An Ethernet controller and four RS-232 ports allow communication with our local area network and attached serial terminals or modems.

The SLS6450 architecture is based on three buses. The 32-bit *memory bus* supports transfer rates up to 26 MB/sec. The second bus, the *I/O bus*, connects the cartridge tape controller and data acquisition subsystem to the memory bus. This industry standard VME bus transfers data up to 18MB/sec. The third and slowest bus (5MB/sec) is the *mass storage bus*. It, too, conforms to industrial standards and is used to connect SCSI storage devices to the memory bus.

The system console is a 19" color monitor with a resolution of 1024x768 8-bit pixels. Its dedicated Texas Instruments TMS34010 graphics processor with 512KB of memory can draw 80,000 2D vectors/sec, 5,000 2D triangles/sec, and supports a 8,000,000 pixel/sec Bitblt rate. Originally, we planned to buy a second monitor identical to the console unit. After some investigation, however, we decided to use the money that would have been spent on a second monitor to buy two Digital color X terminals. Though the Digital terminals are not as fast, we felt that providing two additional color devices out-weighed the speed advantage of the Concurrent product.

Two analog boards were also bought from Concurrent: a 12-bit, four channel digital-to-analog converter (DAC) and a 12-bit, sixteen channel analog-to-digital converter (ADC). Both of these devices provide aggregate conversion rates of 4MHz. A 64-bit, bi-directional, TTL-compatible digital I/O board was purchased from VME Microsystems International Corporation.

3.2 Software

The SLS6450 came with Concurrent's own real-time operating system. Real-Time Unix (RTU) is based on an AT&T System V kernel. In addition to various standard Unix utilities, the system has both a C and Fortran compiler. The command-line user interface supports two "universes" (*att* and *ucb*). This extension allows the user to choose whether to build applications that are compatible with the System V or Berkeley Unix environments. Networking protocols include both TCP/IP and streams. The Network File System (NFS) option was also purchased.

Real-time applications can include functions from RTU's real-time library. Routines are available to perform memory, file, and buffered data acquisition. Sophisticated timing is implemented through the asynchronous system trap (AST) facility. RTU also provides mechanisms for inter-process communication and process synchronization.

4 Advantages of Multi-User System

Multi-user Access   The benefits of the new hardware and software system were immediately apparent. Since the new system allowed simultaneous access, usage of the equipment by students, faculty, and staff increased significantly. Morale among the students improved since they were no longer competing for a single scarce resource.

With the PC system, students could not even edit their programs off-line due to the non-standard ASYST file format. Also, any efforts at data visualization required the built-in graphics module which was only available on the stand-alone machine.

With the new machine, students no longer have to put their names on a "sign-up list" and wait for their chance to use the equipment. Instead, students simply initiate a terminal session to the Concurrent system from a multitude of locations: our departmental labs, various public labs across campus, through the dial-up modem pool provided by Appalachian State, or even from a host anywhere on the Internet.

Multi-Tasking   Another aspect of the Concurrent system enjoyed by our current students is hinted at by the manufacturer's name. Since the real-time machine uses the Unix operating system, students working at the system console and at remote sites can execute multiple programs simultaneously. From the convenient but non-critical use of simple X Windowing System (X11[17]) clients like **xclock** to the running of long compilations or sliding window FFT calculations in the "background," most users find many ways to gain a significant increase in productivity though the underlying multi-tasking operating system.

Networking   The functionality of this multi-user, multi-programming environment is further enhanced by the system's connection to our local area network. In addition, the system interoperates through a "bridge" to the campus fiber "backbone" and via a router to the Internet. What a change from a PC sitting alone on a table in the back of a room! Even though the TCP/IP implementation lacks some standard capabilities such as Unix domain sockets, the most common and useful Internet clients (**finger, telnet, xterm, ftp,** and the so-called Berkeley r* commands) all work with virtually no problems.

Many other benefits result from the Concurrent system's network connection and software. Studies of campus equipment utilization show a significant amount of work is performed during the late evening and early morning hours. Walker Hall, which houses the Computer Science Department, is normally locked from approximately 22:00 in the evening until 07:00 the next day. Accessibility is even more limited on weekends and holidays. Although students must be in the real-time laboratory to use the data acquisition hardware, most other functions of the real-time system are available twenty-four hours a day via the campus network.

Thanks to network accessibility, students working on the system can be monitored remotely by the course instructor. In addition, electronic mail may be sent to and from the machine allowing students to communicate among themselves as well as to share problems with the instructor. A final advantage of the network connection is easy yet secure remote access to documentation, source code, and data sets through the use of **ftp, rcp,** and the Network File System.

None of this was possible when we used the stand-alone PC as the primary lab machine.

Distributed Computer Graphics   Yet another criticism of the earlier system has been overcome by the inclusion of X11. This *de facto* industry-standard distributed windowing environment plays a key role in data visualization. Using **gnuplot** (an excellent public domain graphing application), students produce color, 2- and 3-dimensional plots from the console and two color X terminals. In addition, students may use one of eighteen monochrome X terminals in the department's upper-division X terminal lab. Since many students use *Linux* in their dorm rooms and apartments, they may also access the real-time machine at their convenience in order to visualize raw data they might have acquired earlier the same day.

Familiar Development Environment   After much discussion, research and debate, the Computer Science Faculty decided to use the C programming language in almost all computer science courses and to base most upper-division courses on the Unix operating system. Now that we have fully implemented the change, students taking junior- and senior-level electives like CS4620 have a solid foundation in this software development environment.

In the earlier offerings of *Real-Time Systems*, students were forced to learn a new language, Forth. Though there are benefits to being exposed to different languages, we have provided that experience for years in our *Programming Languages* course. Similar to the situation in *Discrete Simulation* when we used Simscript as the implementation language, too much time was being spent on the idiosyncrasies of the new language rather than on the course subject matter.

With the purchase of the Concurrent system, we were able to provide a familiar development environment. Students can almost immediately begin using the software included in the RTU operating system. Utilities such as **vi**, **elm**, **make**, **lpr**, **lint** and the **csh** and **sh** "shells" are familiar from previous courses. Although most students are more comfortable with versions of Unix derived from the University of California at Berkeley (4BSD), they need little time to adapt to the changes presented by System V.

Industry Standard Software   A final advantage of the new, multi-user real-time system derives from using the same software (C, Unix, TCP/IP, etc.) as others in the Internet community. An example of this was the recent need to obtain spectral analysis software. In particular, we needed a collection of C functions to compute the forward and reverse, real- and complex fast Fourier transforms.

Since all student programs are written in C, many methods for obtaining the functions were available. Although we could have used the FFT code in the newest edition of *Numerical Recipes in C* [14], we instead were easily able to locate, obtain (via anonymous ftp), and install a documented and tested collection of the required C functions within a few minutes by using the software that came with the real-time system. Although there are probably many archives containing Forth versions of the FFT, in general there is much more C source code available on the Internet than Forth.

Other examples of freely available software obtained and installed on the Concurrent machine include **elm**, **gnuplot**, **perl**, **rcs**, and even a version of Forth. Most of these compiled and linked "right out of the box" after a simple configuration. A major factor in the easy installation of these packages is the standard **make** command available on virtually all Unix machines.

5   Course Prerequisites

Students are required to take a significant number of computer science, mathematics, and statistics courses prior to enrolling in *Real-Time Systems*. The "core" computer science curriculum consists of discrete mathematics and introductory computer science theory, programming fundamentals, algorithms, assembly language and machine operation, data structures, programming languages, as well as a two-semester sequence in hardware and software architecture. In addition, the senior real-time students have completed two semesters of calculus, linear algebra, and a probability/statistics course.

Few courses in our department actually use as many of the concepts contained in the prerequisites as *Real-Time Systems*. Besides a firm, practical grasp of advanced programming in C, a strong mathematical background is critical to the understanding and application of signal processing algorithms. Without knowledge of basic operating system concepts such as inter-process communication, file systems, schedulers, virtual memory, etc., our students would be unable to understand and efficiently use the many functions available in Concurrent's real-time library.

Note that there is *no* electronics prerequisite.

6   Laboratory Assignments

The four semester-hour course consists of three hours of lecture and three hours of lab each week. The lab period is a key component. Here the students see how the abstract concepts from lecture are actually applied. Furthermore, the relatively long sessions provide ample time to demonstrate test equipment, electronic devices such as signal-conditioning circuits and anti-aliasing filters, as well as specialized real-time software.

The students are frequently provided with a "skeleton" program incorporating functionality and/or coding techniques that will be needed to complete the week's assignment. For example, in order to optimize direct memory access transfers between the ADC and primary memory, the raw data vector must be "word aligned." It has proved very effective during the three-hour lab period to demonstrate that the sample program does, indeed, work as described.

Overall, the labs are ordered as follows: digital input, digital output, analog output, and analog input. Though we are considering reducing the amount of time spent on the initial digital assignments, there is an advantage in delaying the analog topics. In particular, introductory material (history, applications, real-time modeling, implementation of finite state machines, etc.) must be covered early in the course. In addition, spending a few weeks lecturing on modeling and digital interfacing allows the students to become familiar with RTU's similar but slightly different software development environment – K&R versus ANSI C, for example. It also provides a chance to introduce the theory and operation of the oscilloscope before they need to use the device.

Most of the labs listed below are designed and implemented by each individual student. A few of the more "exploratory" projects are assigned to two-person teams. Students must provide source code listings for all of the labs. Many of the analog labs also require producing graphs with **gnuplot** and writing a discussion of results.

Following are typical lab assignments designed and implemented by the students of *Real-Time Systems*:

- double/single click detection (dscd)

  This lab requires software to be written that will "debounce" two mechanical switches. Then, using a FSM for control, the program recognizes single and double "clicks" on either of the switches.

- rainbow water system (rws)

  Rws mimics a vending machine that sells two different sized cans of water. The switches in *dscd* are used to simulate the entry of nickels, dimes and quarters. A FSM is again used for control.

- seven-segment display driver (ssdd)

  Using a FSM for control, the student's program accesses the digital output ports to directly control a seven-segment display. A simple menu interface is implemented in "raw" terminal mode using **termcap** routines. The two mechanical switches are used to dynamically increase or decrease the frequency of various patterns being displayed.

- simple sound synthesis (sss)

  Sss is usually the second analog assignment. The student must write a program that uses C functions to generate various periodic waveforms, and then outputs those discrete samples to the DAC. The output is verified by connecting the DAC to a stereo amplifier and speaker system.

- Fourier analysis (fa)

  This lab begins by digitizing three waveforms produced by a function generator and creating two waveforms using C functions. After applying a FFT, graphs are produced of the time data and power spectra.

- joint frequency-time analysis (jfta)

  Here, students digitize their first sound data. After ensuring they have captured "good" data, they produce various graphs including "waterfall," surface, and contour plots using the short-time Fourier transform[1, 11].

- speech recognition (sr)

  Students are first placed in two-person groups. A program is written which digitizes each partner saying "yes", "no", and "maybe". After digitizing one of the group members saying one of the three pre-recorded words, their program then determines which partner said which word.

7 Difficulties in Teaching Real-Time

Equipment Cost   The biggest problem we have had offering an undergraduate real-time course has been funding. The cost of a high-performance real-time mini-computer is significantly greater than that of most machines used in an academic setting. Though some of the extra expense can be attributed to the need of a fast CPU, sufficient primary memory, and high speed buses that can transfer data at sufficient speed to support high-speed data acquisition, our experience suggests that most of the extra cost can be attributed to the specialized real-time hardware.

This hardware includes specialized computer graphics accelerators (e.g., the Texas Instruments TMS34010 graphics processor for accelerated X11 primitive rendering); high-speed, high-precision ADCs and DACs; multi-port TTL-compatible digital input and output; and an industry-standard VME backplane which contains the data acquisition boards. A secondary factor contributing to the high cost of multi-user real-time systems is the inflated price of data storage devices (hard disks, tape drives, and CD drives) as compared to very similar devices for personal computers.

Hardware and Software Maintenance Cost   The primary factor contributing to the high price of maintenance of real-time systems is the cost of supporting analog devices. The expense of maintaining the CPU and its subsystems is relatively small compared to that of the ADCs and DACs. In addition, departmental administrators find it difficult to justify the cost arguing that the machine is under-utilized compared to the systems supporting our more general computer science courses.

We were able to save a substantial amount of money on the Concurrent machine's field service contract by designating the course instructor as the on-site engineer. Initial problem isolation and diagnosis is done by him. These additional efforts put extra demands on the faculty member's time (which typically is not considered by the university administration when calculating course loads and committee assignments).

Electronic Technician Support   Many computer science programs still remain sub-disciplines within mathematics departments or are at a university that has no college of engineering. The result is a lack of personnel to perform routine electronic work (calibration, interfacing, cable construction, etc.). Either the course instructor must again stretch his or her already busy schedule, or funds must be found to hire a technician.

System Software Updates   A difficulty in teaching real-time courses arises from the additional time needed by the manufacturers of real-time systems to modify system software. For example, the standard AT&T System V operating system kernel used on the Concurrent system is modified to support real-time process scheduling, ASTs, and contiguous files. Another example derives from needed changes to the standard X Consortium releases of X11 to support real-time processing. It is frustrating having to wait for the new capabilities contained in the standard software releases to finally appear in the company's supported products.

Real-Time Textbooks   Another problem we have found in offering our *Real-Time Systems* course is the lack of suitable real-time textbooks. The books tend to either stress software engineering issues[6, 7, 19] or focus on topics more appropriate to graduate-level courses [13, 15, 18].

Our current[9] and previous[8] textbooks give little coverage to the implementation activity which is appropriate for our introductory, undergraduate course. More applied books have been published, but are too platform-specific[4, 16], lack adequate treatment of data acquisition and data reduction[5], or are soon out of date as new hardware and software become available[3].

Weak Mathematical Skills   Though, as mentioned earlier, our computer science majors are required to take a substantial number of mathematics courses, few of them seem to retain the concepts and techniques presented. At Appalachian State, this is due in part to the fact that they do not use what they have learned in their mathematics classes until late in their academic program. Many of our students are surprised to find

mathematics being used in their junior- and senior-level computer science courses. Instructors of calculus and linear algebra must be encouraged to present examples of using mathematics to solve problems within the field of computer science.

8   Conclusion

Though non-networked, single-user real-time systems are suitable for users of real-time system applications, we have shown the tremendous advantage of the multi-user system in teaching an undergraduate real-time course. The multi-programming features and network accessibility of a modern Unix- and C-based machine contribute significantly to the utility of such a system in an academic setting. We also presented a brief description of the prerequisites and typical labs undertaken by students in our department's *Real-Time Systems* course. We concluded by discussing difficulties encountered in supporting applied real-time computation at a liberal arts university.

Acknowledgment

The new hardware and software system was obtained with support from the National Science Foundation (with matching funds from Appalachian State University) through ILI grant #USE-9050713: *A Modern Undergraduate Real-time Laboratory*.

References

[1] J. B. Allen and L. R. Rabiner. "A Unified Approach to Short Time Fourier Analysis and Synthesis". *Proc. IEEE*, 65:1558-1564, 1977.

[2] L. Brodie. *Starting Forth*, 2nd edition. Prentice Hall, Englewood Cliffs, NJ, 1987.

[3] C. Foster. *Real-Time Programming*. Addison-Wesley, Reading, MA, 1982.

[4] B. Furht, D. Grostick, D. Gluch, G. Rabbat, J. Parker, and M. McRoberts. *Real-Time UNIX Systems Design and Application Guide*. Kluwer Academic, Boston, MA, 1991.

[5] B. O. Gallmeister. *POSIX.4: Programming for the Real World*. O'Reilly & Associates, Sebastopol, CA, 1995.

[6] H. Gomaa. *Software Design Methods for Concurrent and Real-Time Systems*. Addison-Wesley, Reading, MA, 1993.

[7] D. J. Hatley and I. A. Pirbhai. *Strategies for Real-Time System Specification*. Dorset House, New York, NY, 1987.

[8] B. Joseph. *Real-Time Personal Computing*. Prentice Hall, Englewood Cliffs, NJ, 1989.

[9] P. Laplante. *Real-Time Systems Design and Analysis: An Engineer's Handbook*, 2nd edition. IEEE Press/IEEE CS Press, Los Alamitos, CA, 1996.

[10] Macmillan Software Company. *A Brief Introduction to ASYST*. New York, NY, 1985.

[11] J. E. Maisel. "*When* in the time domain a frequency component occurs is as important as its magnitude", *Personal Engineering & Instrumentation News*, pp. 59-61, April, 1993.

[12] National Instruments, Austin, TX, 1996. http://www.natinst.com/.

[13] J. Peterson. *Petri Net Theory and the Modeling of Systems*. Prentice Hall, Englewood Cliffs, NJ, 1981.

[14] W. H. Press, S. A. Teukolsky, W. T. Vetterling, and B. P. Flannery. *Numerical Recipes in C*, 2nd edition. Cambridge University Press, New York, NY, 1992.

[15] W. J. Quirk. *Verification and Validation of Real-Time Software*. Springer-Verlag, Berlin, 1985.

[16] D. L. Ripps. *An Implementation Guide to Real-Time Programming*. Yourdon Press, New York, NY, 1989.

[17] R. W. Scheifler, J. Gettys and R. Newman. *X Windowing System*. Digital Press, Bedford, MA, 1988.

[18] J. A. Stankovic and K. Ramamritham. *Advances in Real-Time Systems*. IEEE Computer Society Press, Los Alamitos, CA, 1993.

[19] P. T. Ward and S. J. Mellor. *Structured Development for Real-Time Systems*. Yourdon Press, New York, NY, 1985.

Graphical Programming and Real-Time Design Instruction

J.-J. Schwarz, J. Skubich, M. Maranzana and R. Aubry
L3i, Département Informatique 502
Institut National des Sciences Appliquées de LYON
F-69621 Villeurbanne Cedex, France
{jjs|skubich|Mathieu.Maranzana|aubry}@if.insa-lyon.fr

Abstract

This paper describes the choices which have been made at the Department of Informatics at the National Institute of Applied Sciences (INSA) de Lyon for teaching real-time systems. The main approach relies upon the use of a graphical tool dedicated to the visual programming of off-the-shelf multitasking real-time operating systems in order to obtain a high quality of the design in actual applications.

1. Introduction

The National Institute for Applied Sciences (INSA) of Lyon is a Higher Education School of Engineering which belongs, in France, to the "Grandes Ecoles d'Ingénieurs". The mission of INSA is three-fold: basic education, research and development, and continuing education. Teaching is vocationally oriented: the aim is to transmit experience as much as knowledge. This explains why the student/teacher ratio is relatively high in an educational institution of such a type; on average it is 10/1. Most of the lecturers are also researchers: there is a strong education/research synergy.

INSA is a polytechnic institute composed of nine departments (faculties), which include the Department of Informatics. After a two-year curriculum dedicated to natural sciences (mathematics, physics, chemistry, and so on), the students can choose to continue studies in one of the nine departments. The duration of studies in their department of specialisation is three more years. Following market needs and the foreseeable evolution of computing, the Department of Informatics has chosen, as its policy, the training of generalists. Thus, instead of defining instruction as being adapted to a specific domain of application in computing sciences, the preferred approach has been to forge a set of basic skills for the students. In this way, they can adapt easily to the requirements of their employers. To achieve this goal, the following fundamental options have been adopted:

- Equal importance is given to each of the different areas studied, thus avoiding specialisation in domains which are liable to significant technical changes in a short term;
- A greater significance is given to requirement analysis, specification and design methods rather than to implementation;
- Students are taught to be designers and architects, so that a multi-domain view is required;
- Students are placed in a semi-professional environment, dealing with projects of increasing complexity, and carried out within student teams;
- Education/research synergy is promoted.

On-going adjustments of the substance of the training programme are made on the basis of the strengths and interests of the research teams and laboratories linked to the Department of Informatics. This approach applies obviously also to real-time systems, and explains some of the choices made in this area.

This paper is organised as follows. Part 2 defines the real-time systems teaching objectives and pre-requisites. Part 3 briefly describes the teaching media, with particular reference to the LACATRE environment. Part 4 describes the methodology used, based on the example of a group project. Finally, some conclusions are drawn evaluating the choices made within this framework.

2. Real-Time systems curriculum

The instruction of real-time techniques takes place within the more general framework of industrial computing and emphasizes the quality of the design, the groupwork and the efficiency of the teaching.

During the design and realisation processes, emphasis is put on the architectural view of the system concerned, and particular attention is given to preliminary design. On the other hand, the detailed design, an obvious necessary step, has been given a higher level of abstraction in order to allow a design which satisfies quality constraints.

This quality approach implies that even for trivial case studies, a set of non-functional features must be taken into account. Among the required quality criteria, some are of greater importance and relate to:

- documentation, which must be reliable, clear and non-ambiguous;
- exception handling, which costs little or nothing during run-time, and which introduces dependability in a natural way;
- modular and structured programming, which promotes reuse (if required) and, above all, simplifies maintainability (direct influence on the maintenance cost of software).

Experience has shown [5] that up to 60% of known errors in real-time systems are introduced during the specification phase. This means that a lot of errors are still due to the design problems. Therefore, it is important to try and improve the quality of the final design. This saves time spent later on tuning and corrective maintenance. The use of standard real-time executives (with a general purpose scheduler based on preemption and priority) rarely offers the possibility of a complete verification of the design before the final target implementation. So, it is rather usual to spend a relatively high amount of time on testing the application within its actual physical environment. An efficient design can reduce this time by attempting to do the verification of the timing constraints.

Groupwork is applicable in this context, because of the following underlying objectives:

- Familiarise the students with groupwork techniques: project management, group communication, and interface definitions. All of the students are aware of the project as a whole, but each of them is responsible for only one technical part. This situation is similar to that encountered in the professional world.
- Allow students to tackle projects with complexity which is close to industrial reality. It allows to distinguish between those parts of the project which are time-critical and those which are not.
- Encourage a pragmatic approach to the solution which favours quality criteria in the groupwork context. Fostering creativity, it also favours blossoming of the solutions. In real-time applications, simple solutions are often the ones which provide better run-time guarantees.

The final aim is the improvement of the productivity of teaching, even if this is not directly measurable. It is important to make the time the lecturer spends "in front of the students" more efficient: transmitting a maximum of methodological concepts within a minimum of time. This is possible only thanks to good lecturer/student communication.

We believe that one approach which assists in the realisation of these goals is to harness the strengths of graphical programming and design [2, 4]. As in other engineering disciplines, the development of real-time applications may greatly benefit from such a method.

The last issue which must be clarified is the set of course prerequisites essential to enable this educational approach.

The students concerned have already attended one year of specialised computer studies, and it may therefore be assumed that they have a good basic knowledge of algorithms, programming techniques (using C and C++), computer architecture (for example, interrupt handling, I/O drivers), operating systems and low-level communication protocols. Moreover, even if the methods currently used in our approach are rather functional (or object based) than object oriented, the students have otherwise a basic training in object oriented methods and languages.

3. The LACATRE environment

Within the framework of this paper, only a brief overview of the characteristics of the LACATRE environment will be given. The reader can find more complete information in [6, 7, 8, 9].

LACATRE is a real-time multitasking application design environment. It relies on a graphical language combining the data- and control-flow approaches and acts, at the lowest level, as a modelling layer to off-the-shelf real-time executives (for example, VRTX, VxWorks, iRMX, etc.). A reduced set of basic real-time objects (task, interrupt, event, message, etc.) and actions (send_to_mailbox, wait_on_sem, etc.), with their own graphical symbolism, is used to represent the main real-time multitasking mechanisms. At the preliminary design level, the designer can model the result of the specification phase in terms of activities using client/server based applicative objects. The symbolism of these objects remains very simple and is inherited from Booch [1]: it is a rectangle with overlapping boxes which are methods (procedure, entry-points, communication ports), specific to these objects. The major feature of LACATRE is that it takes advantage of all the potentials of graphical programming to model and verify the different running phases of an application separately (initialisation, termination, normal running, exception handling). Correctness verification is tackled by means of Shaw's CRSMs (Communicating Real-Time State Machines) [10, 11]. Provision for annotations of timing constraints exists, but is not currently implemented.

The LACATRE environment meets, at least partially, the stated objectives. First of all, it allows a straightforward mode of implementation: the same symbolism is used both by the lecturer to explain how a real-time executive runs and by students to design an application. The pace of comprehension allows a rapid development, while minimising design errors.

It also increases the level of abstraction: the technical details of the implementation are concealed and the designer can focus on issues which are really important.

It also increases the level of abstraction: the technical details of the implementation are concealed and the designer can focus on issues which are really important. Two abstraction levels are provided: one close to the real-time executives, and another one close to the application.

The principle of graphical design allows to produce both components of the design document, the program and its documentation, simultaneously. The former (which is a 2D diagram) is reliable and legible. It is a good communication medium between the members of a team, as well as a good basis for communication between the lecturer and his students. It is therefore relatively easy, for the lecturer, to evaluate and criticise the architecture of a multitasking real-time application designed by the students.

4. Lectures and projects

Because our instruction focuses essentially on projects where expected prerequisite knowledge is not negligible, the part of the time devoted to lectures is relatively small. Lectures consist of a presentation of both a specification method (SART, [3, 12]) and a design method (LACATRE), which simultaneously allow the description of an off-the-shelf real-time executive: iRMX. In fact, the modelling of iRMX is done using LACATRE. With the same formalism, the student learns the use of the real-time executive at the same time as he starts learning the design method. The time gain is significant, and the total time dedicated to lectures is no more then 12 hours.

There are three levels of groupwork (projects) realised progressively in two ways: from learning of basic real-time techniques to the application of quality assurance, and by increasing the complexity of projects. The amount of student work required is equivalent to 16 hours of laboratory work and 20 to 30 hours of individual work per person. Groupwork is performed by teams of 6 students and the task is split into three parts, each realised by a subteam of two. The overall amount of work is therefore approximately 220 to 280 hours per project group. When students are done with the projects, the instruction is completed by taking part in seminars dealing with particular techniques: scheduling methods, reliability, bus architectures, etc. The groupwork presented in the paper is the one at the middle level. It deals with the design of the supervision software for a flexible cell within a production shop (for making data acquisition boards). The equipment being controlled consists of an automatic warehouse, an assembly robot, a test bench (a set of measuring devices connected via an IEEE488 bus) and a conveyor. The three parts of the project are dedicated respectively to:

• the specification of the supervision software (using SART)

• the design of an IEEE488 bus driver

• the design of a remote mailbox mechanism (iRMX)

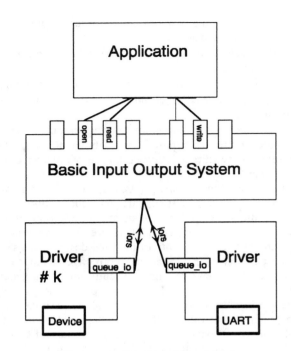

Figure 1. Applicative objects

to allow the distribution of software among several CPUs in a Multibus II machine.

To present a general idea of the practical features of the tool, we are focusing on the design of the driver. The functioning of a driver is presented and explained to the students, first, as well as the basic rules for the driver integration into the file system of the iRMX operating system.

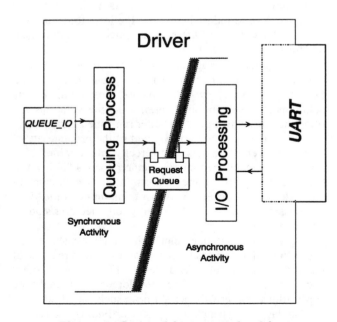

Figure 2. General features of a driver

As the first example, a simple serial link device driver is used, because it does not require a lot of prerequisite knowledge to understand its operation.

Figure 1 shows, with the "applicative objects" of LACATRE, the relative position of the device driver versus the application using it. The application sees the device as a file managed by the native file system (Basic Input Output System, BIOS) thanks to open, read, write, and other system calls (procedures), each being represented by an overlapping box. These calls may be

only one overlapping box is used to represent the services of the driver (Figure 2).

The LACATRE prototype is used by students for the detailed design of the driver. The tool allows splitting of different running phases of the driver (initialisation, nominal running, exception handling, and termination) and associated tracings.

As an example, Figure 3 represents the nominal running phase (kernel phase) in which the queuing of the input-output requests is made by a deposit of the IORS

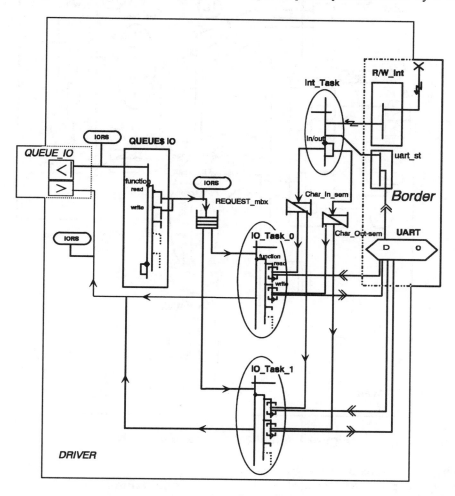

Figure 3. Kernel phase of a driver

considered as services offered by the BIOS for which the application is a client.

At the lower level, BIOS relies upon various device drivers in order to achieve the physical operation. Hence, BIOS is a client of a device driver whose service is to provide both the synchronous queuing of the Input-Output Requests (IORS) and the asynchronous actual I/O Processing. The driver can be asked for different functions, but there is a unique entry-point (the QUEUE_IO procedure) to transmit the request. Thus,

message in the REQUEST_mbx mailbox. This mailbox has been chosen as the simplest way of implementation of the Request Queue object of Figure 2. The interface with the physical environment is made up via a UART (Universal Asynchronous Receiver Transmitter) modelled by the R/W_Int interrupt object and the UART LACATRE resource object.

The interrupt object R/W_Int allows to signal the sending and the receiving of a character (event flow) to the Int_Task task. The semaphores Char_In_sem and

Char_Out_sem are used as event stores for further processing by the two I/O tasks (IO_Task_0 and IO_Task_1). The resource object UART captures the physical read and write operations (data flow), *made by the two I/O tasks*. Ignoring the initialization and the termination phases, this diagram focuses on the essentials.

under preparation will allow this without manual handling of the target code.

The LACATRE diagram is a communication medium between the students and they use it to develop the solution. When the design is finished it can be directly evaluated using the diagrams.

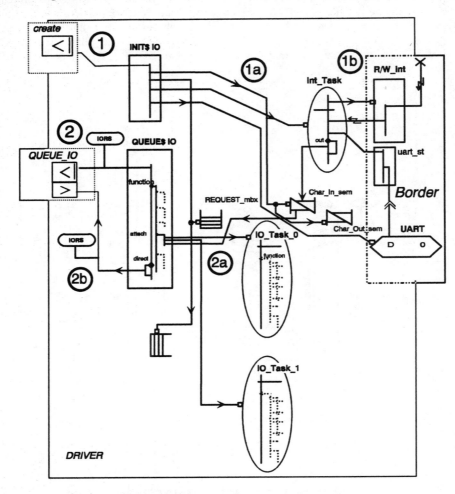

Figure 4. Initialization phase of a driver

It is worth noting that Figures 3 and 4 have been pruned from some textual parameters required for the final design but useless in the context of this paper. The purpose, here, is not to describe a driver understandable to the reader, but simply to give the general look-and-feel and possibilities of the method.

The initialization phase is captured in Figure 4. In order to initialize the driver, BIOS starts with a call to the INIT_IO service. Numbers shown at different steps represent the sequencing of this phase.

Merging of all the tracings (useless to show here) is used for the automatic generation of the skeleton of the program. This code can then be completed with the code related to the data modelling. The LACATRE tool version

5. Conclusion

This teaching platform has been in use for several years and has satisfied all the stated objectives, particularly from the point of view that student employment is a valuable criterion in a vocationally oriented curriculum. The platform continues to evolve with the available technology, but keeps the same general objective: to educate the students in concepts of a real-time architecture. More precisely, current idea is to switch to object oriented methods, and to define an object oriented equivalent of the LACATRE tool devoted to object oriented real-time kernels.

Our position is somewhat peculiar insofar as the real-time technology is taught within the framework of a Computer Engineering Department, whereas such work is usually done in a Department of Electrical or Electronic Engineering. Because of this, our point of view may be considered somewhat biased, although (as noted above) it has met all of the stated course design criteria in the most satisfactory manner.

References

[1] G. Booch. Object-Oriented Development. *IEEE Trans. Software Engineering*, Vol. SE-12, No. 12, December 1986, pp. 211-221.

[2] D. Harel. Statecharts: a visual formalism for complex systems. *Science of Computer Programming*. Vol. 8, 1987, pp. 231-274.

[3] D. Hatley, I. Pirbhai. *Strategies for Real-Time System Specification*. Dorset House, New-York, 1987.

[4] M.G. Hinchey. Visual Methods in Real-Time Programming. *Proc. 19th IFAC/IFIP Workshop on Real-Time Programming*, Reichenau, Germany, June 1994, Pergamon, Oxford, 1994.

[5] L. Motus. Time Concepts in Real-Time Software. *Control Engineering Practice*. Vol. 1, No. 1, February 1993, pp. 21-33.

[6] J.-F. Petit, J.-J. Schwarz, M. Maranzana, J. Skubich. Data Flow Modelling in Real-Time Multitasking Graphical Design. *Proc. 2nd IEEE Workshop on Real-Time Applications*, Washington DC, USA, July 1994, IEEE Computer Society Press, Los Alamitos, California, 1994, pp. 33-38.

[7] J.-J. Schwarz. LACATRE : Langage d'Aide à la Conception d'Applications multitâche Temps REel. *Revue d'Automatique, Productique et Informatique Industrielle*. APII AFCET. Vol. 26, No. 5-6, 1992, pp. 355-384.

[8] J.-J. Schwarz, M. Maranzana, J. Skubich, Y. Martinez. Applicative objects interconnection in a graphical design for real-time applications. *Proc. 20th IFAC/IFIP Workshop on Real-Time Programming*, November 1995, Fort Lauderdale, Florida, USA, Pergamon, Oxford, 1995.

[9] J. Skubich, J.-J. Schwarz, M. Maranzana, T. Szmuc. Time requirement specification in graphical real-time design. *Proc. 3rd IFAC/IFIP Workshop on Algorithms and Architectures for Real-Time Control*, Ostende, Belgium, 31th May-2nd June 1995, Pergamon Press, Oxford, 1995.

[10] A.C. Shaw. Communicating Real-Time State Machines. *IEEE Trans. Software Engineering*, Vol. 18, No. 9, September 1992, pp. 805-816.

[11] T. Szmuc, P. Szwed, J.-J. Schwarz, J. Skubich. Hierarchical Correctness Verification in Multiphase Real-Time Software Design. *Control Engineering Practice*, Vol. 3, No. 6, June 1995, pp. 829-836.

[12] P. Ward, S. Mellor. Structured Development for Real-Time Systems. Prentice Hall, New-York, 1985.

Using ObjecTime to Teach Real-Time Software in the Undergraduate Curriculum

Terry Shepard
Colin Wortley
Department of Electrical and Computer
Engineering
Royal Military College of Canada
Kingston, Ontario, K7K 5L0, Canada
613 541 6000
{shepard, wortley}@rmc.ca

Bran Selic
ObjecTime Ltd.
340 March Road
Kanata, Ontario, K2K 2E2
Canada
613 591 3435
bran@objectime.com

Abstract

Teaching of real-time software techniques has many meanings at the undergraduate level. There is generally not room in the curriculum to teach all the issues that should be taught. There is also a risk that important concepts will get lost in the mass of detail that is intrinsic to real-time software. The approach taken in this paper is that the most important concept is the need to capture and retain design structure for the life of the software. This is taught by showing the students ObjecTime as one specific way to create a design, use it for code generation, and then to preserve the design to protect the code against deterioration caused by changes.

1. Introduction

This paper discusses the teaching of software that controls physical processes. Undergraduates in science and engineering intuitively understand what that means: sensing of values in the environment, typically through some kind of analog to digital interface, calculation of desired values of controlled variables, and output of those values, typically via a digital to analog interface. They may learn about writing such software by working with a few hundred lines of code in C, using a library of routines that interface to a card in a PC that interfaces to a physical device being monitored or controlled. In a more ambitious course, they may learn about one of the traditional real-time design methods [1],[2], perhaps supported with a CASE tool, or they may undertake construction of a larger embedded program, perhaps requiring the writing of several thousand lines of code.

In a one semester course, there is no possiblility of doing the latter while also learning and applying the former - at least a two course sequence is required, and space for that is rarely available in an undergraduate curriculum. Learning the traditional methods as part of a large scale project course is possible, but applying them effectively to the project is not. To make matters worse, there are many practical issues of unexpected complexity that must be dealt with, often with little or no theory to support them, so that the teaching of them is either ignored or is in danger of being overwhelmed by a mass of detail. Among these issues of detail are:

- management of tasks,
- interrupt handling,
- the properties of real-time executive programs,
- host-target development,
- observing and verifying behaviour on the target with minimal perturbation of that behaviour (for example, by using digital logic analyzers and in circuit emulation),
- simulation harnesses to test the software when the process being controlled is not available,
- methods of guaranteeing in the design that performance goals will be met,
- the use of low level code either to improve performance or to gain access to specific hardware features and the effect of that on the integrity of a design, and
- the writing of device drivers.

26

Some compromise is necessary and reasonable, as some of the practical details should be left to be learned after graduation. One of the principal questions addressed in this paper is what material is most important to reduce the risk of ad hoc designs, all too prevalent in current practice.

Whatever approach is taken, it is difficult to convey real understanding of a number of important concepts:

* the complexity inherent in apparently simple embedded software
* the need for appropriate structure at all stages of the software life cycle to effectively manage this complexity
* the difficulty of capturing requirements, and the need for a sound mathematical basis for expressing requirements in a form reviewable by people knowledgeable about the kind of system being controlled - e.g chemical plant, assembly line, airplane, washing machine, etc.
* how time should be dealt during development, and how it is dealt with in practice

The remainder of this paper is concerned with the characteristics of the real-time embedded systems domain, its place in undergraduate curricula, the description of the evolution of a one semester undergraduate course in this domain, and discussion of some of the issues that arise in the context of the design of this course.

2. Characteristics of the Real-Time Embedded Systems Domain

Software for real-time systems always has the first characteristic below, and often has the other four as well [6]:

* Timeliness Actions must be performed by specified times. Making the meaning of this precise characterizes different parts of this domain. In soft real-time systems, deadlines are flexible. In hard real-time, there is no flexibility, and in the hardest of constraints, actions must happen at specific times, not just by a specific time.
* Dynamic internal structure Because desired real-time system behaviour may vary with time (communications links may go down, sensors may fail, some part of a process may have to be changed, changes may have to be made while the software is running, etc.), real-time software must be dynamic, in the sense that it must be capable of coping with this variation.
* Reactiveness Many real-time systems function in an environment in which the order and time of occurrence of external events are not always

predictable. Whatever external events occur, the system must react appropriately.

* Concurrency The physical environment within which a real-time system functions is inherently continuous and concurrent. Therefore, the software that interacts with this world must itself be concurrent, or at least must appear to be. This is often best achieved by rendering the software as a set of concurrent or pseudo-concurrent processes.
* Distribution Many real-time systems (e.g., telecommunications systems) are distributed in the sense that multiple processors at physically distinct sites are connected via a network that is slow compared to the processor speeds. Both processors and communications links may fail spontaneously, and other complications may arise, such as information becoming out of date due to limited network throughput. Solving the problems associated with distribution of computing resources can be the most demanding part of real-time software development.

In general, the focus of this paper is on real-time embedded systems, which are reactive and whose output values are intended to be used in the control of the larger system in which they are embedded. How the five characteristics should be presented to undergraduates will be discussed in greater detail later in the paper.

3. Real-Time Embedded Systems in Undergraduate Curricula

The question is how much material can and should be taught to undergraduates. Because of the detail intensive nature of many aspects of real-time embedded software development, there is a strong case to be made for learning some aspects on the job. This also argues in favour of an apprenticeship style of learning, either in a co-op program, or as an engineer-in-training for several years after graduation. Current practice is based almost entirely on lessons learned and passed on by word of mouth, and to a lesser extent, in professional books and articles. There is very little material oriented toward the support of undergraduate courses in this area. Courses that are offered tend to cover only a portion of the whole domain, so a student may do a course in which most of the effort is put into developing a small real-time executive, and may come away feeling competent to design real-time embedded systems in general. In reality, the student in such a course gets a heavy dose of detail in those issues related to real-time executives, often at the expense of an understanding of other areas that are important to real-time embedded system development.

In which undergraduate curricula might material related to the development of real-time embedded systems be found? It seems most logical in computer engineering, although computer engineers developing such systems will need to work in teams with others who have expertise in the larger system in which the computer and software are being embedded. In computer science, there is no particular reason to emphasize this area, nor do students have the necessary background or time. In other branches of science and engineering, it is a peripheral issue.

One approach to education in this area is to encourage students to take undergraduate degrees in a field not related to computing, and then to do a Master's in software engineering, specializing in real-time embedded software. This has the advantage of creating a team member with an understanding of both the subject area of an application (e.g. a mechanical engineer for engine control) and of how to build good real-time embedded software. At the undergraduate level, such students might pick up some rudimentary understanding of the topic, perhaps enough to realize the need for further education if they are going to work seriously in this area.

On the other hand, many practitioners in these areas have little software background, and little awareness of the need for a deeper understanding of how real-time embedded software should be developed. As well, Master's programs in software engineering are often open only to people with undergraduate degrees in computer science. Thus, while this path is attractive in theory, it may be less so in practice, and it still leaves open the alternative path of a specialization at the undergraduate level, much in the same way that electrical engineers today specialize in power or communications or digital electronics.

The attraction of the undergraduate degree as the sole qualification is that people are out in the work force sooner, and then will find out sooner if their careers really are going to be in the area in which they have been educated. On the other hand, in today's job markets, employers look for and find people with more than the minimum qualifications for the jobs that need doing. The argument in favour of undergraduate specialization is strongest when jobs are plentiful, so people are less likely to do graduate work, and employers are more willing to provide on-the-job training.

4. Description and Evolution of the Course

In the winter term of 1993/94, an undergraduate course entitled Real-Time Embedded System Design was given at RMC for the first time. The emphasis in the course is on software. The calendar description of the course is as follows:

Definition, structure, and properties of embedded real-time systems. Typical applications. Review of related concepts, including tasking models, context switching, interrupts, and the Ada rendez-vous. Specification and design methods for real-time systems and applicable CASE (Computer-Aided-Software-Engineering) tools. Specification and verification of timing. Scheduling and schedulability analysis. Real-time operating systems, kernels, and programming languages. Fault tolerance, critical races, deadlock and livelock. Host-target development. Distributed systems.

The course is 15 weeks long, with 3 periods of lecture and two periods of lab work each week. The course is only available in the software stream of the computer engineering program at RMC [5], and it is offered in the last semester of fourth year, so the students have a relatively strong background in both software and hardware development [5]. They know Ada, C++ and assembly language. They have an understanding of object oriented techniques, elements of several software processes, a variety of software work products, and the properties of operating systems. On the other hand, they are not familiar with many details - for example, what happens when an interrupt is triggered in a multi-tasking real-time executive.

The first two weeks of the course are spent learning and making changes to a small program in assembly language that does context switching triggered by interrupts. The rationale is that by picking one of the many issues that have little theoretical basis and that may be overwhelmed by details, and treating it in a way that displays the details but does not require the students to create every detail themselves, it will be easier to give the students an appreciation of other sources of detail based complexity without taking the time to immerse them in all the details. The time to cover the details is not available in any case. In addition, context switching is not immediate, and the effects of delays may be unexpected, so this exercise introduces the students to the complexities associated with time management in real-time software.

About two weeks is spent on the concept of periodic tasks running at different task rates, and the possibility of using Rate Monotonic Analysis (RMA) to guarantee schedulability of such tasks ([3], Ch. 11). This material is motivated by the presentation of a real example: a high level view of the task set of the CF-188 aircraft [11] (the CF-188 is the Canadian version of the F-18). The CF-188 computer system design is over 20 years old, but its structure is still relevant and interesting for the students, in part because the CF-188 is the principal fighter aircraft of the Canadian Forces. The practical impossibility of applying RMA to the distributed computer system of the CF-188 is discussed in detail. The view taken is that RMA is just one of many ways in which schedulability can be guaranteed, and that better ways are still the subject of active research, so this is one reason schedulability analysis is not widely used in practice. It is important that students see at least one approach to performance guarantees, so that when they design systems later, they will not overlook the possibility out of simple ignorance.

The contents of the remaining 11 weeks of the course changed completely between the first and second offerings of the course.

The first time the course was offered, several analysis and design approaches based on data flow diagram techniques [3], and a sample real-time executive were taught (JNX [4]). A CASE tool (not named, since the version used is now completely out of date) was chosen, partly on the basis of its low cost availability on a PC platform, and partly because it appeared to support the Hatley/Pirbhai [1] and Ward/Mellor [2] analysis and design methods. In practice, the CASE tool chosen turned out to have serious deficiencies from a software engineering perspective, and so using it with the students became primarily an exercise in identifying and understanding the nature of the deficiencies. To give one example, data flow diagram methods depend on maintaining a data dictionary which is tightly bound to the diagrams, and without which, the diagrams lose most of their meaning. The tool provided almost no support for making changes to the data dictionary when parts of a diagram hierarchy were changed. The support that it did provide was just enough to allow the user to make whatever changes were needed by hand, meaning that out-of-date entries could easily be left in the data dictionary. While it is impossible to entirely prevent this possibility, a good tool will make it easy for the user to tidy up the effects of changes in an evolving design.

For the second year of the course, a decision was made that it would be better to teach an alternative real-time design method supported by a CASE tool in a combination that offered better prospects of being useful in real projects. Also, data flow diagram based methods do not support the information hiding principle very well, and in particular, do not reinforce the idea of encapsulating interactions with real world objects in software objects, and require a major change of representation at the implementation stage. The alternative approach chosen was based on Real-Time Object-Oriented Modeling (ROOM) [6]. ROOM is supported by a CASE tool called ObjecTime [7].

ObjecTime is one of the few CASE tools specifically targeted at the real-time embedded software development market, so it was a natural candidate. Also, it is doing well in its market niche, suggesting that the ROOM approach is attractive to practitioners. Another reason for choosing ROOM is that ObjecTime Ltd. offers an excellent university support program. The final reason for choosing ROOM was that it integrates and reinforces a number of concepts the students have seen in their earlier software courses, and provides one particular carefully thought out view of how to organize real-time embedded software. The essential feature of this view is to structure the software as a network of collaborating finite state machines.

5. Discussion of ROOM-based Course Content

ROOM makes particular decisions on how to deal with each of the characteristics of the real-time embedded software domain. These decisions influence the course content, since they provide a reference point for discussions of alternative approaches and of other steps that could be part of the development process. It is important for students to have such a reference point, as otherwise it is easy for them to become confused by the multitude of possiblities. On the other hand, ROOM and ObjecTime are complex, and so the students must spend a significant amount of time becoming familiar with them.

In general terms, ROOM is based on actors (objects with an independent thread of control) connected to each other by binding a port on one actor to a port on a second actor, using a common protocol. An actor can thus communicate independently with two or more other actors. Actor behaviour is defined by a variant of Statecharts [8] called ROOMcharts. One of the important concepts in ROOM is the use of hierarchies. Examples include the possibility of actors containing other actors, actors and protocols inheriting properties from other actors and protocols respectively, and the use of states that may contain other states. Hierarchy in ROOM is more complex than anything the students have seen up to that point, but it is also consistent with what they have learned before. Figures 1, 2 and 3 show parts of sample designs derived from alarm clock requirements [10]. Figure 1 is the top level actor diagram, showing the decompostion of an actor called AlarmSystem into an actor called ClockDisplayAndButtons that represents the user's view of the alarm clock, and another actor called ClockSoftwareAndTimer, which will (in part) contain the software that controls the alarm clock. Figures 2 and 3 show the next level down in the actor hierarchy for

ClockDisplayAndButtons and ClockSoftwareAndTimer respectively. Each of the actors in these three figures contains its own hierarchical behaviour diagram. The three figures show the encapsulation of hardware devices and their supporting software. They also establish a high level context for the design of the rest of the software, which there is no space to show here.

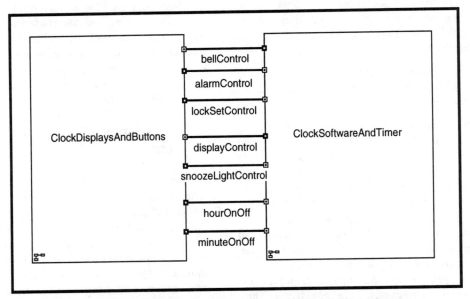

Figure 1. ROOM-based top level decomposition of AlarmSystem

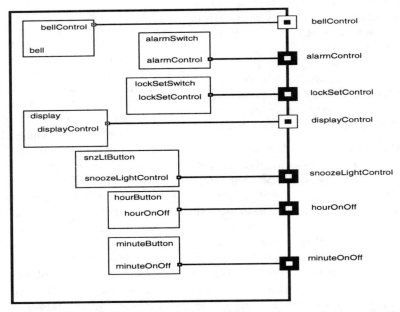

Figure 2. ROOM-based second level decomposition of ClockDisplaysAndButtons

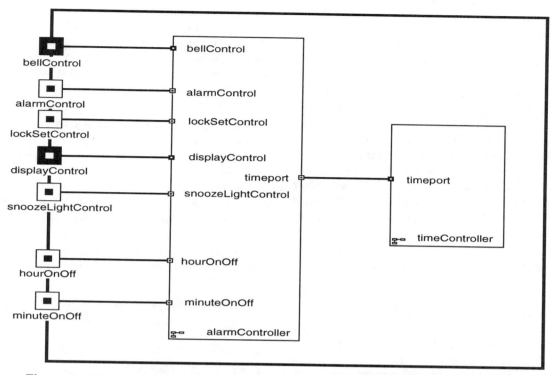

Figure 3. ROOM-based second-level decomposition of ClockSoftwareAndTimer

Following is a discussion of how the five properties (timeliness, dynamic internal structure, reactiveness, concurrency and distribution) that characterize the real-time embedded systems domain are presented in the current version of the course.

5.1. Timeliness, Dynamic Structure and Reactiveness

Timeliness is dealt with in ROOM by providing a well structured design that facilitates early performance estimation, and by providing a timeout service that is most useful in soft real-time systems and in managing fault tolerance. Special support for guaranteeing schedulability of tasks prior to run-time will be provided in future versions of ObjecTime. On the other hand, industry practice today demands this for only a subset of real-time applications. As discussed earlier, two weeks of the course are spent on the RMA approach to guaranteeing schedulability. This is done partly because the CF-188 example used shows what can happen to timing properties as software evolves through use, but primarily to ensure that the students are aware that

performance guarantees are possible for those situations where they are needed.

A dynamic internal structure is provided in ROOM by allowing actors to be created and destroyed at run-time as well as to be dynamically rolled in and out of predefined relationships or "roles". While this is not the only approach to a dynamic internal structure, it is one of the easiest to grasp, and so is attractive for undergraduate teaching. It is difficult in the context of one course to present alternatives, and to explain why alternatives may be difficult to implement. The issues are the possible lack of availability of enough resources needed to keep all options alive at all times, the need to reconfigure and change software on the fly, without shutting the system down, and the difficulty of anticipating prior to run-time all the different patterns that may be needed as the software adapts to changing circumstances. On this latter point, one could argue that good engineering demands such anticipation, and ROOM in fact requires that all valid structural patterns be anticipated at design time. Nonetheless, the level of complexity that arises in real-time embedded software makes it attractive to try to design around the need to expose all possible complexities in the design. These are subtle arguments, and difficult to convey without benefit of experience.

Reactiveness is supported in ROOM by the behaviour model of an actor. Actors react to messages that arrive at their ports. Reaction to a message involves run-to-completion semantics, so the only uncertainty is the availability of the resources needed to allow an actor to respond in a timely fashion to the streams of messages arriving at its ports. In other words, an overload may annul the reactiveness property. One of the advantages of the ROOM approach for undergraduate teaching is that it makes clear that reactiveness is both a global and a local property, in that the whole system's reactiveness depends on the reactivity of individual actors, which in turn depends on global allocation of sufficient resources to each actor.

5.2. Concurrency and Distribution

Concurrency is supported in ROOM by the independent threads of control of the actors. This allows the concurrency of physical processes outside the computer to be modeled in the software. It is important for the students to understand that, at run-time, this concurrency may only be pseudo-concurrency, and to understand how that pseudo-concurrency is achieved. To some extent, this is hidden by the ROOM approach, meaning that the students must be exposed to some of the underlying mechanisms that are needed to support execution of ObjecTime models. The amount of detail that must be presented to do this directly in the ObjecTime context is too large to be manageable in an undergraduate course, so this reinforces the decision to spend the first two weeks of the course on a context switching exercise. On the other hand, it was necessary to drop that part of the course dealing with JNX [4] since there was not enough time to do it and to do ROOM. In partial compensation, ObjecTime contains a Run Time System, and the students become somewhat familiar with that. As well, they learn about the high level synchronization methods available between actors in ROOM.

Actors represent an object-oriented form of tasking. Although tasking in some form is by far the dominant means of handling concurrency in real-time systems, it is not the only way. Its primary disadvantage is that it requires scheduling at execution time. This introduces uncertainties which can be removed by doing the scheduling before run-time. The problem in teaching details of this approach to undergraduates is that it is still the subject of active research, so the ROOM approach may be better pedagogically until the research is further advanced. Scheduling can be handled by estimating

probable loads, as civil engineers do for bridges. The exact arrival times of vehicles don't matter, because the system capacity is engineered for peak load. On the other hand, bank and airline transaction processing systems seem to have solved this problem - perhaps by trial and error over a number of years. However, trial and error is not an acceptable design approach for safety critical real-time systems.

One reason for the lack of the safety margins which are characteristic of classical engineering disciplines is a lack of engineering education/culture among computer professionals, particularly computer scientists. For example, bridge builders tend to use safety margins of 3 to 4, particularly on new types of designs. Such safety margins are unimaginable in most software systems. Another factor is the persistent and overwhelming pressure to add more functionality to an existing system and thus take away any safety factor built into CPU capacity.

The ROOM approach is probably the best approach to handling concurrency in today's practice. As well, there is a need to make concurrency visible in the software while debugging, and this is especially important for undergraduates, who may be having difficulty visualizing what is going on. The ObjecTime tool makes concurrency visible in the static designs by the simple fact of there being multiple actors in nearly all designs. It also provides an ability to execute and monitor ObjecTime models through animation and daemons that can inject and monitor events. This ability to "touch and feel" a model through ObjecTime's run-time environment has enormous potential pedagogical value, but it is difficult to get the full benefit of this potential in a course, since the amount of work needed to build an ObjecTime design and a test harness for that design is considerable. Some of our students did get to that stage in their designs, and those that did were uniformly enthusiastic about it. In future years, we may choose to provide already completed designs and partial test harnesses and ask the students to use them to find flaws in the designs.

Distribution is handled naturally in ROOM by actors. Since actors communicate with each other over defined bindings linking pairs of ports, it makes very little difference conceptually whether the actors are both on one CPU, or whether they are on different CPUs. At the practical, implementation, level, things are not so simple. On the other hand, in an undergraduate course, it is just as well to suppress some of that complexity, since it is necessary to understand how to develop centralized real-time embedded software before trying to deal with the complexities of distributed software. This again makes the ROOM approach attractive for teaching undergraduates.

6. Other Observations

6.1. ROOM, Data-Flow and Tools

Even though the emphasis in the course is on the ROOM approach, it is tempting to keep at least an overview of one of the real-time data flow methods (using [1], [2] or [3]) in the course, on the basis that data flow methods are still widely used, and students should learn something of their strengths and weaknesses, if only to be able to better defend approaches like the ROOM approach. Also, although data flow diagram approaches are hard to apply in practice, they are relatively easy to learn, as are the CASE tools that support them. This makes it possible to consider keeping some data flow based material in the course, although this is risky because of the distraction it creates, and because it reduces the time available to learn ROOM and ObjecTime.

This last issue is a major factor in the course partly because ObjecTime is a professional tool, and so requires extensive use to gain real proficiency. A simplified tool that is intended for use by undergraduates might be an attractive option if it were available. On the other hand, students are used to using compilers and software development environments from companies like Microsoft and Borland, and the students in computer engineering at RMC in particular become familiar with the Mentor Graphics toolset for circuit design, starting with elementary circuits and progressing to VLSI design. They become proficient in the parts of these toolsets that they need, and develop an awareness of the capabilities of other parts. There is a strong argument in favour of this kind of incremental approach to learning about tools in an undergraduate curriculum. The complexities of professional tools then do not come as a surprise, and there is even the possibility that a tool learned up to a certain point as an undergrad will become directly useful in the workplace.

6.2. The Complexity of Real-Time Software

Real-time software is more complex than might initially be expected. The complexity level can be bewildering. For example, the software used to control a modern central office telephone switch typically exceeds 10 million lines of high-level language code. These systems are developed and maintained by teams consisting of hundreds or even thousands of programmers.

To a layman, familiar only with the relatively unsophisticated nature of telephones and telephone usage, such numbers may come as a surprise. Where does this complexity come from? The answer lies in the various characteristics of real-time systems that were described earlier (concurrency, distribution, etc.). For instance, we demand extreme levels of availability and reliability from our telephone service (a standard requirement for availabilty of a telephone switch is that, over a 40 year period, it must not be out of service for a cumulative total of more than 2 hours!). Such stringent requirements imply elaborate software to detect and recover from faults.

6.3. The Need for Structure in Design and Implementation

In many existing real-time embedded systems, the only structure available is whatever there is in the code. One of the virtues of ObjecTime is that it supports the possibility of explicitly preserving the design structure even after system release, so that all modifications can be made at the design level. There are practical difficulties in applying this in many circumstances, but it is important for the students to understand that the possibility exists, so they may be able to bring it to reality in systems that they design later themselves. ROOM provides a particular view of structure which is relatively easy to understand given an understanding of the basic concepts that underlie it. On the other hand, attempting to derive the equivalent of a ROOM structure diagram by examining code may be compared to trying to recreate the Mona Lisa by examining individual molecules of paint. Even for well documented code, it is very difficult to discern high-level structure once it is cast into the form of pointers, compilation modules, and usage dependencies. Much high-level structure actually gets resolved into a decomposition into compilation units; the relationship between these can only be properly established by looking at "make" files. Other forms of structure are appropriate for design recovery. For example, identifying concurrent elements may be very hard, and yet this is the top level of structure in ROOM. In the context of the course, all of the above really means that it is not possible to talk about design recovery.

6.4. Definition of Requirements

There are advantages to using ROOM to capture requirements because requirements for complex real-time systems tend to be incomplete, inconsistent, and, sometimes, technically infeasible. Forcing people into defining requirements operationally (i.e., through executable models) quickly exposes such requirements flaws. It has nearly the same effect as defining requirements using formal mathematical propositions, because executability implies formality. Also, any design that takes place during requirements capture must be considered discardable. Emotional attachment to possibly immature designs only occurs if much effort was expanded in their construction; one of the objectives of ROOM/ObjecTime is to facilitate the creation of lightweight designs, so that there is little reluctance to throw them away if they are inappropriate. On the other hand, experience with even early designs helps to create, in the designers' minds, an intuition and a feel for the problem at hand that can prove invaluable.

On the other hand, for this to work, the users who review the requirements must be able to read them expressed as a high-level design in ObjecTime. At the very least, this requires familiarity with ObjecTime concepts and notations. In some cases, users either will not or cannot acquire such familiarity, and some other form of expression of requirements is necessary. Also, as a matter of practical cost-effectiveness, it may be advantageous to have the requirements influence the design, since if the initial attempt at design is a good choice, it might as well be continued as the basis for the final design.

It is important to make undergraduates understand these issues, and to teach them different ways of expressing requirements, including (in the context of this course) the possibility of expressing them using ObjecTime. Prior to this course, students only see requirements expressed in natural language. In this course, there is an opportunity to teach them that more precise mechanisms for expressing requirements exist by showing them examples. The two examples chosen are requirements capture in ObjecTime, and a design independent method using mathematical logic and functions in tables to express output values in terms of current state and input values.

The design independent method is one developed as part of the Software Cost Reduction (SCR) project at the US Naval Research Labs (NRL) and further refined at Queen's [9]. A small example SCR-style requirements document is provided for a simple alarm clock [10]. The students are only required to read and understand it. In doing so, they learn the basics of the SCR approach. They often start by looking at it only briefly, assuming they know how an alarm clock works, and proceed to design based on their intuitive understanding. Since the precise details given in the SCR style requirements document normally do not correspond to this intuitive

understanding, this becomes a real learning experience. A further element of the learning experience is the need to do actual design: to decide how this relatively precise set of requirements should be mapped on to an ObjecTime design.

6.5. Dealing with Time

In the SCR approach, required timing behaviour is explicitly given. SCR does not specify a design approach. In most design approaches, including ROOM, there are no specific provisions for translating timing requirements into time budgets and forecasts of the expected performance of the finished product. In many cases, an intial estimate is made that the computing resources chosen for the system will be adequate to provide the performance needed to meet timing requirements (which are often not explicitly specified), and then no further attention is paid to this issue until testing of the final implememtation begins.

Good engineering practice would make this whole process more predictable, but there do not seem to be good techniques available today to make the needed predictions. It is thus difficult to teach much about it at the undergraduate level. One option that could be followed is to present ways in which timing simulators can be built and carried through the design process, but to date, this has not been done in the course as offered at RMC, primarily because priority is given to other material and because of the general weakness of available material in this area.

6.6. Comparison of the Two Versions of the Course

Because the class size in this course at RMC is quite small (typically less than 20 students), and because each version of the course has only been offered once at the time of writing, it has not been possible to measure the benefits of approaching the subject one way versus the other. As well, the only real way to judge this would be to measure the effectiveness of those students called on to work in this area in the years after graduation, and it is much too early to do that.

On the other hand, some subjective impressions can be given.

In the first version of the course, the students felt that the different parts of the course were too disparate, and did not relate clearly enough to each other. Also, they were dubious about the value of learning a method that did not seem to be fully supported by the CASE tool used. They were generally willing to accept the fact that better CASE tools were available to support the Ward-Mellor and Hatley-Pirbhai methods, and that it was important to make sure that any tool used was worth the effort of using it.

In the second version of the course, there were complaints about the time needed to really understand how to use ROOM. There were no similar complaints in the first version of the course, as the data flow diagram based methods are much simpler to learn, if not to apply. The basics of ROOM can be learned almost as easily, but ROOM is so much richer that the students tended to feel that they were still just scratching the surface of real understanding even at the end of the course. On the other hand, the strong students in the course were able to make much more effective use of the ObjecTime tool in carrying out the beginnings of a design than was possible with the CASE tool used in the first version of the course.

7. Conclusion

Developing software for real-time embedded systems is quite different from developing software for other domains. Assuming there is sufficient demand for the graduates, there is sufficient domain specific knowledge needed to justify treating it as a specialization at the undergraduate level. On the other hand, design approaches that are known to work well in practice are only just beginning to appear, so undergraduate curricula in this area are anything but stable.

This paper has examined two approaches to teaching good engineering practice in this area, the second of which is relatively novel, and looks very promising. Each of the five characteristics of real-time systems is better addressed in the ROOM-based approach than it was in the first approach. As good practice evolves, a stronger theoretical basis for design will appear, approaches like

ROOM will evolve and improve, and undergraduate curricula will evolve and improve with them.

References

[1]   D.J. Hatley, Pirbhai, I.A., *Strategies for Real-Time System Specification*, Dorset House, New York, 1987

[2]   P.T. Ward, S.J. Mellor, *Structured Development for Real-Time Systems*, Volumes 1, 2 & 3, Yourdon Press, New York, 1985

[3]   H. Gomaa, *Software Design Methods for Concurrent and Real-Time Systems*, Addison-Wesley, Reading, Mass, 1993

[4]   R.J.A. Buhr and D.L. Bailey, *Real-Time Systems*, Draft Text, Carleton University, Ottawa, 1993

[5]   T. Shepard, "Software Engineering in an Undergraduate Computer Engineering Program", Proc. 7th SEI Conference on Software Engineering Education, J. Diaz-Herrera, ed, Springer-Verlag, New York, 1994, pp. 23-34

[6]   B. Selic, G. Gullekson, P. Ward, *Real-Time Object-Oriented Modeling*, John Wiley and Sons, New York, 1994

[7]   ObjecTime 4.2 Document Set, Objectime Ltd., Kanata, Ontario, Canada, 1994

[8]   D. Harel, "On Visual Formalisms", Communications of the ACM, Vol.31, No. 5, May 1988, pp. 514-530

[9]   A. J. Van Schouwen, "The A-7 Requirements Model: Re-examination for Real-Time Systems and an Application to Monitoring Systems", M.Sc. Thesis, Technical Report QUCIS 90-276, Revision 3, Queen's University, Kingston, Ontario, Canada, January 1991

[10]   P. Matelski, J. McKim, "Alarm Clock Requirements", Internal teaching note, Queen's University, Kingston, Ont., Canada, January 11, 1988

[11]   D. Falardeau, "Schedulability Analysis in Rate Monotonic Based Systems with Application to the CF-188", M.Eng Thesis, Royal Military College of Canada, Kingston, Ont., May 1994

Chapter 2
Real-Time Curriculum Issues

A Model for Real-Time Systems Curriculum

Wolfgang A. Halang
Faculty of Electrical Engineering
Fernuniversität
D-58084 Hagen, Germany
wolfgang.halang@fernuni-hagen.de

Janusz Zalewski
Dept. of Computer Science
Embry-Riddle Aeronautical University
Daytona Beach, FL 32114-3900, U.S.A.
zalewski@db.erau.edu

Abstract

An outline of an undergraduate syllabus for the education of real-time systems engineers is given, in a broader context of software engineering, to meet three high-level educational objectives: depth of study, breadth of study, and curriculum flexibility. The model is based on a 4-layer paradigm for course contents, comprising: real-time development methodologies and environments, real-time programming languages, operating system kernels, and real-time hardware architectures. ACM/IEEE-CS "Computing Curricula 1991" framework is used to describe the course contents. Accompanying laboratory work is outlined and suggestions for establishing a laboratory with advanced, but low-cost, hardware and software are provided. Suggestions are also made on prerequisites, course materials, and areas for possible graduate research.

1. Introduction

The significance of real-time systems is rapidly growing. The vast spectrum of these systems can be characterised by just a few examples of increasing complexity: controllers in washing machines, air traffic control and air defense systems, control and safety systems of nuclear power plants, and finally future space borne systems like the Space Station. Furthermore, the competitiveness and prosperity of nations now depends on the early application and efficient utilization of computer integrated manufacturing systems (CIM), of which real-time systems are an essential and decisive part. The importance of such systems on the well-being of people requires considerable effort in research, development and education.

Related job market demands have always been influential in starting curriculum developments. Morover, the observations and own experience of the authors prove that other factors contribute to the general need of having a precisely defined curriculum:

- a gap between EE and CS education particularly from real-time systems point of view
- insufficient students' knowledge of contemporary CASE tools, which have a great potential for real-time systems design
- inadequate knowledge of principles of team work.

In order to catch up with current rapid progress in research, development, and application of real-time systems, it is imperative to provide the best possible education of future real-time engineers. Adequately educated and specialized graduates will be able to effectively strengthen the industries in their countries by innovations and so contribute to the competitiveness of their products and services on the world market. The above arguments underscore why it is timely and important to take a closer look at the education of real-time systems engineers.

The objective of courses for the education of real-time engineers is to discuss topics and problems encountered when developing embedded systems for hard real-time environments. With the latter term industrial, scientific, and military areas of application are meant, which are characterized by strict timing conditions, that must not be violated under any circumstances. In contrast to this, commercial systems, e.g. for automatic banking and airline reservations, only need to fulfill soft real-time requirements, i.e. although they are designed with the objective of timely response, the user may face failure of the completion of his transactions.

Despite the growing demand for real-time systems engineers and growing significance of real-time applications, there is no current published curriculum for this course. In the latest revision of the ACM/IEEE-CS Report "Computing Curricula 1991" [21], which presents detailed descriptions of common requirements and advanced topics for most of the computing subject areas, there is no corresponding description for a Real-Time Systems course, even though the Real-Time Systems area is mentioned twice, as a part of another common requirements topic, and as a separate advanced topic. Also in [4], a separate unit, Embedded Real-Time Systems, is mentioned with merely a few lines of topics description. This paper attempts to build a model of an undergraduate course in Real-Time Systems, in order to provide guidance for those who want to implement such a course.

2. Educational Objectives

When designing a model curriculum, it is particularly important to establish a set of educational goals, which will determine the scope of this model and subsequent decisions on curriculum contents and implementation. All our objectives are dependent on the basic assumption that this course is an upper level undergraduate course nested in the Software Engineering curriculum.

For such a technical subject and highly specialized course as Real-Time Systems, educational goals should be very focused and narrow, on the highest level. In these terms, the goal is to build a course model which can serve as a vehicle to give the students an appropriate amount of professional skills to make them highly competitive on a job market. The emphasis is on a technical component. Thus, in terms of [21], this goal ensures the depth of study.

Because this course is placed in a wider context of Software Engineering courses, it is assumed that students already have sufficient technical background gained in the prerequisite courses. Thus, one natural purpose of real-time systems course is to integrate this knowledge, build on it, and demonstrate how it can be applied. This goal ensures the breadth of study.

On a low level, it is assumed that this model will be used as a template only, to help in designing more specific curricula. One example of expressing objectives in this form, for a real-time systems course, can be found in [4]:

- Comprehension of the significant problems in the analysis, design, and construction of embedded real-time systems.
- Ability to produce small systems that involve interrupt handling, low-level input and output, concurrency, and hard timing requirements, preferably in a high-level language.

Formulating such specific objectives is highly dependent on the nature of local circumstances, and must be left to the implementation of the course. There are two categories of factors, which the model must be prepared

to absorb, in order to allow for successful implementations. First, the audience of the course can vary widely, depending on:

- assumed level of the course
- students' background, their individual goals, and assumed profile for graduates
- differences between preparing students for entry into the professional life, to apply knowledge to solving real life problems, or just preparing them for graduate studies
- decision to increase students' awareness of especially high rate of change in technology of real-time systems
- the desired extent of exposing students to a diversity of stable concepts.

The second category of factors is related to the teaching environment and encompasses all issues which allow to accomodate a variety of departmental preferences and policies, institutional differences, pedagogical priorities, local constraints (like faculty expertise, computing resources, general infrastructure, tools availability, etc.), and last but not least, needs of local industry. To leave enough freedom for future decisions to select proper objectives of that nature, the model must be flexible, to allow for changes, and open to additions.

In summary, the following three objectives are taken into account to create this model:

- content's emphasis on technical issues (depth of study)
- integration of new and former knowledge (breadth of study)
- openness and flexibility.

3. Methodology and the Basic Model

The general framework of the ACM/IEEE-CS "Computing Curricula 1991" [21] forms a very useful vehicle to express a model of curriculum. The entire field of Computing is divided into nine constituents (subject areas). Each subject area is divided into several knowledge units (each covering one important subject), which are further partitioned in a number of lecture topics (smallest modules). The basic idea behind such structure is to allow different academic programs to configure the course in different ways (this ensures flexibility). In addition, for each knowledge unit, several additional attributes are provided to characterize the curriculum: general description, recurring concepts, suggested labs, prerequisites. Unfortunately, in this framework, Real-Time Systems is not a separate subject area. It is included in the Operating Systems subject area, as a knowledge unit named "Distributed and Real-Time Systems", and mentioned additionally as an advanced topic, without providing its contents.

Similar categorization, though limited to the core curriculum of Software Engineering only [4], includes "Embedded Real-Time Systems" as one of twenty one different units (corresponding roughly to knowledge units from [21]), giving a short outline of its topics. In this authors' opinion, the course in Real-Time Systems should ultimately focus on teaching how to develop real-time systems, and as such falls well within the context of Software Engineering curriculum. Therefore the latter categorization is taken here as the basis.

Thus, the basic models of software development cycle are all applicable to Real-Time Systems. There are, however, many peculiarities in real-time systems development, which are normally taken into account very rarely or not at all for traditional software development. Due to very specific timing requirements, which distinguish real-time systems from all other classes of software, and very special reliability and safety concerns, particularly important are the implementation stages: selection and use of appropriate programming languages (bearing real-time constructs), functionality of real-time operating system kernels, and underlying hardware architectures.

This leads to the layered view of the curriculum, presented elsewhere [23] and tested both for real-time systems and general curriculum development [13]. All components of this model must be present to some extent in every curriculum, perhaps unevenly, in different percentage. Every curriculum must integrate software and hardware knowledge and skills in the following four areas:

- Real-Time Specification and Design Methodologies and Environments
- Real-Time Languages' Constructs
- Real-Time Kernels
- Real-Time Hardware Architectures.

Combining the high-level software topics with lower-level architecture topics in one course is indispensable for Real-Time Systems.

It is also assumed that every course, in particular the one on Real-Time Systems, must be a part of a larger course sequence. So, in addition to planning this specific course, one has to consider which particular topics need to be covered in prerequisite courses. Therefore,

in the curriculum there must be room for suggestions for the specific material to be included into lower-level courses corresponding to the above mentioned four key areas. This course in turn will provide background for advanced topics which are out of its scope and should be covered in graduate classes or individual studies, for example: Real-Time Distributed Systems; Fault Tolerance, Reliability, and Safety; Formal Methods; Real-Time Databases and Expert Systems.

Below, the ACM/IEEE-CS framework is applied to the paradigm of the layered model for developing the real-time systems course.

4. Outline of the Syllabus

At the beginning of a course or a series of courses on real-time systems, there should stand a historical survey and an overview about the importance of the subject for industrial applications. Then, the basic requirements with regard to the timing behavior, namely *reponsiveness, timeliness,* and *predictability* [25], and fundamental concepts like real-time mode of computer operation, process types, process coupling, and interrupt systems are introduced, and the time conditions encountered in process control environments are classified. The discussion of the two methods at hand to achieve timely and (quasi-) simultaneous behavior of real-time software, i.e. the cyclic executive approach and asynchronous multitasking, concludes the introduction to the material.

4.1. Development Environment Level

The first major part of the course or course series is dedicated to real-time methodologies and integrated development environments, i.e. software tools, for the realization of embedded and real-time automation projects. They allow for the independent structuring and description of a system and for the specification of the hardware and software architectures, including timing constraints. By taking also hardware and timing aspects into consideration, these tools distinguish themselves from sole software specification and CASE tools, which are covered in computing science courses.

Software tools are introduced which support all phases of engineering work, namely requirements engineering, system design, implementation, verification, and validation, and provide automatically the accompanying documentation. In particular, on one hand, software design objects such as modules, procedures, tasks, data, and interfaces, on the other hand, hardware design objects, such as boards, signals, bus connections, and computers themselves are described, and most importantly, the relations between the software and hardware design objects, i.e. the relations between the logical and the physical structure of a system are presented. Thus, the main difficulties of using separate design tools for the development of software and hardware components can be overcome.

Such integrated project support environments are fully computer supported. Using a specification language and a model suitable for the considered project, which is selected out of a number of available models, the system engineer describes the problem, the objectives, and the methods for realizing the solution.

The knowledge based environments allow for the stepwise refinement of a design and, thus, support various design levels. One of the first such environments was EPOS [12], the most suitable for classroom use due to its advanced integrated development support. There is a whole variety of tools available nowadays, one discussed in this book [17].

4.2. Real-Time Languages

The next major part of the course is dedicated to programming in high-level real-time languages. It starts with describing the requirements of such languages and then follows the different lines of development these languages have taken, namely, extension of existing mathematically oriented constructs by real-time features, definition of new high-level languages, and specialized languages and program generators aimed towards meeting the programming needs in specific application areas.

Subsequently, the major languages in this field are introduced, compared with each other, and evaluated. Then, as an example, one of these languages must be studied more thoroughly. By carrying through a number of programming exercises, the students are to gain proficiency in this language and especially in using its real-time and process control elements.

The selection of a real-time programming language [3, 5, 6, 16, 22] mainly depends on technical features and the availability of appropriate programming systems for educational use. Pearl [14] and Real-Time Euclid [20] appear to be the best suited real-time languages, from the viewpoints of both teaching clean, structured concepts and having expressive power to describe timing behavior for applications in industrial automation.

Ada [1] and Pearl are the only high-level real-time languages readily applicable in industrial control environments, since they have been implemented on a wide range of computers including the major 16- and 32-bit microprocessor series, on which most contemporary process control computers are based. Although unknown in the U.S., Pearl, due to its simple syntax, which resembles Pascal and other structured languages, simplifies teaching for students with some background in programming, since it is sufficient for them to concentrate on real-time specific features.

Furthermore, Pearl and Ada have an additional advantage, because they allow the programming of networks and distributed systems fully within the framework of the language: the various program modules can be assigned to the nodes, logical connections established, and transmission protocols specified. Moreover, language facilities are provided to detail the dynamic reconfiguration of a system in case of errors. For a more detailed justification of the selection of Pearl as the real-time language, the reader is referred to [7], where it is compared with its major competitors and especially with Ada.

One main objective of this part of the course should be to stress that assembly language programming can be renounced, since high-level real-time programming systems have reached a stage which makes their usage feasible for even the most time-critical applications. This can be shown by considering experimental data, which reveal that assembly coding can improve the runtime and storage efficiencies of high-level language programs only by single digit percentages.

4.3. Real-Time Kernels

Initially some notions are briefly summarized, which are already treated in courses on operating systems, but that may still be unfamiliar to students of other disciplines. This includes the notion of a task as a unit of concurrency. Further topics in this context are task scheduling operations and state models, synchronization primitives for organizing the co-operation of tasks, and the timing of task executions. After having discussed the subjects mentioned, structured real-time programming is treated. Initially, this can be carried out in a language-free graphical form, in order to concentrate on the clarification of the intrinsic concepts and on the representation of timing in concurrent systems.

After covering material on real-time programming, real-time operating systems require a significant amount of attention. The coverage commences with the functional description of state of the art real-time operating systems. Special emphasis must be placed on an in-depth comparative treatment of the critical topics of deadlock handling, particularly prevention, synchronization concepts, memory management, and priority and advanced, i.e. time driven, task scheduling strategies for hard time conditions.

In contrast to standard operating system courses, the consideration of each of the topics is to focus on the predictability aspect and that execution time bounds can be guaranteed. The students can gain a very profound knowledge of this subject by carrying out a project of designing and, during laboratory sessions, implementing a small real-time operating system, which should contain the functions for interrupt, time, task, and processor administration, an input/output driver for a slow device, and should provide one or the other advanced feature.

4.4. Real-Time Architecture Level

Turning to hardware, the system structures of real-time computers are treated. This includes local and global bus systems, hardware architectures, especially with regard to achieving fault tolerance, as well as centralized, decentralized, hierarchical, and distributed configurations and their suitability for certain applications. Special emphasis has to be put on the objectives for employing distributed automation structures, which match the hierarchical organization of entire industrial plants, and the criteria for suitable communication structures in such systems.

The main topic of process interfacing and peripherals needs to be introduced with the classification of processes, noise, and signals, and some material on sampling, signal quality, and signal conditioning. The influence of noise must be stressed and a variety of measures for the prevention and reduction of electric disturbances are discussed and studied in laboratory sessions. The purpose of its discussion here is to create awareness for this area of possible major problems in real-time system design.

Then, the structure and principle of operation of process sensors and actuators and the main components of process interfacing are discussed in class and applied in experimental set-ups, namely, analog, digital, and impulse interfaces, multiplexers, various types of analog-to-digital converters, sample-and-hold amplifiers, timers, data acquisition subsystems, and interfaces to certain bus standards like IEEE 488, CAMAC, or VMEbus [26].

The inherent noise suppression properties of inte-grating analog-to-digital converters and the flexibility of microcomputer based programmable process input/output units are to be pointed out. In this part of the course, the students are required to write some specific device driver programs, linking their knowledge of process peripherals with one of the real-time operating systems.

4.5. Additional Topics

As time permits, the next main topic, system reliability, especially of the software, deserves broad attention. The discussion commences with clarifying the terms *reliability* and *safety*, with a characterization of errors and failure situations, and with introducing the concepts of redundancy, in its various forms, and diversity. With regard to the hardware, measures to achieve fail-safe behavior are presented. Then, the students are trained to develop reliable software by writing robust, fault tolerant programs of low complexity observing rigorous development disciplines and by utilizing design tools and diverse approaches.

To prove the reliability of programs, methods for software quality assurance and software verification suitable for real-time environments are described. In this context, procedures for real-time error diagnostics and recovery are also studied. Very important is the discussion of measures to improve the security of realized systems and of methods to carry out the safety licensing of real-time systems.

5. Detailed Course Contents

Following the above assumptions, the contents of this model is presented below, including descriptions of four component units for lecture topics.

5.1. Knowledge Units

Unit 1. Methodologies and Environments for Real-Time Systems Development

Note. The criterion for including a particular development methodology was its industrial maturity, which translates into a book or at least five papers published. The names of principal authors follow some methods.
Topics. Common Notations. Structure Charts, Data Flow Diagrams, State Dependency Diagrams.
Classical Methods. Structured Analysis and Development for Real-Time Systems, SA/RT, SD/RT (Ward/Mellor, Hatley/Pirbhai).
Specification Methods. Statecharts (Harel).

Process-oriented, Applicative and Interpretable Specification Language, PAISLey (Zave). Trace Assertion Method (Parnas). Hierarchical Multistate Specification, HMS (Gabrielian/Franklin). Spec (Berzins/Luqi). Petri Nets. Temporal Logic. Real-Time Logic, RTL (Mok). Formal Methods: Z and VDM (Vienna Development Method).

Design Methods. Design Approach for Real-Time Systems, DARTS (Gomaa). Modular Approach to Software Construction, Operation and Test, MASCOT-3. Jackson System Development, JSD. Real-Time Object-Oriented Methodologies (Booch, HOOD and DRAGOON, MOOD, ROOM). Software Construction by Object-Oriented Pictures, SCOOP-3 (Cherry).

Unit 2. Real-Time Languages

Note. Topics listed below are restricted to Ada. Similar lists can be composed for other languages, such as Pearl, Modula-2, Concurrent C, Occam.

Topics. Ada Tasks and Task Types. Task States: Elaboration, Activation, Completion, Termination. Entries and Rendezvous. Accept and Select Statements. Protected Objects. Delay, Terminate and Abort Statements. Conditional and Timed Entry Calls. Pragma PRIORITY. Package CALENDAR: TIME, DURATION, and CLOCK. Task and Entry Attributes. Exceptions: Declaration, Raising, Handling, Propagation. Partitions and Distributed Computing. Mixed Language Programming and Pragma INTERFACE. Device Registers Representation and Interrupt Handlers.

Unit 3. Real-Time Kernels

Topics. Taxonomy of Kernel Features. Tasking Models, Task States, Services and Transitions. Processes and Threads. Real-Time Scheduling: Round-Robin, FIFO, Priority-Based Preemptive Scheduling. Rate-Monotonic and Deadline-Monotonic Scheduling. Synchronization: Semaphores, Condition Variables and Mutexes. Priority Inversion and Priority Ceiling. Deadlocks. Overview of Interprocess Communication. Message Passing Mechanisms: Queues, Mailboxes, Pipes, Sockets. Events, Signals and Exceptions. Clocks and Timers. Shared Memory, Memory Locking, Memory Allocation, and Garbage Collection. Synchronous and Asynchronous I/O. Real-Time Transactions. Real-Time Files. Device Drivers. Interrupt Handling. Open BIOS. Real-Time Benchmarks: Rhealstone and Hartstone. Standards: Posix.4, Itron.

Unit 4. Real-Time Hardware Architectures

Topics. Overview of Advanced Multiprocessor Buses: VMEbus, Multibus II, Futurebus+, PCI, Scalable Coherent Interface. Static Bus Description: Signal Groups. Dynamic Bus Description: Timing Diagrams. Multiple Masters and Bus Arbitration. Bus Protocols and Data Transfer: Single Transfers, Block Transfers, Broadcasting. Bus Error Handling Mechanisms. Bus Interface Design. Specific Bus Problems: Metastability, Skew, Wired-Or Glitches, Clock Latency, Transceiver Technology. Digital Signal Processors. Microcontrollers. RISC Architectures: Sparc. Cache Coherence Protocols. Real-Time Aspects of Local Area Networks. Real-Time Aspects of Practical Communication Systems (ATM).

5.2. Sample Semester Schedule

The above outlined syllabus is suitable for a one-semester senior or graduate course. It was followed by the present authors, who taught such a course at several universities in the U.S. and elsewhere, and as a continuing education short course. If a second semester is available, then the mentioned topics can be presented in more depth. This holds especially with respect to integrated project development environments, whose application can be practiced in a number of student projects to be presented later in class.

Owing to their increasing importance, the following four software related subjects are studied in the second semester: real-time communications in distributed systems, database organization and programming under real-time conditions (with special emphasis on distributed databases), building expert systems (where all three subjects focus on observing hard deadlines), as well as the utilization of schedulability analysis tools. Aiming at guaranteeing predictable system behavior, the worst case task execution times are to be calculated and evaluated before actual implementation, to see whether a system will meet its timing requirements.

A sample division of the material in two semesters is presented below.

First semester:

- History, importance and basic concepts of computerized process automation
- Real-time software engineering
- Integrated project development support systems
- Programming in high-level real-time languages
- Real-time operating systems with special emphasis on task scheduling
- Hardware architectures and distributed automation structures
- Process interfacing and peripherals

- System reliability and fault-tolerance.

Second semester:

- Advanced topics from the first semester's subject areas, especially on the integrated project development support systems

- Real-time communications in distributed systems

- Organization of (distributed) real-time databases

- Real-time expert systems

- Schedulability analysis

- Design and construction of special purpose process peripherals.

Whereas suitable computers and standard peripherals are usually available off the shelf, the real-time system engineer often has to design and build special purpose interface boards to interconnect the external process to the computer system. This constitutes another topic for detailed study in the advanced course which must, of course, be supplemented by intensive laboratory experiments.

6. Accompanying Laboratory Work

The main feature of the course on real-time systems is that it is accompanied by extensive laboratory sessions providing practical experience on all topics discussed in class. Closed and open labs assure achieving the balance among the three components of the teaching process, recommended in [21]:

- theory is emphasized in lectures

- abstraction is best taught via prototyping in closed labs (both for hardware and software), including experimentation and measurements

- design is stressed in closed labs for hardware exercises and in open labs for software development.

Closed labs are supervised labs for which it is possible to accomplish the task in 3-hours or less. They may be organized in a form of a contest, focusing on a single topic. Two kinds of closed labs are suggested:

- digital design or board design examples

- developing small programs for conducting experiments which involve the use of sensors (analog and digital) and actuators (stepping motors or simple displays), for example in measurement and control applications.

The first kind of a closed lab will allow students to apply concepts learned in the real-time architectures unit. The second kind of application will allow them to use most of the constructs from the real-time kernels unit, and employ a substantial amount of constructs of the real-time programming language.

A number of application programs, e.g. performing process measurements and control, are written in the real-time language selected for the course. Each student has to develop and implement a small operating system or at least a real-time kernel. The computer available in the laboratory is to be connected to various devices and the corresponding driver routines must be developed. Suitable devices for a laboratory environment are models of continuous, discrete, and sequential processes.

A sufficiently general and relatively simple application program for real-time systems, can be formed of four tasks:

- user interface (to enter parameters, activate and kill tasks, display the results, etc.)

- data acquisition (to read data, from inputs like analog-to-digital converters, etc.)

- data handling (to preprocess input data in real time: simple averaging or more involved type of filtering)

- data output (to write data onto a magnetic medium, send into a network, etc.)

Open labs should be available for team projects, to allow students to solve larger problems, hard to accomplish during a 3-hours lab. A project should integrate the entire knowledge from three lower-level units with the real-time development methodologies unit, and incorporate principles of software engineering, including team work. A list of case studies (including references), which can be used for such projects is given elsewhere [9, 23].

The investment to set up a laboratory with the mentioned facilities does not need to be high. Process models are available at low prices; a variety of very useful devices can even be obtained on the market for toys and hobby equipment. Real-time programming systems with appropriate operating systems, as well as the software tools for requirements engineering, are now available on personal computers. Their prices are oriented at the hardware prices, i.e. they are also low. Current information on real-time kernels is available from: `http://www.primenet.com /~ magpub/RTE_vendor_OS.html`. In Germany, both the language Pearl and the requirements engineering tool EPOS, are available for personal computers at a nominal fee for educational institutions.

7. Additional Considerations

7.1. Relation to Other Courses

Since this course can be taken not only by computer science or computer engineering students, but also, for an additional qualification, by senior undergraduate or master students of technical subjects such as chemical, electrical, and mechanical engineering, in order to cope with the heterogeneous knowledge background of the participants, the course covers its area completely. Hence, there are some overlaps with other courses, which some of the students may have already attended. The overlapping material, however, will always be presented with a distinct real-time systems specific emphasis. Besides a good basic knowledge in science and engineering, the only prerequisite required is that the students are proficient in a structured programming language, such as Pascal or C.

7.2. Course Materials

As far as a textbook for the above outlined course(s) is concerned, the first author initially used [11], which was the best book till the early nineties. It had to be complemented by manuals for the language and the other software tools used, as well as by a laboratory handbook describing the function of the process models to be interfaced and controlled. As additional reading, especially for the second course semester and in order to catch up with current research work, the tutorial text [19] and the first author's book [8] represent very good sources of information. The second author used several textbooks, depending on the course focus [2, 10, 15, 18].

7.3. Areas for Graduate Study

The scientific research in real-time systems is presently intensifying, which provides a good opportunity for graduate students to participate in challenging projects. A partial list of actual research areas can read as follows:

- Conceptual foundations of real-time computing
- Predictability and techniques for schedulability analysis
- Requirements engineering and design tools

- Reliability and safety engineering with special emphasis on the quality assurance of real-time software
- High-level languages and their concepts of parallelism synchronization, communication, and time control
- Program transformations to ensure better guarantees
- Real-time operating systems
- Scheduling algorithms
- Distributed, fault tolerant, language and/or operating system oriented innovative computer architectures
- Hardware and software of process interfacing
- Communication systems
- Distributed databases with guaranteed access times
- Artificial intelligence with special emphasis on real-time expert and planning systems
- Practical utilization in process automation and real-time control.

7.4. Other Issues

It is expected that the course can be taught in two ways, as far as the order of topics is considered: using bottom-up or top-down approach. Even though the top-down method (starting from development methodologies through implementation and hardware issues) seems to be more natural to a software engineering view, the bottom-up approach is also legitimate, especially if students have very little background in hardware architectures.

As mentioned in Section 6, the ACM/IEEE-CS "Computing Curricula 1991" [21] further suggests to provide a balance within curriculum contents among the three processes (theory, abstraction and design), which correspond to three complementary approaches employed in teaching, representing mathematics, experimental science, and engineering. To ensure that all three parts of the teaching process are given relatively equal attention in the course, one must provide sufficient resources.

One important aspect of incorporating theory in the teaching process is students' easy access to books and other publications. To incorporate the experimental science aspect, one needs access to more than just traditional computers like VAXes, PC's or Sun workstations. It is absolutely essential to set up a fully blown laboratory, based on one of the standard backplane buses and supported by a commercial real-time kernel and compilers. The incorporation of an engineering requirement can be done through the software development process, via the team project. Crucial for the success of such a project is the availability and use of tools [24].

8. Conclusion

A comprehensive syllabus for a one or two semester course on real-time computer systems engineering for senior undergraduate or master's students of computer science and engineering has been presented. The course(s) may serve as preparation for commencing thesis projects in a field of rapidly intensifying research activity.

The main themes covered in the course(s) are basic concepts of process automation, real-time software engineering and fully integrated project development support systems, programming in high-level real-time languages, real-time operating systems with special emphasis on task scheduling strategies, hardware architectures and particularly distributed automation structures, process interfacing, and optionally, system reliability and fault tolerance. Accompanying course texts are mentioned, and the subjects and goals of laboratory exercises are established.

It is pointed out how a laboratory can be developed with advanced, but low-cost, equipment and software tools. Special consideration is given to the question of selecting a suitable high-level real-time language to be discussed in class and to be used for practical exercises, due to its essential role in the framework of the course(s) and for the application of the material for process control and automation purposes.

The proposed course model is fairly complete. Its implementation may include additional considerations, such as explicit use of recurring concepts [21], exercises, test questions and exams, incorporation of all course materials in lecture notes, etc. One important step which could help to improve this model, is obtaining suggestions and feedback from other academic institutions.

References

[1] Ada Reference Manual. Language and Standard Libraries, International Standard ISO/IEC 8652:1995, ISO, Geneva, January 1995

[2] A. Burns, A. Wellings, Real-Time Systems and Their Programming Languages, Addison-Wesley, Reading, Mass., 1989

[3] J.E. Cooling, Languages for Programming of Real-Time Embedded Systems: A Survey and Comparison, Microprocessors and Microsystems, Vol. 20, 1996, pp. 67-77

[4] G. Ford, 1991 SEI Report on Graduate Software Engineering Education, Report CMU/SEI-91-TR-2, Software Engineering Institute, Pittsburgh, Penn., March 1991

[5] W.A. Halang, On Real-Time Features Available in High-Level Languages and Yet to Be Implemented, Microprocessing and Microprogramming, Vol. 12, No. 2, 1983, pp. 79-87

[6] W.A. Halang, A. Stoyenko, Comparative Evaluation of High-Level Real-Time Programming Languages, Real-Time Systems, Vol. 2, No. 4, November 1990, pp. 365-382

[7] W.A. Halang, A. Stoyenko, Constructing Predictable Real-Time Systems, Kluwer Academic Publishers, Boston, Mass., 1991

[8] W.A. Halang, K.M. Sacha, Real-Time Systems: Implementation of Industrial Computerised Process Automation, World Scientific Publishers, Singapore, 1992

[9] A. Kornecki, J. Zalewski, Projects for Real-Time Systems Classes, Real-Time Systems Education, J. Zalewski, ed., IEEE Computer Society Press, Los Alamitos, Calif., 1996 (this volume)

[10] P. Laplante, Real-Time Systems Design and Analysis. An Engineer's Handbook, IEEE Press, New York, 1993

[11] R. Lauber, Prozessautomatisierung, Vol. 1. 2nd Edition. Springer-Verlag, Berlin, 1989.

[12] R. Lauber, Development Support Systems, IEEE Computer, Vol. 15, No. 5, 1982, pp. 36-46

[13] M. Paprzycki, J. Zalewski, Shaping the Focus of the Undergraduate Curriculum, SIGCSE Bulletin, Vol. 28, No. 3, September 1996, pp. 37-44, 50, 64

[14] Programming Language Pearl, German National Standard, DIN 66253, Parts 1-3, Beuth-Verlag, Berlin, 1981, 1982, 1989

[15] B. Sanden, Software Systems Construction with Examples in Ada, Prentice Hall, Englewood Cliffs, NJ, 1993

[16] H. Sandmayr, A Comparison of Languages: Coral, Pascal, Pearl, Ada and ESL, Computers in Industry, Vol. 2, 1981, pp. 123-132

[17] T. Shepard, C. Wortley, B. Selic, Using Objec-Time to Teach Real-Time Software in the Undergraduate Curriculum, Real-Time Systems Education, J. Zalewski, ed., IEEE Computer Society Press, Los Alamitos, Calif., 1996 (this volume)

[18] K. Shumate, M. Keller, Software Specification and Design. A Disciplined Approach for Real-Time Systems, John Wiley and Sons, New York, 1992

[19] J.A. Stankovic, K. Ramamritham, eds., Hard Real-Time Systems: Tutorial, IEEE Computer Society Press, Los Alamitos, Calif., 1988

[20] A. Stoyenko, E. Kligerman, Real-Time Euclid: A Language for Reliable Real-Time System, IEEE Trans. Software Engineering, Vol. 12, No. 9, September 1986, pp. 941-949

[21] A.B. Tucker, ed., Computing Curricula '91. Report of the ACM/IEEE-CS Joint Curriculum Task Force, ACM/IEEE, New York, 1991

[22] J. Zalewski, Language Selection for Modular Interface Systems. Pt. 2, Computer Physics Communications, Vol. 38, 1985, pp. 295-300

[23] J. Zalewski, A Real-Time Systems Course Based on Ada, Proc. 7th Ann. Ada Software Engineering Education and Training (ASEET) Symp., Monterey, Calif., January 12-14, 1993, pp. 25-49

[24] J. Zalewski, Cohesive Use of Commercial Tools in a Classroom, Proc. 7th SEI Conf. Software Engineering Education, J.L. Diaz-Herrera (Ed.), Springer-Verlag, Berlin, 1994, pp. 65-75

[25] J. Zalewski, What Every Engineer Needs to Know about Rate-Monotonic Scheduling: A Tutorial, Real-Time Magazine (Brussels), Issue 1/95, 1st Quarter 1995, pp. 6-24

[26] J. Zalewski, ed., Advanced Multimicroprocessor Bus Architectures, IEEE Computer Society Press, Los Alamitos, Calif., 1995

Real-Time Systems Education at George Mason University

Bo I. Sandén

Information and Software Systems Engineering

Mail Stop 4A4

George Mason University

Fairfax, VA, 22030-4444

bsanden@gmu.edu

Abstract

The Masters program in Software Systems Engineering at George Mason University has a strong real-time flavor particularly in the Design and Project Laboratory courses. Implementations are usually in Ada (Ada 95). Two design approaches for concurrent real-time systems are taught: ADARTS or CODARTS based on data and control flow, and entity-life modeling (ELM) based on concurrency in the problem domain. ELM has been developed in conjunction with the program and is described here in some detail together with student projects based on the approach.

1. Introduction

The Masters program in Software Systems Engineering at George Mason University (GMU) in Fairfax, Northern Virginia, consists of six core courses plus four electives. The core courses are: Software Construction, Software Design, Software Requirements and Prototyping, Formal Methods and Models, Software Project Management, and Software Project Laboratory. Of these, the Design and Laboratory courses have a slant towards concurrent real-time systems. The Design course, which was first offered in 1991, has a lecture portion and a group project, whose final deliverable is the design of a concurrent real-time system. The Laboratory course involves design and implementation usually of a concurrent real-time system. The standard implementation language is Ada. We are currently migrating to Ada 95.

Over the years, the projects have given us considerable experience with design methods for real-time systems. Teaching and methods development have gone hand in hand. Due to faculty interests, two different approaches to the design of multi-tasking real-time systems are taught. The traditional approach, represented by ADARTS and CODARTS [2], starts with a *data-flow* model that captures how system input is successively transformed into output. Each such *transformation* essentially becomes a task. The other design approach models the task structure in the software on concurrent processes that are inherent in the problem itself. In the following paragraphs, these two approaches are further discussed and compared. One approach to software design based on problem concurrency, called *entity-life modeling (ELM)*, is then described in depth. ELM has largely been developed within the software engineering program at GMU and has been exercised in many student projects, which represent an interesting set of applications of different categories.

1.1. Comparison of design approaches

The data-flow approach [2, 8, 19] considers each input to the system and the successive computations that it entails. The notion is that each computation transforms its input into output that is then the input of another computation. Some transformations produce external output or cause external action. Each transformation is regarded as a potential task. To reduce the number of tasks, heuristics are given for consolidating the transformations before implementing them as tasks. The tasks communicate via some form of shared data, often a queue of messages between the tasks. Each task either executes on a periodic basis or pends on the arrival of a message in the queue. Variations of the data-flow approach include *control transformations* and *control flow* in addition to the data transformations and the data flow. This is the case in ADARTS and CODARTS, which are taught at GMU. (Refer also to [3] in these proceedings.)

Although the data-flow approach is systematic and may result in viable designs, the development process tends to be lengthy and may involve a variety of different notations. This makes the design of even a small and straightforward real-time system into a large undertaking. A concurrency-based approach to the design of real-time software such as ELM tries to overcome this disadvantage by modeling the software directly on concurrency inherent in the problem. The assumption is that all events in the problem domain can be organized into concurrent processes called *threads*. The events within each thread occur one after the other with a certain distance in time. Concurrency is based on the concept of coincidental simultaneity. According to this concept, two threads are concurrent if an event in one thread ever occurs at the same time as an event in the other. The threads form the basis for the tasks in the software.

The concurrency-based approach typically leads to a less fragmented solution with fewer tasks than the data-flow approach. The system's reaction to a given stimulus is described in one place, and the handling of related, successive stimuli appears together in the text of one task. As in the data-flow model, each stimulus may give rise to various computations. But rather than being implemented as separate tasks that hand over their results to each other, all the computations are invoked from the body of the task that received the stimulus. Thus, each task body resembles the main procedure in a sequential program and outlines the entire handling of a thread of events at a certain level of abstraction.

1.2. Approaches to real-time design education

The real-time systems education in the Software Systems Engineering program is primarily centered on the design of concurrent software. It is somewhat abstract in that we have no physical plant that the software can control. Other approaches to real-time education have a much stronger connection to the hardware. On the other hand, this tends to focus the attention on the particular problems that can be illustrated by the existing plant.

While we cover scheduling issues such as rate monotonic theory, the main focus is on softer real-time systems and resource allocation problems. Other approaches to real-time design education are described in [4, 5, 7, 20].

2. Entity-life modeling

Entity-life modeling is discussed in a number of publications [10, 11, 12, 13, 14, 15, 17, 18]. It is based on the assumption that a real-time system must react to (or create) *events* in the problem environment, where each event is without duration but requires a finite amount of processing time. The analyst's concern is to attribute these events to different concurrent threads. To do this, one has to do the following:

- Create an imaginary *trace* by laying out all events that the software has to deal with along a time line. (Include both stimuli to which the software must react, and actions that the software must take.)

- Partition the trace into *threads*, where a thread is a set of events and

  1. each event belongs to exactly one thread

  2. the events within each thread are separated by sufficient time for the processing of each event.

Each thread is an instance of a thread type, which can be described by means of a state-transition diagram or some other notation suitable for a sequential structure.

The set of threads resulting from this partitioning is called a *thread model* of the problem. A thread model is called *minimal* if there is a point in time where an event occurs in each thread. All minimal thread models of a given problem have the same number of threads. This number is the *concurrency level* of the problem and is equal to the maximum number of events that can ever occur simultaneously.

2.1. Threads and tasks

Basically, each thread maps onto a task in the software. By basing the tasks on a thread model of the problem, we make sure that each event is handled by one task, and that no task is inundated with simultaneous events. Such simultaneous events are instead taken care of by different tasks. Threads map smoothly onto tasks in Ada and particularly Ada 95. Tasks are part of the Ada syntax and well integrated with the language.

Each thread model for a given problem is potentially the basis for a software design for that problem. The designer may choose among the different models. While a minimal model results in the smallest number of tasks, there may be reasons to choose a non-minimal model. There are also cases where more tasks are needed than there are threads. This is true when a stimulus cannot be attributed to a thread without further analysis of its associated data. In addition to the tasks, the design contains objects that are shared between the tasks, and other objects that are used exclusively by single tasks.

2.2. Threads and entities

It is usually possible to associate threads with *entities* that are intuitively prominent in the problem, such as an elevator, a robot arm, etc. The thread is then the "life" of the entity. Consider a multi-elevator system where the events are the arrivals and departures of elevators at different floors. We can then identify one thread per elevator since the events associated with each elevator are spaced in time. On the other hand, we cannot include *all* events in the multi-elevator system in one thread, since several events associated with different elevators may occur simultaneously. For the same reason, we cannot associate a thread with each floor, since several elevators may arrive at or depart from a given floor at the same time.

It is particularly useful to look for entities that are either *delayable* or *queuable*:

- A *delayable* entity has events that are triggered by time. This is easily modeled in the software since tasks have the built-in ability to reschedule themselves for later execution. The elevator entities are delayable if, for instance, we want an idle elevator to remain at the floor of its last request for a while before returning to the ground floor.

- *Queuable* entities are *resource users* competing for exclusive access to shared resources. This is of particular interest when an entity needs simultaneous, exclusive access to multiple shared resources. Situations where entities wait for access to shared resources are easily modeled in software based on a task's ability to suspend its activity and queue for access to a resource.

The intuition is that the entities drive the problem with the delayable entities forcing action at specific times, and the queuable entities acquiring and releasing resources. Similarly, the software is driven by tasks modeled on these entities and operating on various passive objects. Each task and the objects on which it operates resemble a sequential program with a main procedure and various modules such as Ada packages. This sequential structure extends naturally to concurrent programs with the difference that there is one "main procedure" per task and that some objects are shared between tasks.

There are similarities between ELM and the *use-case* approach taken in object-oriented analysis [6]. A use case is the sequence of operations on different objects that are initiated by an external *actor* toward a particular goal. The use case is often a dialog between the system and a human operator. It has limited extension in time. Withdrawal of money from an automated teller machine is a simple example of a use case. In the use-case terminology, a withdrawal is a series of *transactions*, each of which completes when the system waits for input stimulus from the actor. In a real-time system, the actors are often inanimate

entities in the problem domain. The entities can be electro-mechanical or electronic systems. As a rule, ELM gives each such entity a task. Typically, one task repeatedly executes one or more use cases.

3. Projects

Over the years, ELM has been applied to a large number of different projects in the Design and Laboratory courses. Students usually come up with their own project ideas along the lines of the many examples used in class. Some student-defined projects have made their way into the text [12]. Many more are included in a curriculum module to be made available through the ASSET depository. (See Conclusions.) The following categories have been identified:

- Periodic problems. These problems rely on the delayability that is built into the task syntax. Examples include:

  - The automatic buoy [1, 9, 12]. A number of tasks periodically sample the water temperature, wind speed, etc. Another task periodically broadcasts the information.
  - The remote temperature sensor [8, 10, 12]. A number of samplers periodically sense the temperature of a set of furnaces.

- Basic state-machine problems. The software controls some entity in the problem that can be described by a finite automaton. External stimuli may change the state and cause external action. Examples include:

  - Control of a power car window [12].
  - Control of an automatic garage door [12].
  - Automobile cruise control. The state of cruising is changed by stimuli coming from the brake and other driver controls. A *regulator task* periodically compares the current and desired speeds and adjusts the throttle according to a control law [12]. This example is also used extensively to illustrate ADARTS and CODARTS [2].

- User-thread systems. These problems are largely structured around a thread that represents the behavior of a human operator. Examples include a supermarket checkout system and various automatic vending systems, which are popular student projects. (Clearly, the user thread is often a part of a larger and more complex system.) The checkout system is also used as a CODARTS project.

A project group suggested a variation on the checkout system that has a credit-card reader attached to the register. This causes additional concurrency since the customer may operate the card reader at the same time as the checker operates the register.

- Assembly-line systems. In these systems, the entities are typically stations between which material or parts flow. Each station–entity operates on a part when it arrives. A good example from a student project is a baggage control system for an airport, where the stations are way-points where a piece of luggage may be routed off the main conveyor onto a baggage pick-up or loading area, or vice versa. Typically, each station becomes one (or more) tasks. For example, one task may be responsible for diverting luggage carts off the main track onto an unloading siding, another for unloading, and a third for merging empty carts back onto the main conveyor at the proper speed.

  Another student project involves an automated coffee shop where coffee cups on trays travel between filling stations for different kinds of coffee, milk, sugar, etc.

- Resource-contention problems. In this kind of system, multiple entities vie for resources. Typically, each entity needs simultaneous exclusive access to more than one resource. The trick is to pose the problem in such a way that the entities are the resource users, and the resources are clearly identified and represented. It is then possible to design away deadlock by means of a variation of static locking order [12].

  Some examples are:

  - The flexible manufacturing system [12, 15, 17], where a *job* that is machined at one workstation after another is a typical entity.
  - The automated switchyard [12], where the switch engines are entities contending for exclusive access to track segments or switches. (This is one of the most elaborate projects that have come out of the Design and Laboratory classes.)
  - Automated parking garages are also popular student projects.

Students have invented a number of more or less fanciful problems in this category. Some involve mobile robots, such as an automatic re-stocker for a grocery store, an automated video rental outlet and various automatic fast-food restaurants.

4. Conclusion

The real-time systems education at GMU has primarily been geared towards the design of concurrent real-time applications, implemented in Ada. It is a drawback that we do not have a physical plant such as a train set [7], a model assembly line or even a micro-mouse maze.

The ADARTS/CODARTS training is mainly centered around a few examples. On the other hand, students have been a bottomless source of projects ideas that have been designed successfully with ELM and sometimes implemented. (Implementation occurs only in the Software Project Laboratory class.) While we lack the means to demonstrate the real-time software on actual laboratory equipment, this also leaves us free to explore ever new problems. Around 50 ELM design projects have been completed. This includes several different solutions to certain popular problems, such as traffic light control, vending, and automated parking.

Around 30 ELM implementations have been completed in the Laboratory class. A few of these have been continuations of design projects completed in the Design course. It is quite rare that a project team can continue from one class to another, since the students progress through the program at individual rates. Continuing a design project in the Laboratory class is quite desirable and usually results in an improved design. Similar improvements also tend to occur when a team tackles a problem attempted earlier by a team in another class.

Although both the data-flow approaches and ELM are language independent in principle, Ada has proven to be a very valuable teaching tool, particularly because of the built-in concurrency features. The design course based on ELM is currently being translated into Ada 95 under a curriculum development grant from DISA (Defense Information Systems Agency) [16]. The resulting material will be made available through the ASSET repository.

The material is also used for external courses. The material on ELM can be covered in 2.5 days in lecture form, without exercises or projects. An additional day is needed to cover the Ada 95 tasking syntax, if this material is new to the audience. (While new Ada-95 concepts such as protected types have replaced some of the Ada 83 syntax, that syntax is still valid and must be covered.)

References

[1] G. Booch. Object-oriented development. *IEEE Transactions on Software Engineering*, 12(2):211–221, February 1986.

[2] H. Gomaa. *Software Design Methods for Concurrent and Real-time Systems*. Addison-Wesley, Reading, MA, 1993.

[3] H. Gomaa. Courses on software design methods for concurrent and real-time systems. In *Proc. Workshop on Real-Time Systems Education, Embry-Riddle Aeronautical University, Daytona Beach, FL*, April 1996.

[4] W. A. Halang. Education of real-time systems engineers. *Microprocessing and Microprogramming*, 25(1-5):71–75, 1989.

[5] W. A. Halang. A curriculum for real-time computer and control systems engineering. *IEEE Trans. on Education*, 33(2):171–178, May 1990.

[6] I. Jacobson. *Object-oriented Software Engineering*. Addison-Wesley, Reading, MA, 1992.

[7] J.W. McCormick. A model railroad for Ada and software engineering. *Communications of the ACM*, 35(11):68–70, November 1992.

[8] K. W. Nielsen and K. Shumate. Designing large real-time systems with Ada. *Communications of the ACM*, 30(8):695–715, August 1987. (Correction: *CACM*, 30(12):1073, December 1987).

[9] B. I. Sandén. The case for eclectic design of real-time software. *IEEE Transactions on Software Engineering*, 15(3):360–362, March 1989.

[10] B. I. Sandén. Entity-life modeling and structured analysis in real-time software design - a comparison. *Communications of the ACM*, 32(12):1458–1466, December 1989.

[11] B. I. Sandén. An entity-life modeling approach to the design of concurrent software. *Communications of the ACM*, 32(3):330–343, March 1989.

[12] B. I. Sandén. *Software Systems Construction with Examples in Ada*. Prentice-Hall, Englewood Cliffs, NJ, 1994.

[13] B. I. Sandén. Design of concurrent software. In *Proc. Seventh Annual Software Technology Conference, Salt Lake City, UT*, April 1995.

[14] B. I. Sandén. Design of concurrent software based on problem concurrency. In M. Toussaint, editor, *Proc. Ada Europe Conference, Frankfurt/Main, Germany*, pages 298–310. Springer Verlag, Berlin, 1995.

[15] B. I. Sandén. Designing control systems with entity-life modeling. *Journal of Systems and Software*, 28:225–237, April 1995.

[16] B. I. Sandén. A course in real-time software design based on Ada 95. In *Proc. Tenth Annual ASEET Symposium*, June 1996.

[17] B. I. Sandén. Entity-life modeling in a distributed environment. In *Proc. Fourth International Workshop on Parallel and Distributed Real-Time Systems, Honolulu, HI*, pages 35–41, April 1996.

[18] B. I. Sandén. Using tasks to capture problem concurrency. *Ada User Journal*, 17(1):25–36, March 1996.

[19] H. Simpson. The MASCOT method. *IEE/BCS Software Engineering Journal*, 1(3):103–120, 1986.

[20] J. Zalewski. A real-time systems course based on Ada. In *Proc. Seventh Annual ASEET Symposium*, pages 25–49, 1993.

A Curriculum Proposal for an Innovative BS/MS Degree in Computer Engineering Emphasizing Real-Time Embedded Systems

T. F. Piatkowski
Dept. of Computer Science
Dept. of Electrical & Computer Engineering
Western Michigan University
Kalamazoo, MI 49008
thomas.piatkowski@wmich.edu

G. Greenwood
Dept. of Electrical & Computer Engineering
Western Michigan University
Kalamazoo, MI 49008
garry.greenwood@wmich.edu

X. (Sharon) Hu
Dept. of Electrical & Computer Engineering
Western Michigan University
Kalamazoo, MI 49008
sharon.hu@wmich.edu

J. Grantner
Dept. of Electrical & Computer Engineering
Western Michigan University
Kalamazoo, MI 49008
janos.grantner@wmich.edu

R. Taylor
Hewlett-Packard Research Labs
Bristol, England
rwt@hplb.hpl.hp.com

Abstract

This paper reports on a curriculum planning study in the Department of Electrical & Computer Engineering at Western Michigan University structuring an accreditable BS degree program and a companion MS degree program, both in Computer Engineering and both emphasizing real-time embedded systems. This curriculum is unique in that, unlike previously proposed programs, it addresses all aspects of real-time, embedded systems design and seamlessly incorporates a 4 year BS with a 5th year MS degree.

1. Introduction

The development of affordable, small, low power, high performance microprocessors has made it possible to substitute digital hardware and software for traditional analog and human control strategies. Digital solutions have major advantages over more traditional approaches including improved function, lower cost, greater flexibility, and better fault tolerance.

The design of such systems is not well supported in traditional engineering curricula. Indeed, the aspects of real-time system design are frequently not even mentioned. Students should be provided with an educational experience which encourages thinking at the systems level and which prepares them for engineering environments in which many of them ultimately will work. Properly addressing such issues de-mands a new look at the way engineering curricula are developed.

In this paper we describe a proposed engineering curriculum that does properly address all areas of real-time embedded system development. This concept is unique as most previously proposed curriculums address only portions of real-time systems (*e.g.*, software development [4]). The program is 5 years in length and awards both a BS and MS degree. The BS degree will be certified by the Accreditation Board of Engineering and Technology (ABET).

The paper is organized as follows. Section 2 provides a description of real-time systems and discusses how their design differs from conventional design. Section 3 describes the proposed curriculum in detail. Section 4 provides some final comments.

2. Real-time Embedded Systems

The emphasis of the proposed programs involves the design of real-time embedded systems (RTES). It is important that a clear understanding of the properties of such systems be established.

Real-time systems must be both *predictable* and *timely*. Predictability ensures that one knows explicitly how the system will respond to any foreseeable operational environment while the timeliness property requires the system to meet all temporal constraints (*e.g.*, task deadlines). This demands that the system be robust, thoroughly tested, and provide a degree of fault tolerance.

Embedded systems encompass a variety of hardware and software components which perform specific functions in host systems (*e.g.*, vehicular systems or medical instrumentation). In addition to guaranteeing timely response to external events, RTES must pay particular attention to expandability, availability, maintainability, and cost effectiveness. All of these aspects must be addressed at the earliest stages of the design process.

Figure 1 shows our view of the various components that make up a RTES. Notice that the design of such systems is inherently interdisciplinary, encompassing the fields of computer, electrical, mechanical, and industrial engineering. Also apparent is a required background in computer science, physics, chemistry and mathematics.

With respect to the specific field of computer engineering, a number of hardware and software technologies are required. A partial list includes:

- Custom digital hardware

- Microprocessors

- Transducer design and application

- Software engineering

- Communications and computer networking

- Control systems theory and applications.

RTES have a wide range of applications including vehicular systems, manufacturing systems, process control systems, robotics, appliances and entertainment systems. Yet, the conventional (ABET accredited) electrical or computer engineering degree available today does not provide all of the background necessary to *effectively* design and analyze such systems [1]. The program described in the next section is intended to correct this situation.

3. Program Description

The program is 5 years in length and results in the award of both a BS and MS degree. An overview of the program structure is shown in Figure 2.

Notice that a number of subject areas span the entire 5 year period while others are restricted to a shorter period. The program attempts to incorporate many of the disciplines identified in the previous sections in a coherent and integrated way. Specific features include:

- Pervasive use of symbolic mathematical tools (*e.g.*, Maple V) beginning with freshman calculus and physics.

- Integrated treatment of mathematics, physical science and systems science.

- Intensive use of computer tools (*e.g.*, Matlab and SimuLink) to support system specification, simulation, validation and optimization.

- Solid introduction to digital electronics, especially as it relates to interfacing and low-level custom digital control design.

- Rigorous treatment of real-time embedded software design methodologies.

- Special focus on transducer design, digital controls and real-time software.

A key element of the program is its extensive use of commercial tools. We feel this particular area will undergo frequent review to insure the students are exposed to current technology. The curriculum is necessarily lab intensive at both the undergraduate and graduate levels. Figure 2 and Table 1 provide details of the laboratories.

The program is designed to provide students with not only a firm background in physical and system science, mathematics and engineering, but also to provide an environment for personal development. Table 2 shows the proposed courses in the 5 year BS/MS program[1]. The interested reader is referred to the appendix where descriptions for several of the key courses are presented.

The 5 year program has total of 163 credit hours. The mathematics courses provide a firm foundation in multivariate calculus, linear algebra, differential equations and complex variables. With this background the student will be adequately prepared for the more advanced theoretical courses particularly at the graduate level.

The 5 year Curriculum is not totally theoretical as it purposely introduces students to current technology. Students must use a variety of programming languages (C++, Matlab, Maple V, VHDL, Ada95), several operating systems (Unix and Unix-based real-time kernels such as LynxOS), network protocols (Ethernet, Token bus) and two processor architectures (the 80196 microcontroller and the ARM60 RISC processor).

Throughout the curriculum are several seminars. These seminars provide a forum for discussing special topics in depth. Rather than using a textbook, the course material will primarily be journal articles, conference papers, trade journal articles, manufacturers' literature, etc. The objective is to have the students present the material and to have the responsible professor monitor an in-class discussion. Each seminar will have a central theme. Example topics include:

- Engineering project management

- Analysis of a real-time system application

- System specification

- Transducers suitable for outer space environments.

Notice that *system specification* is taught as a seminar topic. This should be taught no earlier than the 9th semester. While one might argue this topic should be taught much earlier in the curriculum, we feel it

---

[1]No course numbers are given as they are subject to revision.

cannot be properly taught at the undergraduate level. System specification involves far more than "just a functional description". Indeed, a *proper* system specification (at a minimum) covers:

- System functional description (including a block diagram)

- Any special timing requirements

- Specification of all system inputs and outputs

- Power supply requirements

- Identification of operational and survivability environments (EMI, temperature, humidity, vibration, etc., along with enumeration of the respective standards)

- Any special component requirements (*e.g.*, ICs must be MIL-STD-883B qualified)

- Mechanical (packaging) requirements

- Special design requirements (*e.g.*, need for line terminations or support for automatic testing)

- Design documentation required

- Description of functional tests

- Project development timelines.

Of course, any appropriate tolerances must also be specified. While it might be desirable to cover such topics early on in the program, we feel that undergraduates do not a have sufficient design background to properly address all of these areas in a consistent manner. Teaching this subject in a piecemeal fashion (*i.e.*, spread over several undergraduate courses) would diminish much of its significance. Combining this seminar topic with the Formal System Specification graduate course provides a complete introduction to system specification which is taught during a single semester. Additionally, the students will have achieved a sufficient background to discuss these concepts in some depth.

4. Final Remarks

By its nature, engineering design at its highest levels is an interdisciplinary activity. Additionally, the future of engineering will be dominated by computer-aided tools and computer-aided information systems. This means an engineering curriculum should be interdisciplinary and concentrate on technologies and techniques of the future. Hence, symbolic mathematics and system specification/analysis tools play a major role in the proposed curriculum not only in engineering courses but also in the mathematics and physical science courses. Additionally, optimization techniques (both *ad hoc* and computer-aided) will be introduced early in the program and provide an appropriate setting to conduct design exercises. This philosophy is consistent with the current ABET design criterion [2].

Unfortunately, the real-world is analog in nature and a RTES is forced to operate in such an environment. Status information from this external environment (and signals designed to control it) are frequently not compatible with computing systems. A properly trained engineer must be conversant in *all* aspects of a system designed to operate in the real-world. In the past isolated courses have addressed some of the aspects of RTES design and analysis(*e.g.*, see [3, 4, 6, 7]). Despite its importance, there have been few instances where an entire curriculum has attempted to use RTES as a central theme. Even in those cases there are what we consider to be significant shortfalls. For example, Halang describes a real-time computer and control curriculum [5]. Though it is claimed to be an engineering program, its main orientation is toward computer science. Indeed, a strong emphasis is placed upon real-time programming languages and operating systems. Though interfacing is taught, the key area of transducer systems is conspicuously absent. (Halang even states that concepts such as noise are taught with the computer science student in mind.) Our proposed curriculum is unique since it addresses all aspects of RTES development and does so from an engineering perspective.

Space does not permit the inclusion of many of the ideas associated with this proposal. An 82 page version of the full, original proposal introduced in this paper is available from *thomas.piatkowski@wmich.edu*.

References

[1] Report of *National Science Foundation Workshop on CAD Needs for System Design*, Boulder, CO, April 1995

[2] ABET, *Criteria for Accrediting Programs in Engineering in the United States Effective for Evaluations During the 1996-97 Cycle*

[3] F. DiCesare, S.M. Bunten and P.M. DeRusso, "Microcomputers for Data Acquisition, Control, and Automation - A Laboratory Course for Preengineering Students," *IEEE Trans. on Education*, Vol. 28, No. 2, May 1985, pp. 69-75

[4] B. Goodman Marchewka, "Teaching Software Engineering for Real-Time Design," *Proc. 5th SEI Conference on Software Engineering Education*, J.E. Tomayko (Ed.), Springer-Verlag, Berlin, 1991, pp. 235-244

[5] W. A. Halang, "A Curriculum for Real-Time Computer and Control Systems Engineering," *IEEE Trans. on Education*. Vol. 33, No. 2, May 1990, pp. 171-178

[6] R.E. Seviora, "A Real-Time Project for Software Engineering Course," *Proc. 2nd Int'l Conf. on Software Engineering for Real-Time Systems*, IEE Conf., Publication 309, IEE, London, 1989, pp. 65-69

[7] T. W. Schultz, "Peripheral Hardware and a Hands-on Multitasking Lab," *IEEE Micro*, Vol. 11, No. 1, February 1991, pp. 30-33

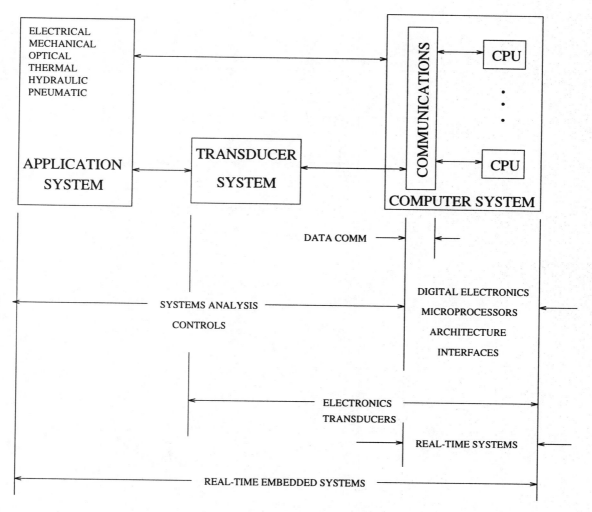

Figure 1: Components of a RTES

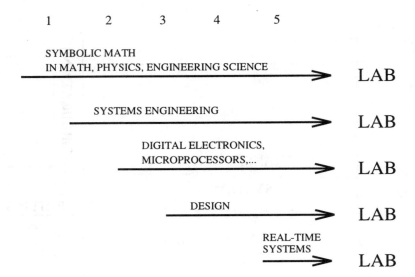

Figure 2: 5 Year Program Overview

YEAR 1	Symbolic math	Hosted on university facilities and student owned personal computers
YEAR 2	Systems engineering	Uses Matlab and SimuLink tools on a department workstation environment. Also conventional introductory electrical/mechanical systems labs.
	Transducer Systems	Provides a wide assortment of commercial transducers and the instrumentation to measure their performance.
YEAR 3	Digital electronics, microprocessors, interfacing	Revitalized labs currently available with incorporation of Xlinx and Mentor Graphics tools, VHDL, etc.
YEAR 4 YEAR 5	Design, communications, distributed systems, embedded systems	Dedicated hands-on studio laboratory incorporating networked workstations with a controllable analog capability providing representative applications environments for RTES.

Table 1: RTES Laboratories

Semester	Course Title	Credit Hours
1	Anatomy of a Modern Computer†	4
	Mathematics I	4
	Writing I	3
	Health Elective	2
	Gen Ed Elective	4
2	Introduction to Real-time System Applications & Issues†	3
	Computer Science I	4
	Mathematics II	4
	Gen Ed Elective	4
3	Environmental Engineering†	4
	Computer Science II	4
	Mathematics III	4
	Physics I	5
4	Introduction to Linear Systems	4
	Digital Logic	4
	Mathematics IV	4
	Physics II	5
5	Advanced Linear Systems†	4
	Analog and Digital Electronics	4
	Formal Reasoning & Structures	3
	Mechanics†	4
6	Introduction to Computer Architecture	3
	Statistical Methods	3
	Transducer Systems†	4
	Gen Ed Elective (ethics)	4
7	Introduction to Microprocessors	4
	Signal Processing	4
	RTES Seminar I†	1
	Computer Science III	4
	Gen Ed Elective (business)	4
8	Computer System Modeling*†	4
	Digital Control Theory	4
	Engineering Design and Project Management	4
	Switching & Finite Automata Theory*	3
9	Formal System Specification*†	4
	Electronic Interfacing†	4
	Real-time Operating Systems†	4
	Communications in RTES*†	4
	RTES Seminar II*†	1
10	Application Specific IC Design*†	4
	Design Factors for Distributed Systems*†	4
	RTES Seminar III*†	1
	Technical Elective*	4
	Technical Elective*	4

Table 2: Proposed courses in 5 year BS/MS program. "*" indicates a graduate level course. Courses marked with "†" are described further in the appendix.

Appendix

This appendix presents catalog descriptions and, where available, text selection for some of the key innovative courses included in the program proposal, presented in the order of their occurrence in Table 2.

Anatomy of a Modern Computer (3-1), 4 hr. An introduction to the history of computer hardware technology. Technical survey of important contemporary computer hardware technologies, such as: keyboards, CPUs, semiconductor memory, floppy disk drives and diskettes, hard drives, CD-ROM, impact printers, laser printers, modems, interfaces, LCD panels, digital cameras, audio input/output, power supplies and batteries. Prerequisites: Freshman standing in engineering, computer science, mathematics, or science.

Text: R. White, *How Computers Work*, Ziff-Davis Press, Emeryville, CA, 1993.

How Computers Work (CD-ROM), Warner New Media, Burbank, CA, 1994.

Technical reference manuals for the target workstation.

An Introduction to Real-Time System Applications and Issues (2-1), 3 hr. Technical survey of the application of digital computers and electronics in the monitoring and control of devices and systems. Examples will be drawn from manufacturing, process control, consumer products, medicine, entertainment, command and control, communications, and transportation among others. Design and optimization issues will be addressed, including: global system behavior and control, transducer and interface systems, communications and distributed computer control systems, control software design, reliability, failure, and cost. Associated engineering analysis and design methodologies and tools will be surveyed. Prerequisites: Anatomy of a Modern Computer and major in computer engineering.

Environmental Engineering (4-0), 4 hr. The chemical, physical, biological, environmental, and economic issues associated with system lifecycles of electrical and electronic equipment and processes. Resource utilization and environmental impacts associated with product and process design, production, operation, and end-of-life disposal. Case studies. Prerequisites: Physics I

Mechanics (4-0), 4 hr. Detailed treatment of the physical principles and practical design considerations in mechanical devices, especially as associated with sensors and actuators in real-time system transducers. Rigid body motion, especially for rotating and linear motion. Strength of materials. Deformation and failure. Vibration, friction, wear, and fatigue. Prerequisites: Physics I

Transducer Systems (3-1), 4 hr. Physical principles and practical design considerations in building and applying computer-to-application interface transducers. Sensor and driver systems studied include interfacing to: electrical, mechanical, thermal, optical, chemical, and biological variables. Recording and transmission media. Noise, errors, and reliability. Special emphasis is placed on selection and application of transducers in practical problems. Corequisites: Advanced Linear Systems and Analog and Digital Electronics

Text: A. D. Khazan, *Transducers and Their Elements*, Prentice-Hall, Englewood Cliffs, NJ, 1994.

H. V. Malmstadt, C. G. Enke and S. R. Crouch, *Microcomputers and Electronic Instrumentation: Making the Right Connection*, American Chemical Society, Washington, DC, 1994

B. R. Barrister and D. G. Whitehead, *Transducers and Interfacing*, Chapman and Hall, London, 1991.

Introduction to Linear Systems (3-1), 4 hr. Unified engineering treatment of mechanical, electrical, fluid, and thermal dynamic systems. Idealized models, response, and analytical description. Prerequisites: Calculus and freshman physics.

Advanced Linear Systems (4-0), 4 hr. A continuation of CprE 220 (Systems I). Contemporary linear systems: continuous and discrete signals and systems. Analysis and design of continuous and discrete control systems. Prerequisites: Introduction to Linear Systems

Computer System Modeling for Performance and Reliability Analysis (4-0), 4 hrs. Concepts and notation for modeling computer systems, especially as networks of queues and servers. Quantification of model performance using analytic and simulation techniques. Hardware and software considerations, small and large systems, free-standing and network systems. Prerequisites: Statistical Methods in Computer Engineering and graduate level competence in computer architecture or computer networking; or permission of instructor.

Text: B. W. Struck and E. Arthurs, *A Computer & Communications Network Performance Analysis Primer*, Prentice-Hall, Englewood Cliffs, NJ, 1985.

E. D. Lazowska, J. Zahorjan, G. S. Graha and K. C. Sevcik, *Quantitative Systems Performance: Computer System Analysis Using Queuing Network Models*, Prentice-Hall, Englewood Cliffs, NJ, 1984.

A. A. B. Pritsker, *Introduction to Simulation and SLAM II*, 4e, John Wiley, New York, 1995.

Formal System Specification (3-1), 4 hr. Survey of formal specification methods for physical systems, communication protocol systems, software systems, and hybrid systems. Concepts and notation for the rigorous mathematical modeling of discrete, continuous, and hybrid systems. Case studies. Specification languages include: μSAN, Eiffel, SETL, Estelle, LOTOS, Petri nets, and VHDL. Special emphasis will be placed on large distributed software and protocol systems and the μSAN specification methodology which introduces a unified theory of combinational function theory, automata theory and control theory. The laboratory includes exercises in development environments for generating and simulating system specifications. Prerequisites: Statistical Methods in Computer Engineering and Switching and Finite Automata Theory and a graduate level competence in computer architecture or computer

networking; or permission of instructor.

Text: T. F. Piatkowski, *Foundations of System Specification and Behavior, Volume 1: Concepts and Notation*, Lecture Notes and Manuscript

Electronic Interfacing (3-1), 4 hr. Analysis and design of microcomputer-based digital systems interfaces. Application oriented hardware and software interface design. Prerequisites: Analog and Digital Electronics and Computer Architecture II

Text: Z. G. Vranesic, S. G. Zaky, *Microcomputer Structures*, Saunders College Publishing, New York, 1989.

Technical data manual for the microprocessors chosen for the course (TBA).

Real-Time Operating Systems (3-1), 4 hr. Operating system theory and practice for real- time embedded systems; scheduling; managing complexity; resource control; clocks; deadlines; fault tolerance and reliability; implementation; Pearl; OS9/000; RTX. Prerequisites: Computer Science III and Switching and Finite Automata Theory.

Text: A. Burns and A. Wellings, *Real Time Systems and their Programming Languages,* Addison-Wesley, Reading , MA, 1992.

Communications in Real-Time Embedded Systems (3-1), 4 hr. Introduction to the hardware and software architecture and protocols of communication systems important to real-time embedded system applications. Communication protocol behavior, implementation examples, performance issues and design trade-offs, including bandwidth, response time, memory requirements, errors, reliability, and cost. Prerequisites: Computer Architecture II. Corequisites: Real-Time System Operating Systems; or permission of the instructor.

Real Time Embedded System Seminar I, II, and III (1-0) each, 1 hr each. A three semester seminar sequence that provides students opportunities to 1) meet with engineering and scientific experts and discuss the theory and practice of RTES design and implementation, and 2) present technical RTES material to a peer group of students and faculty. Prerequisites: For RTES Seminar I : senior standing in computer engineering; for RTES Seminar II : RTES Seminar I; for RTES Seminar III : RTES Seminar II.

Application-Specific Integrated Circuit Design (3-1), 4 hrs. Design, analysis and implementation of Application-Specific Integrated Circuits (ASIC). Emphasis will be placed on programmable designs (including Field Programmable Gate Arrays (FPGA) and Programmable Logic Devices (PLD)). Semi-custom design will also be discussed and full-custom design will be briefly introduced. Introduction to contemporary CAD systems. Prerequisites : Physics II (Electricity and Light) and Digital and Analog Electronics, or permission of the instructor.

Design Factors for Distributed Systems (4-0), 4 hrs. An introduction to distributed computing systems operation and design including interprocessor communication techniques, consensus, distributed control, and fault tolerance with an emphasis on real-time environments. Current publications on distributed computing systems design will be surveyed. Prerequisites: Graduate standing in computer engineering, electrical engineering or computer science, and Computer System Modeling for Performance and Reliability Analysis; or permission of the instructor.

Towards the Creation of the CIC's Real-Time Systems Laboratory

Pedro Mejía and Bárbaro Ferro
Centro Nacional de Cálculo
Instituto Politécnico Nacional.
México. D.F.
cenacpma@pollux.cenac.ipn.mx
bferro@w95.cenac.ipn.mx

Abstract

*The Real-Time Systems Laboratory, at the **Centro de Investigaciones en Computacion: CIC** (Computing Research Center) at the **Instituto Politecnico Nacional** in Mexico has been created to give support to the MSc and PhD programs in Computer Science offered by the CIC. Basic and applied research in this Laboratory covers significant aspects of the analysis, design and implementation of real-time systems.*

This report outlines the most relevant areas of work being developed at the Real-Time System Lab, focusing on course development for the MSc and PhD programs, research projects, research collaboration with other labs within the center, with other universities, and cooperation with the industry in Mexico.

1. Introduction

The *Instituto Politecnico Nacional (IPN)* is the biggest technical University in Mexico composed of a lot of schools, most of them in the field of engineering. The IPN also includes various research centers in Mexico City and other sites, distributed along the national territory.

One of these centers is the *"Centro Nacional de Calculo"* (National Computer Center) with the oldest tradition in graduate education in Computer Science. The Master of Science Program offered by this Center is the oldest one in Latin America with 30 years experience.

Our program has been designed to support full-time and part-time students. Students with a full time schedule take part as assistants in research projects carried out by the faculty.

As part of the educational and research efforts supported by the Government, a new research center named *"Centro de Investigacion en Computacion: CIC"* (Computer Research Center) is being created with faculty members coming from the current National Computer Center and from other centers within the IPN.

The CIC will be offering in next September two Master of Science Programs, one with a software approach and the other focused on computer engineering. Also a PhD program will start in the field of Computer Science in areas such as Real-Time Control Systems, Artificial Intelligence, Software Engineering, Image Processing and others. To support these activities, the CIC is being equipped with state of the art computers, software, instrumentation equipment and a solid network infrastructure.

The research activities in the CIC will be organized in Laboratories as the components of various departments, dedicated to specific areas. Three of these Labs, the Real-Time Systems Lab, the Software Engineering Lab, and the Instrumentation and Control Lab will focus on common research problems characterized by real-time constraints and requirements and the need to develop software solutions and tools. Also these Labs will share hardware and software facilities in order to leverage the development of common industrial application projects and research work carried out by graduate students during their stay at CIC.

As part of this paper we present our approach to graduate education and research in real-time systems. The development of a real-time systems curriculum in Mexico is something new, because there is no single school teaching in this area in their BSc, MSc or PhD programs. This curriculum will include courses such as Real-Time Systems Fundamentals, Real-Time Software Engineering, Real-Time Operating Systems, and Ada95 as the programming language of choice to teach the fundamental concepts of real-time systems [11].

It is important to mention that, there are many real-time and control systems currently running in our industry, but few of them have been designed by Mexican specialists; none of them have been designed using standard real-time methodologies or languages [5,9].

In this report, we also outline the research and academic collaboration with other Labs at CIC as well as the collaboration with foreign universities on common research projects and academic plans. At the beginning, we have started a collaboration with the Computer Science Department of Texas A&M University with which we will develop research projects funded by the NSF and the National Research Council (CONACyT) of Mexico.

2. Research Program

The goals of this Lab are the following:

- Development of innovative research in real-time systems.
- Academic support to the MSc and PhD programs offered by the CIC.
- Applied research, with projects related to Mexican industry and universities.

To fulfill these goals, the Real-Time Systems Lab carries out research on various aspects of the design, implementation, and analysis of real-time systems. Specifically, we are addressing real-time software engineering, scheduling theories, integration of real-time and fault tolerance, kernel design, design and programming tools, embedded real-time systems, distributed systems, and applications. What follows is a detailed description of the research areas that are being carried out by our Lab.

Scheduling: Recent developments in the analysis of fixed priority preemptive scheduling form the basis of an engineering approach to the design, verification and implementation of a hard real-time system. Since the development of the Rate Monotonic Analysis, the real-time systems area has become a mature field for developing reliable and safe applications using this theory.

Based on fixed priority preemptive scheduling schemes, we are developing practical and industrial hard real-time systems. We are interested mainly in integrating scheduling with fault tolerance systems, developing slack scheduling algorithms and using them for aperiodic scheduling and fault tolerance purposes. Also we are carrying research in imprecise computations.

Fault Tolerance: Real-time computing systems are increasingly being used in critical applications where their behavior must not only guarantee the correct operation of a system, but also the timeliness of the results. The need to satisfy simultaneously the criteria of real-time performance and high dependability [8], increases the already difficult task of designing real-time systems. General purpose fault tolerant systems have been designed as a collection of custom-made techniques, which do not guarantee a correct timing execution of the critical tasks of the systems. This has motivated us to carry research in developing a theoretical framework and developing tools for fault tolerant systems with timing constraints.

Real-Time Software Engineering: Most structured design methods claim to address the needs of hard real-time systems, However, few contain abstractions which directly relate the common hard real-time activities such as periodic or sporadic processes. Furthermore, the methods do not constrain the designer to produce systems which can be analyzed for their timing properties. We are concerned with the use of Object-Oriented development methods for designing real-time systems. Actually, we are starting on using HRT-HOOD and ROOM as proven methods for real-time systems development [9].

Real-Time Design and Analysis Tools: With recent advances in Software Engineering there have appeared many tools for designing and prototyping software systems supporting the software development cycle. However, these tools do not include the timing constraints of a real-time system, which makes them not effective when designing systems that involve concurrency and synchronization problems, and the guarantee to meet critical timing requirements. This has motivated us to develop tools for analysis, design and simulation of real-time systems. We are integrating tools for periodic, aperiodic and resource scheduling, synchronization and communication, fault simulation, and distributed environment simulation. Actually we are also designing a real-time tool for teaching purposes.

Real-Time Network Scheduling: Scheduling communications networks is very important, since the communication medium is one of the primary resources of any distributed system. Currently there are some adequate solutions for high speed networks and for low speed and low cost networks as the ones used in the automotive industry. We are interested in carrying research in CAN based networks for their application in our automotive industry. High speed real-time communication networks using FDDI and ATM technologies deserve a special attention.

3. Placement of the Real-Time System Lab and Interactions with other Labs

Figures 1 and 2 below, present the structure of the CIC along with the interaction of the Real-Time Systems Lab with the Software Technology Lab, and with the Control Lab. There is also a common equipment shared among these labs and common research projects.

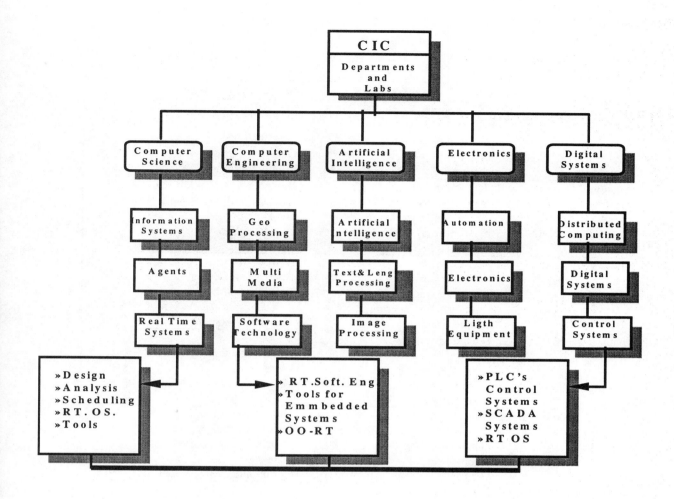

Fig. 1. The CIC's Structure

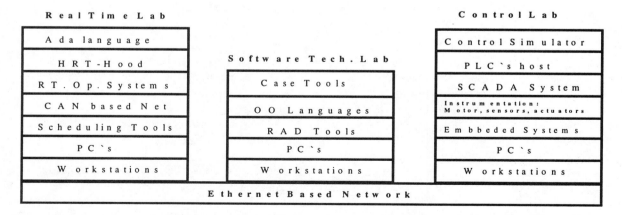

Fig. 2. Equipment of the Real-Time System Lab and equipment shared with other Labs

4. Graduate curriculum

4.1. MSc Program in Computer Science

Major Areas	Mandatory Courses	Optional Courses
Artificial Intelligence	OO Programming AI Logic Programming Math logic Expert Systems	Natural Language Processing Vision. Neural Networks Genetic Algorithms Intelligent Control Systems
Information Systems and Data Bases	OO Programming Operating Systems Distributed Systems Data Base Systems Design Information Systems	Implementation of DBMS Interoperability of Data Bases OO Data Bases Data base Management Systems
System Programming and Software Technology	OO Programming Operating Systems Languages and Automata Software Engineering Data Bases	Algorithms Distributed Software Compilers Soft. Eng. for the Design of RTS Real-Time Systems
Computer Graphics, Pattern Recognition and Image Processing	OO Programming AI Image Processing Pattern Recognition Computer Graphics	Vision Fuzzy logic techniques Multimedia Testors theory Algebraic logic
Distributed and Parallel Computing	OO Programming Operating Systems Distributed Systems Networking Parallel Computer Architectures	Parallel Programming Languages and Algorithms Distributed Operating Systems Data Bases Communication protocols
Real-Time Control Systems	Operating Systems Software Engineering Ada Programming Real-Time Systems Control Systems Engineering	Automation Intelligent Control Systems OO Programming Soft. Eng. for the Design of RTS Data Bases

Fig. 3. Graduate curriculum of the CIC's Laboratories

The average time for completion of the MSc program is two years. The student must take the mandatory courses in the above table together with some of the optional courses to complete 80 units or credits, according to the major area selected. The student must submit an acceptable thesis under the supervision of his advisor and approved by a thesis committee.

4.2. PhD Program in Computer Science

Major areas of study in the PhD program are:

- Artificial Intelligence
- Information Systems and Data Bases
- System Programming and Software Technology
- Computer Graphics, Pattern Recognition and Image Processing
- Distributed and Parallel Computing
- Real-Time Control Systems

Students may apply directly to the PhD program without a master's degree. Students entering the doctoral program without a MSc degree may be required to take some of the mandatory courses which are selected by an admission committee after a screening examination. In normal cases, a set of courses constituting a major area of study must be completed.

The major area examination tests the student's knowledge of his proposed major area. After passing this examination the student must prepare a dissertation proposal. Such a proposal must describe the main topics as well as the accumulated background in his area. The final examination is the defense of the student's dissertation. It must be an original research in the selected field.

4.3. Courses provided by the Real-Time Systems Lab

The Real-Time Systems Lab supports the MSc and PhD programs with a set of courses as well as research projects. Some of the courses described below may be taken by students with a major area other than the Real-Time Control Systems. Most of them are designed for master or doctoral students with interests in real-time. We only present a description of the fundamental courses taught by the Lab:

- Real-Time Systems.
- Software Engineering for the Design of Real-Time Systems: An Object-Oriented Approach.
- Real-Time Systems Programming in Ada95.
- Critical Real-Time Systems Development.

Course: Real -Time Systems

Number of hours: 60 (including Lab Assignments).

Course Description

A real-time computer system must respond to external stimuli within specified time [7,8]. If it fails to respond within this time, it is considered incorrect. Real-time systems are getting more and more important with the increasing use of computer-based control in industry processes, transportation and communication systems, and home appliances. Many of the Mexican industries, including the Federal Commission of Electricity (CFE), and the National Petroleum Company (PEMEX), design and manufacture products and services based on large and complex real-time control systems. Often these real-time systems control safety critical systems and must therefore be verified to be correct and fault tolerant.

The aim of this course is to present and discuss the main issues in the design of real-time systems [3,6].

Contents

- Introduction to Real-Time Systems: Basic concepts, the concurrency problem, the scheduling problem.
- Design of a Safety Critical Real-Time System: Specification of real-time constraints and verification of timing correctness, system design process, modeling, prototyping, testing and software quality assurance.
- Scheduling Approaches: Cyclic scheduling, RMA, Dynamic scheduling, Best effort scheduling. Extensions of scheduling (synchronization, jitter, mode changes), Imprecise computation.
- Reliability and Fault Tolerance of Real-Time Systems: Basic concepts of Fault Tolerance, Integration of Real-Time and Fault Tolerance, Redundancy management, Scheduling and Fault Tolerance.
- Distributed Real-Time Systems: Architectures for Distributed Real-Time Systems, Real-Time Network Scheduling problem, Network models (IEEE 802.5 Token Ring, FDDI, ATM), the MARS approach, the MARUTI approach.
- Performance Evaluation: Modeling, measurement and evaluation.
- Sample Real-Time Applications: SCADA systems, robotics and manufacturing, Distributed real-time systems.

Prerequisites

Computer Architecture, Operating Systems and some experience of programming in C, Ada or Pascal.

Textbooks

A. Burns and A.Wellings, *Real-Time Systems and Their Programming Languages*, Addison-Wesley, 1989.

M.Klein et al, *A Practitioner's Handbook for Real Time Analysis: Guide to Rate Monotonic Analysis*, Kluwer Academic Publishers, 1993.

J. Laprie, *Dependability, Basic Concepts and Terminology*, Springer-Verlag, 1991.

Course: Software Engineering for the Design of Real-Time Systems: An Object-Oriented Approach

Number of hours: 60 (including Lab Assignments).

Course Description

Since its introduction with Simula, Object-Oriented Programming and consequently Object-Oriented

Analysis and Design (formerly used in other engineering disciplines) have become a popular and widespread software paradigm for research and industrial use. The object paradigm presents a range of advantages over classical structural analysis and design [4, 10]:

- Better conceptual modeling: The objects in the computer closely resemble objects of the real world.
- Objects as software machines are inherently concurrent and may be combined to realize a specific system and be reused in other similar systems. In a concurrent system, objects can be assigned a thread of control to capture their behavior.
- Objects present a natural independence and therefore are good candidates for distributed systems showing autonomy and decoupling.
- Abstraction and incremental modeling are best supported with the object paradigm.
- Easy to add new modeling concepts to the object models to deal with real-time requirements such as timeliness, reactiveness, concurrency, dynamic reconfiguration and task distributions.

The purpose of this course is to teach the analysis, design and construction of real-time systems from an object-oriented perspective. The first part of the course deals with the main principles of software development in the real-time world and tries to explain why the object-oriented approach is adequate to realize such systems.

The second part introduces the ROOM methodology as an accepted tool to construct real-time systems.

Contents

- The specification, design and implementation of large complex software systems.
- Object-oriented technology as a useful engineering discipline for the construction of quality software systems.
- The characterization of real-time systems.
- The fundamental drawbacks of using a general-purpose methodology for real-time systems development.
- The principles of software engineering focused on the real-time domain: the main elements of a real-time methodology.
- Augmenting general purpose methodologies for application to real-time.
- An Object-Oriented Approach for real-time systems development.
- The Fundamental concepts in the object paradigm: classes, objects, encapsulation, inheritance, polymorphism, messages, etc.

- The integration of timeliness, dynamic internal structure, reactiveness, concurrency, distribution and other real-time concepts into object-oriented modeling.
- Concurrency and synchronization in Object-Oriented Programming.
- ROOM as a modeling language for real-time systems development.
- An Overview of the ROOM Modeling Language.
- The definition of the ROOM Modeling Language.
- Learning by examples: the description of sample projects.
- Tools to support the ROOM methodology: The ObjecTime Toolset.

Prerequisites

An introductory course on Fundamentals of Real-Time.

An introductory course on Object-Oriented Analysis and Design.

Textbooks

G. Booch, *Object-Oriented Analysis and Design with Applications*, Benjamin Cummings, 1994.

B. Selic et al, *Real-Time Object-Oriented Modeling*, John Wiley and Sons, 1994.

Course: Real-Time Systems Programming in Ada95

Number of hours: 60 (including Lab Assignments).

Course Description

As the complexity of real-time systems increases, high demand is being placed on the programming abstractions provided by languages. Currently Ada95 is evolving with advances in the specification techniques, logic, and theory underlying real-time systems.

Ada95 has been designed to support real-time safety applications and is intended to support priority driven scheduling [1, 2]. Some of the characteristics of the language include:

- Predictability and Determinism.
- Support for the management of time.
- Priority scheduling and schedulability checking.
- Reusable real-time modules.
- Support for fault tolerance and distributed programming.

The aim of this course is to present and discuss the main issues in the programming of real-time systems with Ada95 [3,6] .

Contents

- Programming in the small. Create the main program along with the supporting subprograms; Strong typing, declarations and ellaborations, statements, subprograms (specification, parameter passing, structure, recursion); Compiling a main subprogram with predefined packages for I/O, numeric, characters, strings; Subtypes for specifying constraints, type conversion, exception handling.
- Programming in the large. This part deals with programming with new and existing modules of software. Module specification and bodies (interface management and information hiding); Subunits; Scope and visibility and overloading; Library and compilation unit management; Hierarchical libraries (concept, clients and servers, views); Generics (concept, specification and instantiation, package parameters and generic "signatures", generic hierarchical libraries, renaming, organization of pre-defined environment).
- Abstract data types and OOP. This part deals with abstract data types, where types are defined by only their operations, leaving type structure hidden. ADT's are provided by private and limited privates types. Also, this part deals with object oriented programming with Ada95. Included in this part are concepts such as, inheritance and polymorphism, initialization, finalization and assignment, multiple inheritance, tasking and OOP.
- Interfacing with hardware and software systems. Aliased objects and general access types, access to subprograms, representation concept (logical versus physical, pragmas, attributes), support for software and hardware interfaces.
- Concurrent programming. Tasks (threads of control, specification and body, lifetime management), protected types, communication and synchronization (protected operations, rendezvous, shared data), re-queuing, exception handling and tasking, abortion, asynchronous transfer of control, deffering abortion.
- Real-time programming. Time services and delay statement, interrupts, task ids, TCB extensions, priorities for task and protected objects and priority management, priority ceiling and mode changes, performance specifications, restrictions pragma, synchronous and asynchronous task control. Support for interrupt handlers, handling missed deadlines and

solutions to time overruns. Partial computations. User defined scheduling.
- Distributed programming with Ada95. Concepts covered in this part are: Programs, partitions and environment tasks; Role of Ada95 in distributed systems programming; Active and passive partitions; Creating and mapping partitions; Executing multiple partition program; Communication among partitions.

Prerequisites

An introductory course on Fundamentals of Real-Time.

Textbooks

J. Barnes, *Programming in Ada95*, Addison-Wesley, 1996.

A. Burns and A.Wellings, *Real-Time Systems and Their Programming Languages*, Addison-Wesley, 1989.

Course: Critical Real-Time Systems Development

Number of hours: 24.

Course Description

This short course focuses on critical real-time systems where critical systems are either those on which an organization depends or those whose failure can cause harm or damage to the whole system or its environment [5]. The course has several practical assignments.

Contents

- Systems Engineering: An overview of software-based systems engineering for the development of real-time software.
- Requirements Definition: What a system should do from the point of view of the user and system procurer, to understand the place of requirements definition in the software process and to be able to write simple requirements definitions.
- Requirements Specification: Some insights into the production of a detailed requirements specification in real-time systems development which can serve as the basis of a contract for a system development project.
- Prototyping: The role of prototyping in the requirements process and introduction of several approaches to rapid prototyping in real-time systems. When a prototype should be developed and why the suggested techniques are appropriate for rapid prototyping.

- Software Quality Assurance: The role of quality assurance in the software development process of real-time systems. Quality assurance procedures which are currently used in industrial software development. Which quality assurance methods contribute to the development of real-time critical systems.
- Reliability: Introducing the complex notion of reliability when applied to real-time software systems and some metrics for specifying reliability and techniques for modeling and predicting reliability. The methods used for reliability measurement and assessment. The techniques used to develop reliable systems and reliability growth models are discussed.
- Safety-critical software: Some of the factors which affect the specification and the development of real-time safety-critical software systems.

Prerequisites

Computer Architecture, Operating Systems and some experience of programming in C, Ada or Pascal.

Textbooks

I. Somerville, *Software Engineering, 5th Edition.* Addison-Wesley, 1996.

A. Burns and A.Wellings, *Real-Time Systems and Their Programming Languages*, Addison-Wesley, 1989.

J.Laprie, *Dependability, Basic Concepts and Terminology*, Springer -Verlag, 1991.

5. Conclusion

The authors believe that Real-Time Systems is nowadays a fundamental part of the curriculum of the undergraduate and graduate programs of many schools and universities in developed countries. One of the reasons to leverage research and education in this area is the growing presence of embedded control systems in the industry implemented with powerful hardware which satisfy real-time requirements, once found only in laboratories. Conventional software systems are being equipped with "real-time modules" in distributed and networked applications which face timing problems such as concurrency, synchronization, timeliness, dynamic configurations and tasks distributions.

In Mexico, there is no tradition in real-time systems education, and one of our goals in designing a graduate program (for both MSc and PhD) is to bring students with noticeable interests in this field into our Lab in order to participate in basic and applied research projects, whose results might be used in the national industry.

Together with other laboratories at CIC, other courses have been designed focused on other major areas with concerns in real-time fundamentals. What this paper has presented is an attempt to fill the gap in graduate education on real-time systems in Mexico.

References

[1] J. Barnes, *Programacion en Ada,* ED Diaz de Santos, Madrid. 1987.
[2] J.Barnes, *Programming in Ada95*, Addison-Wesley, Reading, MA, 1996.
[3] A. Burns and A.Wellings, *Real-Time Systems and Their Programming Languages*, Addison-Wesley, Reading, MA, 1989.
[4] G. Booch, *Object-Oriented Analysis and Design with Applications*, Benjamin Cummings, Redwood City, CA, 1994.
[5] H. Gomma, *Software Design Methods for Concurrent and Real-Time Systems*, Addison-Wesley, Reading, MA 1993.
[6] M. Gonzalez Harbour, et-al, Course Notes. Real-Time Systems Programming. Xi Laredo Summer Courses, Universidad de Cantabria, Spain,1995.
[7] M.Klein et al, *A Practitioner's Handbook for Real-Time Analysis: Guide to Rate Monotonic Analysis*, Kluwer Academic Publishers, Boston, MA, 1993.
[8] J.Laprie, *Dependability, Basic Concepts and Terminology.* Springer-Verlag, Berlin, 1991.
[9] B. Selic et al, *Real-Time Object-Oriented Modeling*, John Wiley and Sons, New York, 1994.
[10] I. Somerville, *Software Engineering, 5th Edition.* Addison-Wesley, Reading, MA, 1996.
[11] J. Zalewski, Cohesive Use of Commercial Tools in a Classroom. 7th SEI Conference of Software Engineering Education, pp. 65-75, San Antonio, TX, Springer-Verlag, Berlin, 1994.

Chapter 3
Real~Time Systems Education at Embry~Riddle

Real-Time Laboratory in a Computer Science/Engineering Program

Andrew J. Kornecki & Janusz Zalewski
Dept. of Computer Science
Embry-Riddle Aeronautical University
Daytona Beach, FL 32114-3900, U.S.A.
+1 (904) 226-6690
{korn, zalewski}@db.erau.edu

Abstract

There has been an ongoing discussion on the merit of using a hardware laboratory in software-oriented undergraduate computer science curricula. We challenge the view that the hardware is to be studied only in the computer engineering or electrical engineering programs. This view is obviously taking into consideration the existence or lack of laboratory space, computer science faculty background, and the organization of curriculum. This paper discusses the problems to prepare graduates to meet the needs of industry seeking individuals with software engineering knowledge and a good deal of hardware experience (as related to the development of software). The solution is in the modification of a standard curriculum, by adding elements of real-time system implementation to the software engineering oriented curriculum. The paper presents the educational objectives and describes the laboratory set-up designed to provide a platform to accomplish the required objectives.

1. Introduction

The progress in computer applications has widened the gap between real-world software development needs and experiences of undergraduates in most computer science and engineering programs. College courses in computer science programs tend to stress theoretical foundations and programming skills. The latter are mostly limited to data manipulation with standard input/output and rarely consider the operating system environment and timing. In the computer and electrical engineering programs the focus is on hardware, leaving the software development process and the quality of software artifacts as issues of marginal importance.

At the same time, the majority of industrial applications require knowledge of the software development lifecycle for time-critical and reactive systems and the ability to utilize operating system resources. The required topics include programming with interrupts, concurrency and scheduling, memory management, input and output devices, interfacing different systems and programming platforms. The knowledge and skills in these areas, required by the industry, is rarely taught at the university level. For parts of the software industry, it is imperative to get college graduates with not only a general computer science background but also software engineering skills and related hardware experience.

To meet such a demand, a real-time laboratory has been created. Easy access to a well equipped real-time software development laboratory is needed to provide students with hands-on experience in the areas of microprocessor-based software, computer interfacing, and utilization of operating system resources in a time-critical software development.

2. Description of the Program

Since 1989, the Computer Science undergraduate program at Embry-Riddle Aeronautical University (ERAU) has been based on an innovative approach, termed "a Domain Centered Curriculum" [3], which is essentially software oriented and follows the ACM/IEEE Curriculum 91 guidelines [8]. Currently, the program has ten full time faculty, nine holding doctoral degrees, and approximately 200 undergraduate students. The department also offers minors in Computer Science, Computer Applications, as well as service courses for the other programs. In 1993, ERAU introduced a Master of Software Engineering program which presently enrolls 45 graduate students.

Although software-oriented, the undergraduate program includes more hardware-oriented courses than the typical computer science curriculum. Modifications introduced to the curriculum replaced the older courses on digital logic, assembly programming, and microprocessors with a sequence of two courses on Computer Organization (CS211 and CS311). The sequence covers such topics as number systems, digital logic, digital system analysis and design, organization of computer systems, microprocessor and assembly language concepts, input/output and interrupt interfacing, memory organization and management [4]. In the senior year, the hardware sequence is capped by the computer architecture course (CS470) which discusses various architectures, bus standards, and elements of operating systems. Two additional elective courses on interfacing (CS445) and telecommunication (CS460) also address selected hardware aspects of computing.

In parallel to the above, two computer science courses (CS115, CS215) introduce fundamentals of computer science with problem solving, elements of personal software process, and software development lifecycle principles. The students learn about software requirements specification, design, implementation, and testing using Ada as the programming language. These topics are expanded in the freshman/junior level course on software engineering. Some other courses in the program include: discrete math, data structures, data bases, programming languages and operating systems, computer graphics, simulation, artificial intelligence, etc.

In the senior year, students take a real-time systems course (CS450). It covers topics of concurrency as well as time critical and reactive programming with external interfaces, including utilization of system resources and interprocess communication. The curriculum is capped with a senior team project course (CS465), during which students develop various software artifacts.

Until now, the available laboratory resources have only allowed us to offer the real-time class within the constraints of "soft" real-time [5]. The implementation platform is a network of Sun workstations with simulated external sources of data and interrupts. The students worked on a semester-long team project collecting requirements, preparing the design and implementing software capable of acquiring the external data, reacting to interrupts and user input, and generating output conforming to pre-defined timing specifications. The projects allow exploration of such topics as concurrency, intertask communication, and interface with the operating system software. The implementation language was Ada with its tasking and run-time libraries supporting the course material. Examples of class projects are a "dog fight" aviation video game, a reconfigurable aircraft instrument panel, space shut-

tle launch control panel, and a program for monitoring airport ground traffic from a Global Navigation Satellite System feed. Utilizing the resources of the ERAU Airway Science Simulation Laboratory, selected groups of students have developed projects on non-standard platforms. Examples of those include: PC-based real-time data acquisition and processing from a Kavouras weather station, Silicon Graphics flight simulator with instrument panel, and a visual display controlled from a modified Boeing 707 flight procedure trainer. Details of some of these projects are presented in [6].

3. Why Do We Need a Hard-Real-Time Laboratory?

Despite very positive reactions from both the students and the industry, there is evidence that the offering could be significantly improved by introducing the "hard" aspects of real-time software development. The input from industries employing our graduates suggests that the omission of these aspects is a serious deficiency of the undergraduate education in computer science and engineering. We feel strongly that this deficiency can be resolved by offering access to a laboratory focusing on computer organization and hardware underpinning of software issues.

To ensure that the computer science program and a newly developed computer engineering program will produce students capable of understanding and applying real-time concepts used in industrial practice, it is evident that ERAU must modify the curriculum by putting more emphasis on the hardware and real-time component of the software development process [1, 2, 7, 11]. This approach can be used as a blueprint for other computer science and engineering programs across the country that may already have access to a laboratory with digital trainers and/or microprocessor boards.

In 1995, the Computer Science department moved into the "new" Science and Technology Building with significantly increased laboratory space. In this new building we have established the Real-Time Software Development (RTSD) laboratory. The real-time lab has been funded by the Instrumentation and Laboratory Improvement Grant from the National Science Foundation to equip the laboratory to support the computer organization and real-time part of our undergraduate curriculum.

There are two basic components of the currently developed RTSD lab. The first concentrates on the fundamentals of computer organization and interfacing. The second supports the development of real-time software in both self-hosted and host-target configurations conforming to the specific timing and interfacing constraints.

Based on contacts with industry, published literature and previous work [9, 10], we assumed that in order for the students to obtain complete understanding of real-time software development, they need to get instruction in the following four areas:

- System specification and design on a host computer.

- Implementation and testing on a host computer.

- Downloading and cross-testing on a target backplane bus system with real-time operating system kernel.

- Testing the real-time operation with connected external equipment and actual timing constraints.

The expansion of a new laboratory requires equipment that can support development of "hard" real-time software systems (including real-time operating system kernels, downloading, testing, and the execution on a target system). This expansion creates an environment allowing to get hands-on experience also in the computer organization classes with microprocessor interfacing, to prepare students for playing supporting roles in the real-time software development.

The previous offering of the real-time systems course has supported the instruction within the limit of the first two areas listed above. The team projects in currently offered real-time class require students to build requirements and a specification document using CASE tools, real-time specification and design methodologies. Subsequently, the projects are implemented on Sun workstations running non-real-time Unix and SunAda with only "soft" real-time support.

The new laboratory infrastructure is designed to support instruction in the two remaining areas, and significantly improve student knowledge and skills in the software development in a realistic real-time industrial environment, which has thus far been neglected in college education [1, 7].

4. Educational Objectives

The overall objective for an effective education of a real-time software developer can be defined as empowering him with an ability to apply a rigorous development process and individual activities in engineering time-critical and reactive software within the constraints of the implementation platform hardware and the operating system environment. On the other hand, to meet industrial and academic standards, we have identified a list of "a-to-z" real-time related topics to be taught. The list focuses on those hardware aspects of real-time computing that are related to an efficient software development process. Keeping in mind the overall objective, the list of topics has been reshaped and is presented in Table 1.

a. Digital logic gates and circuits

b. Computer components and organization

c. Computer operations and code representation

d. Bus architecture, signals, and timing

e. Assembly language concepts

f. Assembling, linking, loading and executing of programs

g. Interrupt concept

h. Input/output interface concept

i. Interrupt and input/output programming

j. Operating system basics

k. Real-time features of an operating system

l. Reactive and time-critical programming concepts

m. Requirement analysis for real-time software

n. Design of real-time software

o. Concurrency of programming tasks

p. Signals and operating system interface

q. Programming languages and environments for real-time

r. Resource contention constructs

s. Implementation of concurrent programs

t. Multiprocess and multithread applications

u. Multiprocessor operations

v. Communication protocols

w. Cross-development environment and tools

x. Debugging on target system

y. Timing and performance analysis

z. Bus analysis and industrial standards

Table 1: List of Educational Objectives
in Real-Time Software Development

To meet the objectives, we have identified two subsequent steps, which are described in the next sections:

- assign the topics to the individual courses in the curriculum, and
- identify the laboratory hardware/software infrastructure to support the individual topics.

5. Allocation of Topics to Courses

A minimal sequence of courses to meet the above real-time educational objectives and cover the topics list is composed of the following five courses:

- Computer Organization I
- Computer Organization II
- Programming with Operating Systems
- Software Engineering
- Real-Time Systems

The following elective courses add an additional dimension to the offering:

- Interfacing
- Computer Architecture
- Distributed Computing and Networking

The list of required topics to be taught in order to cover the real-time spectrum of instruction is allocated individually to each course. The topic allocation is non-exclusive, i.e. the same topic may be listed in more than one course. In such case, the breadth and/or depth of the topic coverage is expanded in the next course in sequence. The proposed allocation is being tested in some of the current and the future course offerings in ERAU computer science program discussed below. In the description presented, the letters denoting particular topics refer to the overall "a-to-z" topics list from Table 1.

Computer Organization I

The objective of the first computer organization course is to introduce the students to the basic concepts of digital hardware and computer operation:

a. Digital logic gates and circuits

b. Computer components and organization

c. Computer operations and code representation

d. Bus architecture, signals, and timing

To support this objective, the lab experiments cover familiarization with the number systems, logic gate operations, memory devices, medium scale integration devices, and the design and implementation of a moderate size sequential circuit. In the current ERAU offering, CS211 (Computer Organization I) fully conforms to the above description.

Computer Organization II

The second computer organization class explores computer organization and programming with focus on interrupt and input-output interface:

c. Computer operations and code representation

d. Bus architecture, signals, and timing

e. Assembly language concepts

f. Assembling and executing of programs

g. Interrupt concept

h. Input/output interface concept

i. Interrupt and input/output programming

To support these objectives, the lab experiments deal with developing and testing microprocessor assembly and machine level language programs. The experiments also include simple input-output and interrupt interfacing, analysis of signals and timing. In the current ERAU offering, CS311 (Computer Organization II) fully conforms to the above description.

In an additional elective course on interfacing, the lab experiments utilize the concepts learned above, adding the design and implementation of more sophisticated systems interfacing microprocessors, using a variety of combinational and sequential circuits, A/D and D/A converters, concepts of digital signal processing, and also external hardware interfacing (sensors, switches, displays, stepping motors).

Programming with Operating Systems

This course offered in the junior year is based on the student's familiarity with high-level language programming and data structures. The course addresses issues of system programming, features of operating systems used in application programs, resource allocation, interprocess communication and operating system constructs. From the real-time list of topics, we include the following:

j. Operating system basics

k. Real-time features of operating systems

p. Signals and operating system interface

r. Resource contention constructs

t. Multiprocess and multithread applications

u. Multiprocessor operations

v. Communication protocols

In the current ERAU catalog, there are two courses oriented toward teaching these concepts: the required course CS344 (C and Unix) and an elective CS420 (Operating Systems). In currently offered CS344 course, most of the time is spent on teaching C programming, leaving not enough time to cover the material described by items: j, k, p, r, t, u, and v. In the future, the basic knowledge of C programming shall be a pre-requisite for this course, thus allowing for adequate coverage of other topics. The CS420 course will provide an in-depth coverage.

Software Engineering

The junior year course on software engineering is based on the introductory instruction delivered in the freshmen computer science classes, i.e. knowledge of the software development lifecycle and the personal software process. The course introduces concepts of team development, managing the development process, details of software lifecycle, CASE tools, and the format of software artifacts to be produced. From the real-time list, the following items are being taught (even though the course emphasis is not on real-time):

m. Requirement analysis for real-time software

n. Design of real-time software

In the current offering, CS431 course (Software Engineering) is used to teach these concepts.

Real-Time Systems

This senior level course's focus is on the development of time-critical and reactive software. The real-time topics covered in this course include:

k. Real-time features of operating systems

l. Reactive and time critical programming concepts

m. Requirement analysis for real-time software

n. Design of real-time software

o. Concurrency of programming tasks

p. Signals and operating system interface

q. Programming languages for real-time

r. Resource contention constructs

w. Cross-development environment and tools

x. Debugging on target systems

y. Timing and performance analysis

The list is rather long and the breadth of coverage takes precedence over the depth. Some of the material is covered in more depth in other courses, such as elective courses on interfacing, computer architecture, and distributed computing (topics listed in Table 1, as items: j, o, p, r, s, t, u, v, y, and z). In the current ERAU offering, CS450 (Real Time Systems) fully conforms to the above description.

6. Laboratory Infrastructure

To support the educational objectives presented in Section 4, a minimal laboratory infrastructure is required. Both hardware and software components of such a lab are listed in Table 2.

The selection process focused on various hardware and software configurations to accomplish the proposed educational objectives. After careful investigation and analysis of the existing tools, a decision was made to replace the digital logic hardware experiments by the simulated environment in a familiar multiuser MS Windows setup. More emphasis has been put on the real-time software development aspects in a multiuser and multiprocessor environment and interfacing with realistic signal sources as defined by the military bus MIL-STD-1553 or avionics bus ARINC429 standards. We selected industry-recognized real-time operating systems (LynxOS, QNX, Solaris, Linux with RT extensions, VxWorks, AIX) to be installed and used in the classroom settings. They provide not only concurrency mechanisms (such as semaphores, mailboxes, signals, etc.), but also Unix/Posix-compliant real-time scheduling mechanisms (such as rate-monotonic or deadline-monotonic scheduling, priority inheritance) compatible with languages of our choice (C, C++, Ada).

1. Digital Logic/Breadboard Simulator

2. Microprocessor Development Boards with I/O hardware

3. Microprocessor Compiler, Assembler, and Debugger

4. Signal/Bus Analysis Hardware and Software

5. CASE Tools with Real-Time Extensions

6. Real-Time Self-Host Development System

7. Real-Time Host-Target Cross Development System

8. VMEbus Powered Enclosure with CPU and Controller Boards

9. DAQ (Data Acquisition) Software and Hardware

10. Real Time Performance Analysis Software

Table 2: Elements of Laboratory Infrastructure

The complete laboratory environment includes the following two sections.

A. Computer Organization Section

In the computer organization section of the lab, we have about a dozen Intel-based microcomputers used as the lab stations applied in experiments with the microprocessor boards and hardware interfacing. In addition, students have access to the networked software (for digital circuit simulation and assembly language development) from a university-wide microcomputer network. Using this environment, the laboratory shall provide:

- Digital logic and circuits simulation on a microcomputer network.
- Microprocessor development boards with associated assembling, linking, downloading, and debugging utilities on the microcomputer platform.
- Interrupt and I/O interfacing experiments to be used with the microprocessor development boards.
- Data acquisition tools on Intel-based MS Windows platform (e.g. National Instruments LabView, Feedback)

B. Real-Time Software Section

In the real-time section of the lab, we are in the process of putting several workstations on the network, including eight Intel-based machines with native real-time operating systems, two RS6000 and two PowerPC workstations running AIX, two Sun Sparc machines: a server running SunOS and the VxWorks development system, and a separate workstation running Solaris. All these machines are connected to the university wide Unix network and to the six VMEbus enclosures with Motorola target processors and controllers. The complete laboratory set-up is presented below:

- Networked workstations for development of self-hosted real-time software using dedicated real-time kernels (QNX, LynxOS, Solaris) and programming environments (C, C++, X window system, Motif).
- Unix server with a real-time cross-development environment (e.g. VxWorks) including multilanguage development system (C, C++, Ada), target downloading, and debugging utilities.
- VMEbus target systems with compatible real-time kernel software on the network for software downloading, debugging, and performance analysis (e.g. VxWorks, SDS Single Step or Cross Code)

- CASE tools on the network for project planning, developing real-time requirements, specifications, and designs (e.g. Cadre Teamwork, MS Windows Project)
- Tools for real-time scheduling analysis (e.g. iRAT rate-monotonic analysis tool for MS Windows)
- Tools for bus/signal analysis (e.g. logic analyzer, software tools under MS Windows).

Table 3 presents the cross-reference between the elements of a real-time laboratory hardware and software infrastructure (items 1-10, as presented in Table 2) and the educational objectives (items a-z, as presented in Table 1). This laboratory infrastructure is indispensible to meet the educational objectives and provides for a valuable hands-on experience amplifying the concepts learned. The selected laboratory equipment broadly covers the entire list of real-time topics.

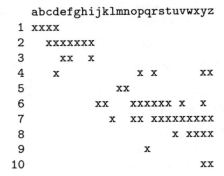

Table 3. Laboratory Components
Facilitating Instructional Objectives

7. Conclusion

The presented laboratory set-up forms a base for a distributed network environment, where students can do the software development virtually from any university workstation (since the installed real-time development systems are accessible from the entire Unix network). The lab allows students to get hands-on experience in dealing with "hard" real-time systems implementation, downloading, monitoring, and software testing on a target computer. The concepts of real-time operating system kernels, scheduling, task prioritization are all the subjects of laboratory experimentation. The laboratory assignments will allow us to demonstrate real-time behavior in real-life environment, analyze the response time and visualize the impact of context switching for various scheduling protocols. Examples of the future real-time projects include: data acquisition, temperature control, liquid level control, multiprocessor simulation of an aircraft trajectory, etc.

In addition to the real-time computing equipment, we are planning to add some additional hardware to be controlled. Examples of such equipment that exists at other departments, at ERAU, includes the meteorological equipment, avionics and global positioning satellite system, aircraft and air traffic control simulators.

Using such a sophisticated equipment may be a challenge for undergraduate students. However a stepwise approach, already tested in the classroom [9], based on demos, class exercises, homework assignments, and team projects helps to alleviate any significant problems. In a demo, the instructor shows to the class a simple example and its solution, using a tool. In an exercise, the student is assigned to modify slightly the example presented in the demo and see and explain the results, under the instructor's supervision. In a homework assignment, the student is assigned a problem to solve individually, in an open lab, using the tool. In a team project, a group of students is assigned a problem to solve, using the skills acquired in three former steps.

The presented lab structure is currently under development. The selection has been made for all of the components. The purchase and installation is in progress. The integration and testing has started this summer, and will continue over the academic year 1996/97. The lab is planned to become fully operational by the beginning of the Fall'97 term.

Acknowledgements

This work has been supported by the 1995/96 National Science Fundation Instrumentation and Laboratory Improvement IP Grant. Educational support from Quantum Software and Green Hill Systems is greatly appreciated.

References

[1] W.A. Halang, A Curriculum for Real-Time Computer and Control Systems Engineering, IEEE Trans. on Education. Vol. 33, No. 2, May 1990, pp. 171-178

[2] T. Hilburn, I. Hirmanpour, A. Kornecki, The Integration of Software Engineering into a Computer Science Curriculum, Proc. 8th SEI Conf. on Software Engineering Education, R.L. Ibrahim, Ed., Springer-Verlag, Berlin, 1995, pp. 87-95

[3] I. Hirmanpour, T. Hilburn, A. Kornecki, A Domain Centered Curriculum: An Alternative Approach to Computing Education, SIGCSE Bulletin, Vol 27, No. 1, 1995, pp. 126-130

[4] A. Kornecki, Microprocessor Laboratory in a Software Oriented Computer Science College Program, Proc. National Educational Computing Conference, NECC'88, Dallas, TX, 1988, p. 237

[5] A. Kornecki, Global Positioning System as a Real-Time Software Engineering Project in an Undergraduate CS Curriculum, Proc. Conf. Software Engineering Research in Florida, SERF'93, R. Guha, Ed., Orlando, FL, 1993, pp. 126-129

[6] A. Kornecki, J. Zalewski, Projects for Real-Time Systems Classes, Workshop on Real-Time Systems Education, Daytona Beach, FL, April 20, 1996

[7] J.W. McCormick, A Laboratory for Teaching the Development of Real-Time Software Systems, SIGCSE Bulletin, Vol. 23, No.1, March 1991, pp. 260-264

[8] A. Tucker, Ed., Computing Curricula 1991, Communications of the ACM, Vol. 34, No. 6, June 1991, pp. pp. 68-84

[9] J. Zalewski, A Real-Time Systems Course Based on Ada, Proc. ASEET 7th Ann. Ada Software Engineering Education and Training Symp., Monterey, CA, January 12-14, 1993, pp. 25-49

[10] J. Zalewski, Cohesive Use of Commercial Tools in a Classroom, Proc. 7th SEI Conf. on Software Engineering Education, J.L. Diaz-Herrera, Ed., Springer-Verlag, Berlin, 1994, pp. 65-75

[11] R.M. Zobel, Real-Time Systems Education in Computer Science at Manchester University, Microprocessing and Microprogramming, Vol. 24, 1988, pp. 835-840

Projects for Real-Time Systems Classes

Andrew J. Kornecki & Janusz Zalewski
Dept. of Computer Science
Embry-Riddle Aeronautical University
Daytona Beach, FL 32114-3900, U.S.A.
+1 (904) 226-6690
{korn, zalewski}@db.erau.edu

Abstract

This paper presents authors' experiences with running individual and team projects for real-time systems classes. Demos, exercises, and individual assignments precede the actual work on bigger projects. Each project is conducted in a number of phases. Both undergraduate and graduate class projects are discussed.

1. Introduction

The authors' approach to class projects encompasses different steps in helping students to acquire knowledge to design real-time systems: demos and exercises followed by assignments first, and team projects next. This approach can be characterized as follows: watch and repeat the demos, then work individually on simple exercises and assignments, and finally work in teams to solve a significant problem.

Demos may include short one- or two-page programs on multitasking or multithreading. Their purpose is to cover, in one program, a set of primary language concepts, for example: task types, task scheduling, rendezvous, time slicing, delay and abort statements, task priorities and attributes, and exceptions. They may include a presentation of a well understood example. A good example of a bigger problem to start with is the cruise control system, because it is well described in several publications and is delivered as a sample problem with several tool sets. It can be presented first in a lecture and then students can work on it individually in the lab learning how to use the tool.

For a typical real-time programming exercise, a specification or a design is given and discussed, and the students write an implementation. This kind of application should allow the students to use most of the concepts and constructs for concurrency, as well as employ a substantial amount of real-time constructs of programming languages or operating systems. As exercises one can use relatively simple, individual projects based on concepts of concurrent programming, such as those discussed in [10, 20] or more involved projects, which build on this knowledge, such as multitasking simulation of Ethernet, network synchronization in Ada, data acquisition benchmark, or more advanced ones, requiring some special knowledge, such as trie search. The selection depends on the level of the student group, and is more clear after first demos and exercises are done. An important consideration is that students have several presented exercises to choose from. They are also allowed to work in pairs, building the groundwork for the team project later on. An exercise can be extended to a full assignment. One example of such is the multithreaded program presented in Appendix. It contains an incorrect program handed to students, who are requested to correct it in several steps. The gas station controller written in Ada is another example [20].

Regarding more complex projects, which are the ultimate goal of a real-time systems class, there are plenty of different realistic examples. They vary from a simple vending machine to a complex air traffic control system, and are relatively well described in the literature (see Section 2). Team projects to develop software for real life applications should incorporate principles of software engineering, with focus on team work. Methodologies used in these projects, some explicitly oriented towards Ada, include: SSEM [16], SCOOP-3 [4], or Spec [1] for specifications, and DARTS [6] or HOOD [13] for designs.

The principal idea behind structuring the material into demos first, exercises and assignments next, and team projects last, is that concurrent programming skills and style of thinking are most crucial for software development in real-time systems, and acquiring them should precede all other activities in such a course.

2. Sample Projects

Below, typical projects are listed, as found in the literature, and one generic project is described applicable in a variety of circumstances.

2.1. Typical Projects

A list of case studies (inluding references), which can be used for student projects is given below:

- Automobile Management System [7]
- Home Heating System [7]
- Vending Machine [7]
- Cruise Control System [4, 18]
- Bottle Filling System [18]
- Defect Inspection System [18]
- Single Lane Bridge Traffic Control [12]
- Mine Drainage Control System [3]
- Robot Controller [9]
- Air Traffic Control System [9]
- Remote Temperature Sensor [15]
- Combination Lock [4]
- Digital Watch [2]
- Elevator Control [2]
- Flexible Manufacturing System [14]
- Data Acquisition and Shuttle Launch Control [5]
- Weather/Environment Monitor [19].

Some of these are described in our previous publications [10, 20]: the gas station controller (that allows the students to use the Ada rendezvous with dynamic task creation and deletion (to simulate arriving and leaving customers), and realize the danger of deadlocks (due to incorrect specifications), the single-lane bridge lights controller (that demonstrates a danger of starvation and its consequences), and a tunnel control (that can check students' understanding of mutual exclusion problems and their solutions).

2.2. Generic Project

A sufficiently general and relatively simple application program for real-time systems, which can be used in both undergraduate and graduate classes, is a data acquisition system composed of the following tasks:

- user interface (to enter parameters, activate and kill tasks, display the results, etc.)

- data acquisition (to read data, from inputs like ADCs, etc.)
- data handling (to preprocess input data in real time, by simple averaging or more involved type of filtering)
- data output (to write data onto a magnetic medium, send into a network, etc.).

It has an advantage that virtually every real-time system met in practice has these four components, although due to its simplicity it does not include communication and control components.

3. Original Projects for Undergrads

The five projects A through E listed below were used at Embry-Riddle to be implemented as Ada programs on Sun workstations using a provided data generator package. User interfaces are implemented using the C *curses* library (ported to SunAda). The external data are to be read from ports, files, or shared memory (or as direct data from the data generator package tasks). The external events are implemented in a form of Unix signals to which the program is to react.

Other projects could be added to the list. In the past, we had projects processing meteorological data from the Kavouras weather station, flight data from Frasca simulators, interfacing to the Boeing 707 flight simulator, imitating operation of a ground based satellite Global Positioning System.

Students, after discussion among the classmates and with an instructor, decide the topic and the team composition. We suggest a team to consist of at least three and at most five students. The activities included working on the requirements, design, implementation, and testing. Ideally a team needs a person with a leadership skills, a document writer with technical writing skills, a problem solver with analytical skills, a code hacker with Unix/Ada/C wizardry, and a difficult to satisfy but well organized tester. Despite this role playing all team members are responsible for the entire project, but the particular individual tasks are reflected in the project grade. The team keeps a detailed report of their activities, meetings, work done, and deliverables.

The description of projects is rather vague and resembles the actual statement of work as obtained from the customer. It is the team's responsibility to pinpoint the system requirements and, in the first phase of the project, produce a simplified software requirements specification (SRS) document to be a base for the design and implementation. This activity may require further studies such as talking to faculty and students from the aviation part of the campus and identifying the scope of the system to be implemented.

Although we speed-up through the entire software development cycle, the main emphasis is on the design and implementation – this is the point of concentration of this class. Each team member is required to work on the implementation and understand the issues of task interfaces and timing. Writing Ada packages or C modules and using intertask and interprocess communication is the main objective of this exercise.

A list of projects and their descriptions are presented in the next section, followed by brief descriptions of development phases as done in class (for Ada as an implementation language).

3.1. List of Projects

Project A: Instruments Display System

Aircraft instrument display system acquiring external data (e.g. representing velocity, pitch, yaw, and bank) and displaying them on the screen, responding to the user input to reconfigure the presentation.

Input

- external data (velocity, pitch, bank, and yaw)
- external events (engine failure, stall)
- asynchronous user keyboard input requesting one of the four possible presentations

Output

- display of the instrument panel in various configurations with the updated data and event messages

Project B: Navigation Display System

Aircraft navigation display system acquiring external data (e.g. representing horizontal and vertical speed) and displaying the aircraft position on the screen in relation to the selected navigational aids.

Input

- external data (horizontal/vertical speed, heading)
- external events (equipment failure, windshear)
- asynchronous user keyboard input selecting navigational aid frequencies and operation modes

Output

- display of navigation instruments with the updated data and event messages

Project C: Radar Display System

Acquisition of target position data from a simulated air-traffic control (ATC) radar. Displaying the data block and updating it on the screen. Responding to user input representing various ATC operations (handouts, data block manipulations, track association).

Input

- external data representing the aircraft (ID, x, y, alt)
- external events representing handoff-request, alerts, etc.
- asynchronous controller keyboard input representing such actions as: handoff acceptance/execution, data block modification, etc.

Output

- radar display with aircraft data block, timely updated and reacting to the controller inputs

Project D: Dog-Fight System

Dog-fight system acquiring the data representing position of the enemy aircraft and responding to the pilot input attempting to target and fire the weapon in an optimal condition.

Input

- position of the target (e.g. x, y, alt, status/fof - "friend-or-foe") from the external data
- external events (enemy fire, equipment malfunction)
- asynchronous pilot keyboard input (up, down, right, left, slow, fast, firing button)

Output

- a radar-like display with positions of the target, control messages and the outcome of the pursuit when the firing occurs (hit/miss probability)

Project E: Weapon Targeting System

Weapon targeting system acquiring the data representing position of an unknown target, detecting the target intentions and generating advice and control for the air defense.

Input

- position of the target (e.g. x, y, alt, status/fof) from the external data
- external events (enemy fire, equipment malfunction)
- asynchronous operator keyboard input (fof inquiry, change range, change operation mode, fire)

Output

- a radar-like display with positions of the target, control messages and the outcome of the target track evaluation and action taken (hit/miss probability)

3.2. Phase 1

The first phase of a project shall address the specification and requirement phase extended to an early design. The required deliverables are:

(a) introduction and the problem statement (including a narrative description of the project, rationale, background, and a detailed context diagram with description of the environment terminals and the system functionality)

(b) initial identification of timing requirements for the system with an analysis and clarification of the time constraints (response time, data acquisition time, update time, etc.)

(c) system Data Flow Diagram (DFD), first and second level, with identification of data stores and interfacing flows

(d) State Transition Diagrams (STD) for the related Control Processes with explanations including Event List and description of normal and abnormal states

(e) Control/Data Flow Diagram (C/DFD) resulting from steps (c) and (d)

(f) Data Dictionary (DD) with detailed description of all data and control flows and their specification

(g) Process and Control Specifications (PSPECS) for each of the lowest level processes

(h) initial identification of tasks (an initial Ada Task Diagram) to be revised in the second phase of the project.

The project front page shall describe project, class, instructor, term, team, and date. Separate pages shall describe all activities with dates, names, and the scope of work done. All the team meetings shall have a record describing time, place, participants, item discussed, action items, and responsible team member. Each of the above deliverables (items a through h) shall be clearly identified and in order.

Separately, each team member shall send via e-mail a brief statement describing the team co-operation and evaluation of the other team members (possible categories are: contributing, cooperating, attending, non-cooperating, missing).

The document to be prepared is to be clear, consistent, and easy to modify. The class materials are placed on library reserve desk and include items useful for the task accomplishment.

For the Sun-based projects, the source of input data is provided as an Ada package generating a continuous stream of integer data written to predefined ports/files. The system developed shall read these ports/files at a specified rate, using timing from CALENDAR package. Additionally, the provided package generates two interrupts (Unix signals) which the system developed shall intercept and respond to. The format of the data is discussed in detail in class.

3.3. Phase 2

The second phase of a project should include the following:

- upgrade of the first phase including necessary interfaces between the data processes

- identification of timing requirements for the system with a detailed analysis and clarification of the time constraints (response time, data acquisition time, update time, etc.)

- identification of interfacing processes (to include internal data stores) with analysis of the data flows directions and the caller/callee definitions

- Ada task graph and packaging decisions

- a first draft of Ada code including all specifications and interfaces (seperated into packages)

- a brief description of hardware requirements and constraints.

Students may consider submitting revisions of the first phase including problem background, purpose, context diagram, etc. The grading of the second phase will concentrate on:

(a) updated D/CFD of required depth considering concurrency of processes

(b) updated STD of the control processes

(c) consistent and updated DD with all data/control flows,

(d) identification of the interfacing processes (assumption is that the data "writer" is responsible for the interface), i.e. replacing data stores by equivalent processes

(e) Ada Task Graph and packaging diagrams, defining definition, helper, and application packages

(f) first draft of Ada code including all specifications and interfaces (consistent with the rest of documentation)

(g) a write-up related to hardware/software requirements and description of the hardware/software base used for the project implementation based on the input data and display description (including the timing discussion).

The format of incoming data is known and available. There is package provided imitating the "real-time" data for the students to use. Provided is also information describing the data generator package and the ways to incorporate it into the program.

3.4. Phase 3

Phase 2 of the project identified the top-down components of the system, updated the requirement and specification document with selected artifacts (D/CFD, DD, STD, PSPECS, etc.). It has defined the Ada packages and specification for procedures, tasks, and inter-module interfaces.

The third phase of the project should include the following:

(a) operational Ada code with all specifications, bodies, and interfaces using proper software standards with headers, comments and formatting; each package, procedure, function, task, and module must have a header with clear identification of the purpose, interface, author, time, changes, etc.

(b) a manual describing the system operations in an acceptable tutorial-like format

(c) discussion of timing requirements based on program testing (changing display rate, data input rate, etc.).

The grading is concentrated on the working code – solutions have to be proven by using a test-bed for running the system. Some designated team members should re-visit the documentation and study the Software Development Manual to be found in class directories. Students are urged to use the hints and recommendation from the manual to guide them on the documentation format.

3.5. Phase 4

The final project must be submitted in a clean and professional format and contain the following deliverables:

(a) title page with student names, class, semester, instructor, project title, etc.

(b) schedule of events describing student activities on the project (date, activity, meeting reports – an appendix attached to the project)

(c) table of contents and list of references

(d) an introduction and a narrative description of the system (i.e. background of the project)

(e) a general problem statement with the overall system Context Diagram

(f) a detailed problem statement for the system including user interface "look" (if applicable) and description of operations (i.e. system functionality)

(g) Event List and a note on timing requirements and assumptions (this section must be re-visited, as new information is now available related to the implementation; all comments and data on the system speed, response time, performance, future improvements, etc., are to be included)

(h) Data/Control Flow Diagrams for the system up to the required depth (to identify the processes to be implemented as separate code entities); consistency between the D/CFD and the tasks in the Ada Task Diagram must be checked

(i) State Transition Diagrams for the relevant subsystems

(j) Process/Control Specifications at the lowest level including process name, input, output, processing, timing

(k) a consistent Data Dictionary identifying all internal variables in the subsystem and all variables shared by the subsystems

(l) identification of interfacing processes with names of calling and called processes, and the list of data to be interchanged (with the timing requirements - see (g) above)

(m) process Ada Task Diagram and packaging decisions (providing consistency between the diagram and the specification part of the code; which tasks are callers and which are callees; and the directions of data interfaces)

(n) the complete listing of Ada code including all specifications, bodies, interfaces (with description and formats of all data files created and/or used by the program); the program should adhere to acceptable coding standards; a `read.me` file describing all source files in the program and the compilation/linking process needs to be provided

(o) a brief write-up related to hardware and software requirements and description of the hardware/software base used for the project implementation, all graphic files, used tools, and other elements of software development

(p) a narrative description of testing of the system; how to proceed with the testing, what is the input, output, what leads to the conclusion that the system works correctly

(q) a working version of the system placed in the class directory: all source files, applicable data files, and the executable code

(r) a conclusion section identifying the problems encountered, lessons learned, and suggestions for the future project offerings

(s) separately, via e-mail, each team member shall send a personal evaluation of his team giving each teammate a score (within the suggested categories: leading, contributing, participating, showing, missing).

The grading is based on the overall deliverables for the project, internal consistency of the text, and quality of the above items (a–s) and the class presentation. For the presentation, 4-6 transparencies are suggested to include:

- title page (class, project title, authors)
- system description (input, output, processes, behavior, layout)
- context diagram and the first level D/CFD
- Ada Task Graph
- conclusions and lessons learned.

During the presentation the program should be run to demonstrate the system behavior. The presentation usually does not exceed 15 minutes. Copies of presentation transparencies shall be included as an appendix in the project report. The presentation is usually in the last week of classes and is an important component of the final project grade.

4. Graduate Projects

The authors' own industrial experience concentrated on safety related applications; similar lab projects were also developed for graduate projects:

- Traffic Alert and Collision Avoidance System (TCAS)
- Water Boiler Controller [8]
- Radiation Detection System [20]
- Message Broadcast System [17].

4.1. TCAS System

The project is designed to produce software artifacts representing the core operational part of the airborne TCAS system. The following is a brief description of the project. Information for the software development is based on the available documents, textbooks, handouts, and the domain expert knowledge.

The project deliverables are as follows:

- Project Plan
- Software Requirement Specification Document
- Initial Design Document
- Detailed Design
- Testing Plan
- Implementation
- User and Developer Documentation
- Project Presentation.

4.1.1. TCAS System Information

The purpose of this system is to monitor the traffic in the vicinity of the aircraft. The information about the traffic is collected by avionics hardware from antennas and is available in a computer readable format. At any given time the system can read an external data buffer representing the most current information about the adjacent air traffic (see next section). The information for each target will include the following items: identification, range, bearing, and altitude. There could be up to N targets tracked at any given time. Asynchronously, the system will receive external messages representing coordination from other TCAS aircraft including identification and the intent of the maneuver. From the aircraft's own avionics the system can read a buffer including such information as altitude and selected equipment sensitivity.

The system operator (pilot) can set the equipment in four operational modes: Off, Standby, Traffic Advisories Only (TA), and Resolution Advisories (RA). The equipment sensitivity in advisory modes is based on the aircraft altitude (or can be overriden manually) according to the TCAS specification.

The system shall keep monitoring the traffic, processing the data and issuing appropriate advisories. When working in RA mode, the system must additionally output and broadcast a coordination message. The traffic and advisories shall be displayed in an appropriate format using symbols and text strings described in the TCAS specification.

4.1.2. Scaffolding Simulation Software

In order to implement the TCAS system there is a need to develop a simplistic simulator for the TCAS aircraft combined with the target aircraft. The simulation system is continuosly generating the aircraft position and altitude, determined by initial position, speed, heading, and climb/descend rate parameters (to be controlled from the keyboard). The system, in a similar manner, generates the position and altitude of targets according to predefined parameters. The parameter values may change randomly within some predefined range.

The simulation system, based on the position of the TCAS aircraft and the targets, shall compute and generate in synchronous intervals the data buffer with target information (identification, range, bearing, altitude). To add realism, in certain time intervals some of the targets are not included into the buffer. The same system provides information about the TCAS aircraft altitude (in a separate buffer). The coordination messages from other TCAS aircraft are generated randomly and placed in yet another buffer for reading by the system.

4.2. Water Boiler Controller

A water boiler controller, as a part of an entire power generating station, is to be developed from scratch, implemented and tested using a simplified boiler simulator obtained from the Institute of Risk Research [8].

The objective of this project is to develop a working software controller compliant with the specification. In addition to the real-time control aspect, inherent to the problem there is a safety aspect: too low or too high water level could cause boiler overheating and drying out or downstream damage, respectively.

The approach taken to solve this problem is a combination of two design methods: a general method of software design, and an enhancement to the general method based on the specific safety model. Thus the methodology selected to solve the problem may include two basic components:

- an application of a typical real-time development methodology, tailored towards solving real-time problems [6]
- a specific safety related method [11], applied on top the traditional real-time method.

First, a systematic real-time software design method, called DARTS (Design Approach for Real-Time Systems) is used [6]. Next, the EWICS model of safety-related system development, presented in [11], involving a process-based methodology to enhance system safety, is applied. It covers safety aspects of the following stages of system development: project management, system requirements specification, design, coding and hardware construction, hardware/software integration, verification and validation, qualification, operation and maintenance. In particular, each step of the design process using DARTS is associated with the following phases of the Design for Safety guidelines:

(a) Overall Safety Analysis

(b) Analysis of the Functional Specification

(c) Designing for Safety

(d) Validation of Design.

4.3. Radiation Protection System

A Radiation Detection System design was developed earlier [19] without tools, using SCOOP-3 [4] methodology, and implemented in Ada and C++, on the VAX/VMS. It is a good vehicle for comparison with a newer HOOD [13] design and Ada implementation for LynxOS real-time kernel, as an alternative to replace the cruise control example used as a bigger demo.

The purpose of this project is to develop a software system in which a network of microcomputer controlled measuring devices gathers radiological information. Each measuring device reports to a medium level computer, which collates local information, periodically transmitting the information to the central computer for final processing, presentation, and long term storage.

Data are gathered according to the following timing classification:

- measured every 500 ms are air temperature (in the range of -20 to 120 degrees Fahrenheit), ground temperature (-20 to 120 degrees Fahrenheit), wind speed (0 to 150 mph), relative humidity (0% to 100%), barometric pressure (0 to 1500 mm/mercury), visibility (0 to 1000 m), and radiation (in counts of alpha particles)
- measured every 30 s is the wind direction (range: 0 to 360 degrees)
- measured every 30 min is the rainfall (0 to 100 mm).

For measurements with the smallest time interval, exact timing information shall be provided, such that for 100 consecutive measurements a 2% error shall not be exceeded. Automatic corrections shall be conducted for errors greater then 2%.

For each of the above mentioned measurements a variable representing the maximum, minimum, and mean measurements will be provided with the exception of the measurement for wind direction. The data are presented as described in an additional documentation. The user interface shall be insensitive to operator input errors and shall provide direct access to user documentation via the help command.

For radiation measurements, the maximum number of alpha particles in a given time is given (simulating the allowed dose) and the maximum count expected is 20,000,000. Exceeding these values should cause an alarm to be generated. For the gathering of other meteorological information the allowed maximum and minimum limits will be determined by the geographic location of the measuring devices. Any excess of these values should also cause respective alarms.

4.4. Message Broadcast System

The Superconducting Super Collider (SSC) was supposed to consist of six accelerators: a linac, three boosters, and two intersecting, contra-rotating synchrotrons that make up the collider itself. It was estimated that 20,000 digital devices would be needed to support remote control and interrogation to operate the SSC and diagnose its condition. A message broadcast system (MBS) has been proposed for distribution of medium-time critical commands and data. Physically, it has one message generation system, which contains a sequence generator and six message formatters, one for each of the six accelerator machines comprising the SSC. Because of the large cycle time difference among these six machines, separate message broadcast channel is needed for each machine. Therefore there are six message transport systems along with their own receivers. The ATS (Asynchronous Time Sharing) message scheduling algorithm has been developed for message passing between the sequence generator and these six machines, considered as six separate channels receiving messages.

The entire system is operated as follows. The sequence generator translates the high level requests, which are predefined by physisicts and stored in a database, to suitable low-level messages to be sent out. After these messages have been translated, they are passed on to a common RAM, where each formatter is assigned a block accessible only to this formatter and the generator. The formatter reads messages from its block continuously, encapsulating and transmitting them to the transport system. Attached to the transport system is a broadcast message receiver, which monitors all the message broadcasts to its channel and recognizes the messages specific to one particular device. After the receiver recognizes one particular message, it sends a signal indicating a message has arrived to that device along with the message headers and parameters. The device will then interpret the message and perform required action.

The purpose of this project is to design and implement Message Broadcast System software, assuming a system architecture described above, the ATS message scheduling algorithm, and three classes of messages of different priorities (high, medium, and low) for each of the six accelerator machines. Because no true messages are available, simulation of message generation according to Poisson distribution shall be assumed. Details are described in [17].

5. Summary

Project descriptions for undergraduate and graduate real-time systems classes have been presented. They are a culmination of a sequence composed of demos, exercises, and assignments. Real projects follow these preliminary stages and are usually composed of four, separately graded, development phases. A sample preparation program, stressing acquisition of implementation skills, is presented in Appendix.

References

[1] V. Berzins, Luqi, Software Engineering with Abstractions, Addison-Wesley, Reading, Mass., 1991

[2] R.J.A. Buhr, Practical Visual Techniques in System Design with Applications to Ada, Prentice Hall, Englewood Cliffs, NJ, 1990

[3] A. Burns, A. Wellings, Real-Time Systems and Their Programming Languages, Addison-Wesley, Reading, Mass., 1989

[4] G. Cherry, Software Construction by Object-Oriented Pictures - Specifying Reactive and Interactive Systems, Thought Tools, Canandaigua, NY, 1990

[5] B. Furht et al., Real-Time Unix Systems: A Design and Application Guide, Kluwer Academic Publishers, Boston, Mass., 1991

[6] H. Gomaa, Software Design Methods for Concurrent and Real-Time Systems, Addison-Wesley, Reading, Mass., 1993

[7] D.J. Hatley, I.A. Pirbhai, Strategies for Real-Time System Specification, Dorset House, New York, 1988

[8] IRR, Specification for a Software Program for a Boiler Water Content Monitor and Control System, Institute for Risk Research, Waterloo, Ontario, Canada, January 1992

[9] K. Nielsen, Ada in Distributed Real-Time Systems, Mc Graw-Hill, New York, 1990

[10] M. Paprzycki, J. Zalewski. Teaching Parallel Computing without a Separate Course, Proc. NSF Workshop on Parallel Computing for Undergraduates, Colgate University, Hamilton, NY, June 22-24, 1994, C. Nevison (Ed.), pp. 19/1-18

[11] F. Redmill, ed., Dependability of Critical Computer Systems, Vols 1/2, Elsevier Science Publishers, London, 1988/89

[12] D.L. Ripps, An Implementation Guide to Real-Time Programming, Prentice Hall, Englewood Cliffs, NJ, 1989

[13] P.J. Robinson, Hierarchical Object-Oriented Design, Prentice Hall, Englewood Cliffs, NJ, 1992

[14] B. Sanden, Software Systems Construction with Examples in Ada, Prentice Hall, Englewood Cliffs, NJ, 1994

[15] K. Shumate, Understanding Concurrency in Ada, McGraw-Hill, New York, 1988

[16] K. Shumate, M. Keller, Software Specification and Design, John Wiley and Sons, New York, 1992

[17] K.-C. Wann, J. Zalewski, Scheduling Messages in Real-Time with Application to the SSC Message Broadcast System, IEEE Trans. on Nuclear Science, Vol. 41, No. 1, February 1994, pp. 213-215

[18] P.T. Ward, S.J. Mellor, Structured Development for Real-Time Systems, Vols. 1-3, Prentice Hall, Englewood Cliffs, NJ, 1985/86

[19] J. Zalewski, IEEE Draft P-1074 Mapped on a Parallel Model: A Teaching Vehicle for Software Development, Proc. Workshop Directions in Software Engineering Education, L. Werth, J. Werth, eds., 13th Int'l Conf. Software Engineering, Austin, Tex., May 12-16, 1991, pp. 125-134

[20] J. Zalewski, A Real-Time Systems Course Based on Ada. Proc. 7th ASEET Ann. Ada Software Engineering Education and Training Symposium, Monterey, Calif., January 12-14, 1993, pp. 25-49

Appendix

```c
/* Original code provided to students. Under
   AIX, contains errors to be corrected.  */
#include <stdio.h>
#include <sys/shm.h>
#include <pthread.h>
#include <unistd.h>

int SHMID, KILL;
void * first(void *str)
{
    printf("\tThis is one: %s\n",(char *)str);
    printf("One SHMID = %d\n", SHMID);
    KILL = shmctl(SHMID, IPC_RMID, 0);
    pthread_exit(NULL);
}
void * second(void *str)
{
    printf("\tThis is two: %s\n",(char *)str);
    printf("Two SHMID = %d\n", SHMID);
    KILL = shmctl(SHMID, IPC_RMID, 0);
    pthread_exit(NULL);
}
main()
{
    int * SHM_PTR;

    pthread_attr_t attr;
    char *str = "Hello, Jonny  ";
    int thread1, thread2;
    pthread_t one, two;
    int NUM=0, x=1;

    pthread_attr_init(&attr);

    thread1 = pthread_create
            (&one, NULL, first, (void *)str);
    printf("thread1 = %x\n", one);
    if (thread1 < 0)
        printf("error in one\n");

    thread2 = pthread_create
            (&two, NULL, second, (void *)str);
    printf("thread2 = %x\n", two);
    if (thread2 <0)
        printf("error in one\n");

    if ((SHMID = shmget(IPC_PRIVATE,
                sizeof(int), IPC_CREAT)) < 0)
        printf("Shmget Error\n");
    if ((SHM_PTR = shmat(SHMID, 0, 0)) < 0)
        printf("Shmat Error\n");
    printf("Main SHMID = %d\n", SHMID);
    KILL = shmctl(SHMID, IPC_RMID, 0);
    printf("Main SHMID = %d\n", SHMID);
}
```

```
/* Former program corrected in several steps:

   Step 1. Minor adjustments.
   Step 2. Attempt to join threads (to prevent
           terminating them when the main()
           terminates).
   Step 3. Checking attribute JOINABLE
           (to see why join cannot succeed).
   Step 4. Fixing the thread attribute JOINABLE
           via explicit change (and determina-
           tion that the actual value is not
           PTHREAD_CREATE_JOINABLE, required by
           Posix, but PTHREAD_CREATE_UNDETACHED
           -- AIX-specific).
   Step 5. Adding synchronization via mutexes.
   Step 6. Initializing mutex correctly.
*/

#include <stdio.h>
#include <sys/shm.h>
#include <pthread.h>
#include <unistd.h>

int SHMID, KILL;
pthread_attr_t  attr;
pthread_mutex_t mPtr=PTHREAD_MUTEX_INITIALIZER;

void * first(void *str)
{
    int detState[1];

    printf("\tThis is One: %s\n", (char *)str);
    pthread_mutex_lock(&mPtr);
    printf("\tOne SHMID = %d\n", SHMID);
    pthread_mutex_unlock(&mPtr);
    sleep(2);
    pthread_attr_getdetachstate(&attr,detState);
    printf("\tAfter sleep One detState = %d\n",
                                      *detState);
    pthread_exit(NULL);
}

void * second(void *str)
{
    int detState[1];

    printf("\tThis is Two: %s\n", (char *)str);
    pthread_mutex_lock(&mPtr);
    printf("\tTwo SHMID = %d\n", SHMID);
    pthread_mutex_unlock(&mPtr);
    /* sleep(2); */
    pthread_attr_getdetachstate(&attr,detState);
    printf("\tAfter sleep Two detState = %d\n",
                                      *detState);
    pthread_exit(NULL);
}

main()
{
    int * SHM_PTR;
    char * str = "Hello, Jonny...";
    int thread1, thread2;
    pthread_t one, two;
    int retVal;
    int NUM = 0, x = 1;
    int detState[1];

/* Testing if Posix semaphores are implemented
   (-1, if not supported).
   printf("\nSemaphores: %d\n\n",
          sysconf(_SC_SEMAPHORES));
*/
    if (pthread_attr_init(&attr) != 0) printf
       ("\nThread attr. object not created!\n");

    if ((retVal=pthread_mutex_lock(&mPtr)) != 0)
       printf("mutexLock failed: %d\n", retVal);

    pthread_attr_getdetachstate(&attr,detState);
    printf("JOINABLE = %d; DETACHED = %d\n",
           PTHREAD_CREATE_UNDETACHED,
           PTHREAD_CREATE_DETACHED);
    if (pthread_attr_setdetachstate(&attr,
              PTHREAD_CREATE_UNDETACHED) != 0)
       printf("Setting attr. unsuccessful!\n");

    thread1 = pthread_create(&one, &attr,
                             first, (void *)str);
    printf("thread1 = %x\n", one);

    thread2 = pthread_create(&two, &attr,
                             second, (void *)str);
    printf("thread2 = %x\n", two);

    if ((SHMID = shmget(IPC_PRIVATE,sizeof(int),
                   IPC_CREAT)) < 0)
       printf("Shmget Error\n");
    if ((retVal=pthread_mutex_unlock(&mPtr))!=0)
      printf("mutexUnlock failed: %d\n",retVal);
    if ((SHM_PTR = shmat(SHMID, 0, 0)) < 0)
        printf("Shmat Error\n");

    printf("Main SHMID = %d\n", SHMID);

    /* Error = 3 means unidentified thread. */
    if ((retVal=pthread_join(one, NULL)) != 0)
       printf("Join 1 failed!: %d\n", retVal);
    if ((retVal=pthread_join(two, NULL)) != 0)
       printf("Join 2 failed!: %d\n", retVal);

    KILL = shmctl(SHMID, IPC_RMID, 0);
    printf("Main SHMID = %d\n", SHMID);
}
```

A Real-Time Systems Track in the Master of Software Engineering Program

Andrew J. Kornecki & Janusz Zalewski

Dept. of Computer Science

Embry-Riddle Aeronautical University

Daytona Beach, FL 32114-3900, U.S.A.

+1 (904) 226-6690

{korn, zalewski}@db.erau.edu

Abstract

This paper discusses the Real-Time Systems track in the Master of Software Engineering (MSE) program, at Embry-Ridle Aeronautical University. It presents outlines of four courses in this track: Concurrent and Distributed Systems, Specification and Design for Real-Time Systems, Software Safety, and Performance Analysis of Real-Time Systems. The outlines include: course descriptions and goals, performance objectives, required and supplemental texts, topic outlines and principles of assessment. Background information leading to track development is discussed and some initial experience, after two years of running the MSE program, is presented.

1. Introduction

The MSE program at Embry-Riddle started two years ago [2], originally with emphasis on the software process. At this point, it includes core courses and electives, plus courses with Process focus and courses with Real-Time focus. This paper concentrates on four courses forming the Real-Time Systems track.

Catalog descriptions of all four courses are given below. The detailed outlines are presented in the next section. Early experiences are discussed in the final section.

MSE 640 Concurrent and Distributed Systems

This course covers the principles, methodology, tools, and techniques as applied to concurrent and distributed systems. The concepts of concurrent programming, various synchronization and communication mechanisms, programming paradigms, implementation issues, and techniques to understand and de-velop correct programs are surveyed and studied. Applications of distributed and concurrent systems in aviation/aerospace are presented, discussed and studied.

MSE 595 Specification and Design for Real-Time Systems

The objective of this course is to teach the principles of domain specific software development, applied to real-time systems. Various specification and design methodologies are presented, including structured development methods, such as Ward/Mellor, Hatley/Pirbhai, DARTS, and object-oriented approaches such as HOOD and ROOM. Specific analytic techniques, such as rate-monotonic and deadline-monotonic scheduling, are presented and applied to practical problems. An essential element of this course is a semester-long team project, supported by the use of professional software development tools.

MSE 590 Software Safety

This course covers the principles, methods, techniques and tools, as applied to the development of safe software systems. The concepts of safety related issues in software specification, design, and implementation for mission critical applications are surveyed and studied. Application of software safety concepts in aviation/aerospace and other industries are presented, discussed, and explored.

MSE 599 Performance Analysis of Real-Time Systems

This course covers the principles, methods, techniques and tools, as applied to the modeling and analysis of performance of real-time systems. The fundamental concepts of performance analysis at the design and implementation levels are discussed, with practical examples. Applications of performance analysis in mission critical systems are studied.

90

2. Course Outlines

The detailed outlines of four courses in the Real-Time Systems track are presented below.

2.1. Concurrent and Distributed Systems

Course No. MSE 640
Credit Hours: 3
Lecture Hours: 42
Lab Hours: 0

Course Description

The objective of this course is to teach principles of software development for concurrent and distributed systems. Specification, design and implementation techniques are described and illustrated by examples and practical exercises. Principles and practices of concurrent programming, including synchronization and communication issues, and a survey of languages suitable for implementing concurrent solutions. An essential element of this course is an individual project on the development of concurrent/distributed software, including its design, implementation, and testing.

Goals

Provide students with practical knowledge and understanding of concurrent and distributed software development. Students are exposed to the most crucial phases of the development process, including specification, design, implementation, and verification, with emphasis on implementation techniques. In addition, students learn how to use industrial quality software development tools.

Performance Objectives

Upon completion of this course, students should be able to:

- describe the essential elements of concurrent and distributed systems
- discuss the major problems in development of concurrent/distributed software
- propose and select a method, techniques, and tools to solve a particular application problem
- use a selected method to develop and evaluate the specification of a concurrent/distributed application
- develop, analyze and evaluate a design for a concurrent/distributed application
- use a variety of synchronization and communication concepts to implement concurrent/distributed software
- determine the major criteria (in terms of safety and liveness properties) and assess the quality of the implementation
- use modern software tools and environments for developing concurrent and distributed systems.

Required Text

Ben-Ari M., Principles of Concurrent and Distributed Programming, Prentice-Hall, Englewood Cliffs, NJ, 1990

Supplemental Texts

Andrews G., Concurrent Programming. Principles and Practices, Benjamin/Cummings, Redwood City (CA), 1991

Andrews G., R.A. Olsson, The SR Programming Language: Concurrency in Practice, Benjamin/Cummings, Redwood City (CA), 1993

Axford T., Concurrent Programming - Fundamental Techniques for Real-Time and Parallel Software Design, John Wiley and Sons, New York, 1989

Bustard D., J. Elder, J. Welsh, Concurrent Program Structures, Prentice-Hall, Englewood Cliffs (NJ), 1988

Coulouris G. et al., Distributed Systems: Concepts and Design. Second Edition, Addison-Wesley, Reading (MA), 1994

Fleischmann A., Distributed Systems: Software Design and Implementation, Springer-Verlag, Berlin, 1994

Gehani N., Ada - Concurrent Programming. Second Edition, Silicon Press, Summit (NJ), 1991

Gehani N., A.D. McGettrick (Eds.), Concurrent Programming, Addison-Wesley, Reading (MA), 1988

Hartley S., Operating Systems Programming: The SR Programming Language, Oxford University Press, New York, 1995

Mullender S. (Ed.), Distributed Systems. Second Edition, Addison-Wesley, Reading (MA), 1993

Shatz S.M., Development of Distributed Software: Concepts and Tools, Macmillan, New York, 1993

Snow C.R., Concurrent Programming, Cambridge University Press, London, 1991

Topic Outline   Approx. Hours

1. General Overview. What is a Concurrent and/or Distributed System? — 3

2. Software Engineering Principles Applied to Concurrent and Distributed Systems — 3

3. Formal Approaches to Program Specification and Verification: Petri Nets, Temporal Logic, etc. — 6

4. Properties of Concurrent Programs: Liveness and Safety   3

5. Concurrent and Distributed Program Design: DARTS, HOOD, etc.   3

6. Concurrency Mechanisms: Multitasking and Multithreading, Task Interaction and Mutual Exclusion   3

7. Task Allocation and Scheduling   3

8. Concurrent and Distributed Languages: Ada, Concurrent C++, etc.   3

9. Shared Variables, Critical Regions, Semaphores, Message Passing (Asynchronous, Synchronous, Rendezvous)   3

10. Selection of Standard Problems: Producer-Consumer, Bounded Buffer, Readers and Writers, Dining Philosophers   3

11. Fault Tolerance and Real-Time Communication   3

12. Review of Typical Applications in Aviation and Aerospace   6

Assignments and Assessment

Assignments include the following: development of a documentation for an individual project, oral and written reports on selected aspects of concurrent/distributed software development, exercises based on practical examples and concerned with using a variety of implementation techniques. The final evaluation is based on an individual project, submission of a report/documentation, an in-class presentation, a two-hour comprehensive test, and the final exam.

2.2. Specification and Design for Real-Time Systems

Course No. MSE 595
Credit Hours: 3
Lecture Hours: 42
Lab Hours: 0

Course Description

This course addresses basic concepts and methods used in software specification and design of concurrent and real-time systems. The characteristics of concurrent and real-time systems, and the role of software design in software development are discussed. A number of software design methods specifically suited for concurrent and real-time systems is reviewed and compared. Two of the methods are analyzed in detail and case studies illustrate the design process. The course may require to do research of real-time aspects of software design and produce appropriate reports.

Goals

The purpose of the course is to have students understand the software lifecycle considerations for concurrent and real-time systems with particular emphasis on prototyping, incremental development and variants of the spiral model. Students survey various software design methods to become familiar with available approaches. The course concentrates on design approaches for real-time systems and gives an opportunity to study in depth the notation and process, and apply this knowledge in a simple case study.

Performance Objectives

Upon completion of this course, students should be able to:

- describe specifics of concurrent and real-time applications
- understand the software lifecycle considerations for real-time systems
- describe and understand various software design methods
- understand the conceptual foundation for major design approaches for real-time systems
- describe performance models and analyze performance of concurrent and real-time software designs
- build the environmental and behavioral models for real-time systems
- perform task structuring and develop the task architecture
- map the tasking design into architectural design.

Required Text

Gomaa H., Software Design Methods for Concurrent and Real-Time Systems, Addison-Wesley, Reading (MA), 1993

Supplemental Texts

Cooling J.E., Software Design for Real-Time Systems, Chapman and Hall, London, 1991

Edwards K., Real-Time Structured Methods: System Analysis, John Wiley and Sons, New York, 1993

Goldsmith S., A Practical Guide to Real-Time Systems Development, Prentice Hall, Englewood Cliffs, (NJ), 1993

Halang W., Stoyenko A. Constructing Predictable Real-Time Systems, Kluwer Academic Publishers, Boston (MA), 1993

Hatley D.J., I.A. Pirbhai, Strategies for Real-Time System Specification, Dorset House, New York, 1988

Heller P., Real-Time Software Design – A Guide for Microprocessor Systems Birkhäuser, Boston (MA), 1987

Kavi K. (Ed.), Real-Time Systems: Abstraction, Languages, and Design Methodologies, IEEE Computer Society Press, Los Alamitos (MA), 1993

Levi S., Agrawala A., Real-Time System Design, McGraw-Hill, New York, 1990

Nielsen K., Object-Oriented Design with Ada: Maximizing Reusability for Real-Time Systems, Bantam Books, New York, 1992

Nielsen K., Shumate K., Designing Large Real-Time Systems with Ada, McGraw Hill, New York, 1988

Shumate K., Keller M., Software Specification and Design: A Disciplined Approach for Real-Time Systems, John Wiley and Sons, New York, 1992

Ward P.T., S.J. Mellor, Structured Development for Real-Time Systems, Prentice Hall, Englewood Cliffs (NJ), 1985

Topic Outline

	Approx. Hours
1. Concurrent and Real-Time System Concepts	1
2. Software Life Cycle for Real-Time Systems	3
3. Software Design Concepts	3
4. Survey of Software Design Methods	3
5. Performance Analysis of Concurrent and Real-Time Software Designs	3
6. Overview of ADARTS and CODARTS	3
7. Analysis and Modeling	6
8. Task and Module Structuring	6
9. Task Integration and Ada-based Design	6
10. Case Studies and Implementation Issues	8

Assignments and Assessment

Assignments include the following: oral and written reports on various aspects of software design for concurrent and real-time systems, and a case study (project) with specified software artifacts related to a time-critical application. The final evaluation is based on a number of in-class quizzes and a two-hour comprehensive final exam, as well as on the completeness and quality of all assignments.

2.3. Software Safety

Course No. MSE 590
Credit Hours: 3
Lecture Hours: 42
Lab Hours: 0

Course Description

The objective of this course is to teach the unique methods and techniques of software development for critical applications, that is, applications whose failure may involve loss of human life or property (e.g. nuclear power plants, air-traffic control, medical devices). The most important notions of critical system properties, such as dependability, reliability, safety, and security are explained, and respective techniques presented to achieve high levels of confidence in safe operation. Principles of building software, with emphasis on safety, in all stages of software development are analyzed, stressing the use of formal description and modeling. Programming language constructs are also analyzed, in this respect. An essential element of this course is a group project on the development of safety related software, including its design, implementation, and testing.

Goals

Provide students with practical knowledge and understanding of software development for safety and mission critical systems. Students are exposed to the most crucial phases of the development process to ensure software safety, including specification, design, implementation, and verification techniques. In addition, students learn how to use formal methods and tools supporting them.

Performance Objectives

Upon completion of this course, students should be able to:

- identify safety concerns in software and distinguish them from other dependability properties

- describe the essential elements of safety related software

- discuss the major problems in development of safety related software

- propose and select a method, techniques, and tools to solve a particular application problem

- use a selected method to develop and evaluate the specification of a safety related application

- develop, analyze and evaluate a design for a safety related application

- use a variety of modern implementation techniques to implement safety related software

- determine the major safety criteria and assess the quality of the implementation

- use modern software tools and environments for developing safety related software.

Required Text

Leveson N., Safeware: System Safety and Computers, Addison-Wesley, Reading (MA), 1995

Supplemental Texts

Bennett P. (Ed.), Safety Aspects of Computer Control, Butterworth-Heinemann, Oxford, 1993

Craigen D., S. Gerhart, T. Ralston, Industrial Applications of Formal Methods to Model, Design and Analyze Computer Systems, Noyes Data Corp., Park Ridge (NJ), 1994

Del Bel Belluz D., H.C. Ratz (Eds.), Design and Review of Sofware Controlled Safety Related Systems, Institute of Risk Research, Waterloo (Ont.), 1995

Friedman M.A., J.M. Voas, Software Assessment: Reliability, Safety, Testability, John Wiley and Sons, New York, 1995

Halang W. et al., A Safety Licensable Computing Architecture, World Scientific, Singapore, 1993

Hatton L., Safer C: Developing S/W for High-Integrity & Safety-Critical Systems, McGraw-Hill, London, 1995

Jalote P., Fault Tolerance in Distributed Systems, Prentice Hall, Englewood Cliffs (NJ), 1994

Koob G.M., C.G. Lau (Eds.), Foundations of Dependable Computing, Vols. 1-3, Kluwer Academic Publishers, Boston (MA), 1994,

Langmaack H., W.-P. de Roever, J. Vytopil (Eds.), Formal Techniques in Real-Time and Fault-Tolerant Systems, Springer-Verlag, Berlin, 1994

Lyu M.R. (Ed.), Software Fault Tolerance, John Wiley and Sons, New York, 1995

Lyu M.R. (Ed.), The Handbook of Software Reliability Engineering, McGraw-Hill, New York, 1996

Neumann P., Computer Related Risks, Addison Wesley, Reading (MA), 1995

Pham H. (Ed.), Software Reliability and Testing, IEEE Computer Society Press, Los Alamitos (CA), 1995

Redmill F. (Ed.), Dependability of Critical Computer Systems, Vols. 1/2, Elsevier Science Publishers, London, 1989

Vytopil J. (Ed.), Formal Techniques in Real-Time and Fault-Tolerant Systems, Kluwer Academic Publishers, Boston (MA), 1993

Wallace I.G., Developing Effective Safety Systems, Gulf Publishing Company, Houston (TX), 1995

Topic Outline	Approx. Hours
1. General Overview: Dependability Properties. What is Software Safety vs. Reliability and Security?	3
2. Fault Tolerance as a Means to Implement Safety	3
3. Design for Safety: The Approach of the European Workshop on Industrial Computer Systems	3
4. Programming Language Constructs and Safety	3
5. Software Safety on the Operating System Level: Mutual Exclusion and Deadlock Avoidance	3
6. N-Version Programming and Recovery Blocks	3
7. Formal Approaches to Software Safety	3
8. Software Tools to Support Formal Approaches	3
9. Safety Analysis Techniques: PHA, HAZOP, FMEA, Fault Trees, Reviews, Inspections	3
10. Software Safety Standards: Military, Avionics, Nuclear	6
11. Program Testing, Verification, Validation, and Metrics to Achieve Safety	3
12. Fault Tolerance in Real-Time Communication	3
13. Review of Safety-Related Applications in Aviation/Aerospace	3

Assignments and Assessment

Assignments include the following: development of a documentation for an individual project, oral and written reports on selected aspects of safety-related software development, exercises based on practical examples and concerned with using a variety of implementation techniques. The final evaluation is based on a group project, submission of a report/documentation, an in-class presentation, a two-hour comprehensive test, and the final exam.

2.4. Performance Analysis of Real-Time Systems

Course No. MSE 599
Credit Hours: 3
Lecture Hours: 42
Lab Hours: 0

Course Description

The objective of this course is to teach principles of performance analysis of real-time systems on the design and implementation levels. Performance modeling and analysis techniques are described and illustrated by examples and practical exercises. Principles and practices of software development to achieve required or optimal performance, including design analysis and assessment of the implementation, are addressed. An actual project in instrumentation of software for performance evaluation is an essential element of this course.

Goals

Provide students with practical knowledge and understanding of performance analysis and evaluation of real-time software. Students are exposed to the most important concepts of real-time performance, including program instrumentation, timing analysis, benchmarks, rate-monotonic analysis, modeling and simulation techniques. Students learn how to use modern engineering tools supporting performance evaluation.

Performance Objectives

Upon completion of this course, students should be able to:

- describe the essential concepts of computer performance analysis and evaluation

- discuss the major problems in analyzing performance of real-time applications

- determine the major criteria to assess the quality of a real-time system

- propose and select a method, techniques, and tools to solve a particular performance analysis problem

- use a selected method to evaluate the design or implementation of a real-time system

- use modern software tools and environments for performance evaluation of real-time systems.

Required Text <to be determined>

Supplemental Texts

Halang W., A. Stoyenko (Eds.), Real-Time Computing, Springer-Verlag, Berlin, 1994

Joseph M. (Ed.), Real-Time Systems: Specification, Verification and Analysis, Prentice Hall, London, 1996

Lee Y.H., C.M. Krishna (Eds.), Readings in Real-Time Systems, IEEE Computer Society Press, Los Alamitos (CA), 1993

Motus L., M. Rodd, Timing Analysis of Real-Time Software, Elsevier, Oxford, 1994

Rus T., C. Rattray (Eds.), Theories and Experience for Real-Time System Development, World Scientific, Singapore, 1994

Son S.H. (Ed.), Advances in Real-Time Systems, Prentice Hall, Englewood Cliffs (NJ), 1995

Stankovic J., K. Ramamritham (Eds.), Tutorial: Hard Real-Time Systems, IEEE Computer Society Press, Los Alamitos (CA), 1988

Stankovic J., K. Ramamritham (Eds.), Advances in

Real-Time Systems, IEEE Computer Society Press, Los Alamitos (CA), 1993

Topic Outline	Approx. Hours
1. General Overview: Computer Hardware and Software Performance Analysis	3
2. Program Instrumentation to Evaluate Performance	3
3. Principles of Analyzing and Timing Computer Programs	3
4. Evaluating Primary Safety and Liveness Properties	3
5. Fundamentals of Rate-Monotonic and Deadline-Monotonic Analysis	6
6. Rate-Monotonic Analysis of Multiprocessor Systems	3
7. Formal Approaches to Modeling Real-Time Behavior	3
8. Simulation and Modeling Tools, and Their Use	3
9. Performance Analysis of Real-Time Computer Architectures	6
10. Timing Analysis and Real-Time Benchmarks	3
11. Performance Analysis of Real-Time Communication	3
12. Review of Real-Time Performance Issues in Aviation and Aerospace	3

Assignments and Assessment

Assignments include the following:

- a project based on development of an instrumentation for real-time software and taking actual timing measurements

- a modeling and simulation project to analyze behavior of a real-time computer architecture (hardware or software)

- oral and written reports on projects completion

- exercises based on practical examples and use of various modeling and analysis techniques.

The final evaluation is based on group projects, submission of a report or documentation, an in-class presentation, a two-hour comprehensive test, and the final exam.

2.5 Prerequisites and Resources

A prerequisite for all courses is MSE 500 Software Engineering Concepts. In additon, for MSE 595, basic knowledge of specification and design of software systems, Ada/C programming, and successful completion of MSE 640 Concurrent and Distributed Systems are required.

Resource requirements for all courses include a computer laboratory with Unix-based/X window system workstations and modern integrated CASE tools. In addition, Internet access, Ada/C environment and real-time kernel are required for the first two courses.

The role of supplemental texts is to provide material for reference reading. In a graduate program, it is rather difficult to base the entire course on a single textbook. Therefore we include an extensive list of additional readings to provide students with a choice and make them aware of the breadth of the issues associated with the class material. Selected chapters of the supplemental texts are discussed in lectures. Other chapters are assigned for individual reading in relation to specific projects.

3. Discussion of Experiences

3.1. Background Information

As can be easily recognized, this MSE track is a result of a long development history, including both efforts at Embry-Riddle and personal experiences of the authors elsewhere. Embry-Riddle is a domain centered institution with a focus on aviation and aerospace. This application area has always been in demand of skilled real-time software engineers. It has been observed that aviation and aerospace companies are eagerly looking for graduates with respective knowledge and skills. Therefore our sequence of courses in the real-time track is closely related to the needs of industry and follows some of the recommendations of the MSE Industrial Advisory Board, whose members represent these companies.

One aspect which cannot be neglected is that the background of both authors is in control engineering. This implies a natural approach to developing reactive and feedback systems that have been usually considered of predominant importance in the students' future professional careers, at least for this application domain.

In addition to that, one of the authors has had previous extensive experience in developing real-time systems at nuclear research laboratories, as well as in helping develop a real-time concentration in the graduate program at another university [5], since the early nineties. This concentration had a pattern similar to the current MSE real-time track and was carefully

planned to consist of four courses:

- CS5349 – Concurrent Programming
- CS5350 – Dependability of Computer Systems
- CS5352 – Distributed Computing
- CS5364 – Advanced Real-Time Computing Applications.

It was proved that students who have taken a couple of intensive courses in this track were able to pursue interesting research and practical work [6, 7].

3.2. Lessons Learned

At Embry-Riddle, thus far, there were two classes of MSE 640 offered in the springs of '95 and '96. They emphasized individual work on implementing distributed systems software, including interprocess and network communication mechanisms [4], such as System V and Posix semaphores, message queues, and shared memory segments, combination of sockets, TLI (Transport Layer Interface) and RPC (Remote Procedure Calls), and two thread-based constructs: mutexes and condition variables. A number of software packages for parallel and distributed programming were installed and investigated in individual projects, such as Mentat, MPI (Message Passing Interface), PVM (Parallel Virtual Machine), Parallaxis. In addition to traditional languages, such as C and Ada, newer languages were exploited in individual projects: SR (Synchronizing Resources), Java, Occam, as well as smaller packages, such as Multi-Pascal, Pascal-FC, Multi-C. The latter three, while providing functionality equivalent to the others, are PC-based and therefore much simpler to use, which makes some students more comfortable to deal with such tools. Keeping the diversity of tools was one of the major paradigms in making the course interesting.

The Software Safety course, MSE 590, was offered once with emphasis on hazard analysis and methods to analyze safety, such as fault trees, FMEA (Fault Modes and Effects Analysis), HAZOP (Hazards and Operability Analysis), and others. The primary problem in this course was to make students realize how safety differs from properties such as reliability and security, and that fault-tolerance is not a property in itself but just a means to implement other properties, such as safety. An attempt to introduce automatic tools to support the use of formal methods was not extremely successful due to the necessity to spend a significant amount of class time on explaining theoretical foundations. However, three public domain tools were installed as a part of team projects: PVS (Prototype Verification System, `ftp.csl.sri.com:/pub/pvs`), SMV (Symbolic Model Verifier, `emc.cs.cmu.edu:/pub`), and *murphi* (`snooze.stanford.edu:/pub/murphi`). Their usefulness in the safety process and possible future class projects supporting formal approaches was investigated.

The recent offering of MSE 595 was based on a class project to develop the Traffic Alert and Collision Avoidance System (TCAS) software. The objective of the project is to simulate the functionality of TCAS within the environment to provide a base for testing. After many simplifications limiting the scope and complexity of the system, two teams developed the requirements document, designed and implemented the system prototype. In the process, the students researched various design methodologies and applied established notations. The specifics of the system resulted in a design with multiple tasks implemented as threads using real-time extensions of AIX operating system.

One team designed the simulation with scaffolding external software generating the radar data. The second team presented the simulation on a client/server basis, where each user on the network would control his own aircraft. The short time frame and the team size made the project rather difficult, leaving not enough time for feedback and required modifications. For the development it was decided to use the sandwiched approach (part of the team doing top-down design, another part prototyping the system functionality and the real-time implementation details). The educational objective was to identify real-time characteristics of software, explore issues of concurrency and intertask communication while building various software artifacts. The three phases of the project resulted in formal reviews of the requirements, design, and implementation. The team presented the complete project, including the prototype demonstration, at the end of class. More information can be found in [3].

MSE 599 has not been offered yet, although an extensive use of simulation and analysis tools, such as Modsim language or iRAT tool for rate-monotonic analysis, has been planned. The course material is also to review the issues related to experiment planning and statistical analysis of experiment results. The textbook [1] is currently under consideration.

The projects are discussed in class in a format ranging from an informal discussion to a formal review meeting. The final project is prepared in a written form including deliverable components identified in the formulation of the assignment. The presentation is open to faculty and graduate students. The teams present their work using slides and transparencies (to be included as project deliverables). The presentation is given in the laboratory which allows also for the demonstration of software.

4. Conclusion

The presented description is based on the past and current course offering in the Real-Time Systems track. The experience of the last year provides enough material to look into potential improvements in terms of content modifications, sequencing, and better utilization of the laboratory infrastructure.

There is still some work to be done regarding better coordination of courses and designing the prerequisite structure. The MSE students very often have a diverse background with varying experiences and level of mastery in computer programming and hardware proficiency. Such situation requires us to work on proper sequencing of courses in the Real-Time Systems track and appropriate coordination with the core MSE courses.

References

[1] R. Jain, The Art of Computer Systems Performance Analysis: Techniques for Experimental Design, Measurement, Simulation, and Modeling, John Wiley and Sons, New York, 1991

[2] S. Khajenoori, Process-Oriented Software Education, IEEE Software, Vol. 11, No. 6, November 1994, pp. 99-101

[3] A. Kornecki, J. Zalewski, Projects for Real-Time Systems Classes, Workshop on Real-Time Systems Education, Daytona Beach, FL, April 20, 1996

[4] M. Paprzycki, R. Wasniowski, J. Zalewski, Parallel and Distributed Computing Education: A Software Engineering Approach, Proc. 8th SEI Conf. on Software Engineering Education, R.L. Ibrahim (Ed.), Springer-Verlag, Berlin, 1995, pp. 187-204

[5] Southwest Texas State University, Computer Science Deptartment, San Marcos, Tex., `http://www.cs.swt.edu/courses/grad_courses.html`

[6] B. Tchouaffe, J. Zalewski, Fully Deterministic Real-Time Protocol for a CSMA/CD Type Local Area Network, Informatica, Vol. 19, No. 1, February 1995, pp. 123-132

[7] K.C. Wann, J. Zalewski, Scheduling Messages in Real Time with Application to the SSC Message Broadcast System, IEEE Trans. on Nuclear Science, Vol. 41, No. 1, February 1994, pp. 213-215

A Course on Safety-Related Real-Time Computing Systems

Wolfgang A. Halang
Faculty of Electrical Engineering
Fernuniversität
58084 Hagen, Germany
wolfgang.halang@fernuni-hagen.de

Janusz Zalewski
Dept. of Computer Science
Embry-Riddle Aeronautical University
Daytona Beach, FL 32114-3900, U.S.A.
zalewski@db.erau.edu

Abstract

This paper presents an outline of a course on safety-related real-time systems, with two implementations at the authors' parent institutions. It starts with a general introduction to safety-related systems and discusses basic notions and didactic concepts. Then, it overviews related courses in North America and the United Kingdom, and presents the details of specific courses developed by the authors.

1. Introduction

In society, there is a growing concern about safety and environmental issues producing an increasing demand for dependable technical systems in order not to endanger human lives and to prevent environmental disasters. Computerized technical systems are increasingly being applied for both control and automation functions under real-time constraints to give industry a competitive edge by enhancing productivity, flexibility, and quality. In contrast to other technical systems, computers have the special property that they consist of hardware and software. This has important consequences for the assessment of computer-controlled systems.

A large part of real-time computer control applications are safety-related. Such applications heavily depend on the correctness of hardware and software and may cause large losses, such as human lives, property, etc., in case of hardware or software defects. Examples of such systems include airplane control, nuclear reactors, medical devices, or even car control and telecommunication systems (it's a tremendous loss of money for businesses, if a large telephone network goes down even for a minute).

Hardware is subject to wear and to faults occurring at random and which may be of a transient nature. To a very large extent, these sources of non-dependability can successfully be coped with by applying a wide spectrum of redundancy and fault-tolerance methods. In software, on the other hand, there are no faults caused by aging, environmental events, etc. Instead, all errors are design errors, i.e., of systematic nature, and their causes are always (latently) present. Hence, dependability of software cannot be achieved by reducing the number of errors contained by testing, checks, or other heuristic methods to a low level, which is generally greater than zero, but only by rigorously proving that it is defect-free. One has now begun to realize these inherent safety problems associated with software. Since it appears unrealistic to abandon the use of computers for safety-related control purposes — on the contrary, there is no doubt that their utilization in such applications is going to increase considerably — the problem of software dependability is becoming more and more urgent.

The above considerations imply the importance and the educational needs of a completely new field in science and engineering, which can be called safety-related real-time systems. This field stands at the very beginning of its treatment in research and education [8]. Its development aims to reach the state that real-time computing systems can be constructed with a sufficient degree of confidence in their dependability that enables their licensing for safety-critical tasks.

To deal with such situations, special techniques are required to ensure that software is defect-free or that the system still performs its function if a software fault occurs. Such techniques are usually applied in software development cycle, beginning at the specification level and continuing for design, implementation, including other proceses such as project management, verification and validation, etc.

Since the engineers involved in the specification, design, implementation, and maintenance of such systems lack a thorough understanding of the underlying principles, there is an urgent educational need to fill this gap.

2. Basic Notions

The principal notions of safety-related systems involve two categories: those associated with hazards and risk, and those associated with faults, errors, and failures. The latest versions of these terms have been defined in [12], Part 4. A *hazard* is a physical situation with a potential of human injury. A *risk* is the probable rate of occurrence of a hazard causing harm, and the degree of severity of the harm. Degrees of severity need to be defined separately. A *fault*, as defined there, is the cause of an error. An *error* is traditionally defined in measurement theory as a deviation from the correct value. Errors lead to failures. A *failure*, according to the above mentioned document, is the effect of an error on the intended service. If one adds to this that a *mistake* is a human action that may lead to a fault, the four notions form a classification that characterizes the erroneous behavior of technical systems. Defining a consistent set of critical system properties, including safety, is more difficult.

2.1. Safety and Related Properties

Considering critical system properties, we usually require guarantees on system behavior, requesting specifically that "nothing bad will happen." If we ask the question, what harm is done to the computer system or its environment due to a computer failure, we may have the following answers [25]:

1. Failure does not lead to severe consequences to the environment or a computer system, nevertheless improving the failure rate is of principal concern (the notion of *reliability*).

2. Failure leads to severe consequences to the environment, and later, maybe, to the computer system (the notion of *safety*).

3. Failure leads to severe consequences to the computer system itself, and later, possibly, also to the environment (the notion of *security*).

In other words, reliability means minimizing undesired situations and their effects, and safety and security mean preventing the environment or computer system, respectively, from undesired situations and their effects.

To achieve reliability, safety, security, and possibly other critical system properties, special techniques are necessary. One such technique commonly used is fault tolerance. *Fault tolerance* is a means to achieve high assurance (high integrity, dependability, trustworthiness) in system behavior but it is not a separate property.

Similar view of mutual relationships among critical system properties that constitute the highest level property, *dependability*, has been presented earlier [15, 22, 23]. It is consistent with other views, such as the German industry standard [1], where safety is defined as a status whose risk does not exceed the limit risk, with the latter being the highest, still justifiable, specific risk of a technical process or state.

2.2. Real-Time Properties

It is characteristic for real-time systems that their correctness does not only depend on the processing results, but also on the instants, when these results become available. In case of error situations, the user expects predictable system behavior, such as graceful degradation of performance.

The principle of real-time operation and behavior, to react on time, in a technical language means meeting deadlines (timing constraints). This requirement has several distinct components. Before reacting, a computer system has to notice that an event has occured. A respective property is called *responsiveness*. It is characterized by the worst-case time that elapses from the occurence of a particular event to the start of its processing. Only after noticing an event, a computer system has a chance to react, and react on time to meet timing requirements. A respective property is called *timeliness*. It is characterized by the worst-case time that is needed for processing of a perceived event.

The requirement to meet deadlines gives rise to another important property, *schedulability*: the property of a set of tasks that ensures that the tasks all meet their deadlines. But the requirement to meet deadlines is not as strict as one would think. If a set of tasks is not schedulable, a respective computer system can be still working fine in real time and meeting the requirements. This is because it has been designed in a way that guarantees the critical tasks to meet their deadlines, with non-critical tasks occasionally missing them. In this sense, a real-time system demonstrates a predictable behavior, and a respective property is called *predictability*: the property characterized by an upper bound on the overall reaction time – of each task in the system – to external stimuli. Even if deadlines are missed, the overall response is predictable. The critical part of the system can be still operational, with some tasks predictably failing.

Thus, from the analytical point of view, outlined above, there are four real-time properties that need to be considered: responsiveness, timeliness, schedulability and predictability [24].

3. The Didactic Concept

A key issue in developing real-time safety-critical systems is to ensure and verify that the system exhibits respective critical properties. To understand the nature of verification, which is neither a scientific nor a technical, but a social process, its clear and distinct *comprehension by humans* is necessary. This holds for mathematical proofs as well, whose correctness is based on a consensus of members of the mathematical community that certain chains of reasoning lead to given conclusions. Applied to safety-related systems, and considering their importance to human lives and health, but also to the environment and capital investments, this consensus ought to be as wide as possible. Hence, systems must be simple, and appropriate safety-licensing methods must be easily understandable for non-experts without compromising rigor.

Based on this human-centred approach to safety-licensing, the didactic concept of the course on safety-related real-time computing systems presented here differs considerably from other courses on related subjects, such as fault-tolerance, safe software, or formal methods, because it is comprehensive. Usually, courses taught individually on any of these subjects fall short in demonstrating to be both applicable on an industrial scale and by engineers working there.

Fault-tolerance methods often apply to rather small problems only, and are frequently characterized by too simplistic fault models. Most available software verification and validation methods are neither sufficiently rigorous, nor can they cope with complex software systems. The corresponding national and international standards are voluminous, but vague and lack concrete guidance to practically working engineers, thus leaving them confused and without real help. Formal methods have only proven to be useful in toy applications so far, and could not find wider acceptance in the engineering world due to their mathematical appearance and requirements for special expertise.

For these reasons, the course emphasizes industrially workable and proven methods, supported by the results of our own research directed towards developing more such methods. Whereas selective courses take the approach of teaching methods to assure that given systems are safe, our course features an engineering approach, i.e. focuses on methods to achieve safety and verifiability already by design. In other words, a more suggestive synthetic approach is taken versus the common analytical one which, although requiring considerable mathematical apparatus and effort, has not led to the desired state of the art, yet.

4. Emphasis on Software

Since hardware has already achieved a rather high degree of dependability, the course devotes particular attention to the problem of safe software. When used in safety-related applications, software must be rigorously verified, i.e., safety-licensed, which is a very difficult and not yet satisfactorily solved task. The intrinsic problems and fundamental principles of safety-licensing software are shown and the importance of the human element in this process is stressed.

The classical techniques are covered, which include formal and empirical analytical methods for a posteriori software verification. Since their performance is not fully satisfactory, the course concept puts emphasis on holistic approaches to hardware *and* software development whose design principles are oriented at ergonomic criteria and which achieve system verifiability and, hence, safety by design. These engineering paradigms feature simple, inherently safe programming and design integrated verification not only having the quality of mathematical rigor, but also oriented at the comprehension capabilities of non-experts, to replace testing in safety-licensing. Verification regarded as a social process of reaching a consensus is facilitated by such features as graphical programming, reuse of prefabricated and certified components, specification level programming by filling in decision tables and, generally, striving for utmost simplicity. In particular, the use of two software development paradigms especially suitable for safety-critical control systems and easy verification, namely, function block diagrams and cause-effect tables, is advocated for.

Function block diagrams as defined in the standard [11] have already a long tradition in control engineering. Graphical programming in form of function block diagrams is well established in automation technology. Solving an application problem in form of a function block diagram is straightforward. The procedure closely resembles the conventional process of assembling control systems of traditional elements and devices. By programming in form of function block diagrams, specifications are directly mapped onto sequences of procedure invocations. The invoked procedures implement the functionality of individual function blocks, drawn from a library and verified only once during their lifetime with well-established formal specification and program verification techniques. In the course, two case studies on the implementation of the function block paradigm for safety-related real-time computing are elaborated.

Software for protection systems, such as emergency

shut-down systems, which are charged with the safety responsibility in dangerous technical systems, is usually represented in form of fill-in decision tables, called *cause-effect tables*. Cause-effect tables are the ideal form of programming safety-related systems, because specifications are formulated in a commonly understandable, but nevertheless formal way, as decision tables. Specifications can easily be checked and verified by (social) consensus, and specified operations can be directly interpreted and executed by a machine without requiring complicated transformations. For these reasons, the course presents this method as a last resort when systems developed with other techniques cannot be safety-licensed, but also as the method of choice meeting highest safety requirements. Following the concept of teaching holistic approaches, a corresponding especially tailored execution platform is described in the framework of a case study.

Consequently, the courses based on this approach emphasize industrially workable and proven methods, and stress human-centered and holistic engineering techniques for achieving safety and verifiability by design. For proper background, before discussing our implementations, we present in the Appendix descriptions of similar courses by other educators, without real-time focus. They are reviewed in terms of course objectives, prerequisites, and a course outline. General issues of system safety in education are discussed in [9].

5. Implementation at Embry-Riddle

A graduate course on Software Safety, MSE 590, was offered once during the Fall '95, focusing on methods to analyze safety, including the use of automatic software tools and team work. It is described in the accompanying paper [14], in this volume.

After experiences during this edition, it was decided to revise the course with regard to two aspects: a slightly different focus and a different way of instruction. The lack of emphasis on real-time systems was this course's one real deficiency. Consequently, it is felt that in addition to the only prerequisite, MSE 500, Software Engineering Concepts, a new prerequisite, MSE 595, Specification and Design for Real-Time Systems, needs to be added. Furthermore, changes in the course contents are needed to reflect a new focus. This includes several aspects discussed in Section 4, as well as programmable logic controllers (PLC) and implementation languages [6, 7], that replace the part on safety aspects of operating systems moved to MSE 640, Concurrent and Distributed Systems, and the part on formal verification, taken care of by a separate course.

Course Outline – New
MSE 650 Software Safety

- General Overview: Critical System Properties
- Thorough Discussion of Real-Time Properties
- Fault Tolerance as a Means to Implement Safety
- Programmable Logic Controllers and Their Role in Safety Systems
- Design for Safety: The Approach of the European Workshop on Industrial Computer Systems
- Function Charts and Cause-Effect Tables
- Programming Language Constructs and Safety
- N-Version Programming and Recovery Blocks
- Formal Approaches and Tools
- Safety Analysis Techniques: PHA, HAZOP, FMEA, Fault Trees, Reviews, Inspections
- Software Safety Standards
- Program Testing, Verification, Validation, and Metrics to Achieve Safety
- Certification and Licensing
- Review of Real-Time Safety-Related Applications

The other deficiency observed in the former edition was the insufficient coordination of project work. Rather than having a number of independent projects, all students in class will now work on various aspects of one bigger safety-related project. Their assignments will be composed of two elements: a literature study on a selected method to deal with safety aspects, and an implementation part to apply this method in a real project, both accomplished in three phases listed below.

- Phase 1. Writing a research report on the method dealing with safety, selected from a preapproved list.
- Phase 2. Applying the method in a real safety-related project, including the implementation.
- Phase 3. A class presentation.

The report should have the following structure: Introduction; Problem Description; Method Description (as a solution to the problem); Example of Application; Conclusion; Literature. Drafts of the report should be discussed with instructor, on a weekly basis, before final submission is made. A sample list of literature on methods to choose from is given below.

- Software Development and Documentation, MIL-STD-498, Draft 2, 2 October 1994

- Software Requirements. Guidance and Control Software Development Specification, NASA Contractor Report 182058, June 1990

- Software Reliability, ANSI/AIAA Recommended Practice R-013-1992

- Software Safety Standard, NASA Report NSS 1740.13, June 1994

- High Integrity Software for Nuclear Power Plants, Report NUREG/CR-6263, Vol. 2, June 1995

- Guidelines on Achieving Safety in Distributed Systems, EWICS WP 705/7, August 1994

- IEC Draft 1508 Functional Safety: Safety-Related Systems, 1995

- IEEE Standard for Software Productivity Metrics, IEEE Std 1045-1992

- Software Reliability and Safety in Nuclear Reactor Protection Systems, Report UCRL-ID-114839

- Fault Tree Analysis, IEC Pub 1025, 1990

An additional (book) literature on safety-related systems is provided in `http://erau.db.erau.edu/~zalewski/HAS.ps`.

After the report has been submitted, a class presentation is scheduled. Presentations normally take half an hour each. At the time of presentation all students in class should be provided with copies of each report (by e-mail or with paper copies). The talk should basically follow the structure of the report, that is:

- Explain the problem
- Describe the solution to this problem (the method)
- Illustrate the solution with an application
- Conclude and leave some time for discussion.

6. Implementation in a Distance Teaching Environment at Fernuniversität

After having successfully completed already a number of research projects [3, 4, 5] in this area, the Chair for Real-Time Systems in the Faculty of Electrical Engineering at Fernuniversität Hagen is now addressing safety-related real-time systems in teaching as well (see: `http://www.fernuni-hagen.de/IT`). Fernuniversität is a public university of North-Rhine Westphalia, the biggest state within the Federal Republic of Germany. As the only German language institution of distance education at the university level, i.e., granting doctoral degrees and habilitations, it has some 56,000 students, who are distributed over almost all countries

on earth. It maintains 67 study centres: 30 in North-Rhine Westphalia, 31 in the other German states, 3 in Austria, 2 in Switzerland and 1 in Hungary. Engineering curricula are offered by the Faculties of Computer Science and of Electrical Engineering with some 5,000 or 2,000 students enrolled, respectively.

Presently, the course in form of two consecutive parts of 3 credit hours each on the subject as outlined below is being developed, and will be launched in the winter semester 1996/97 and the summer semester 1997, respectively. In the regular curriculum of electrical engineering it can be taken as elective on the graduate level. Due to the practical significance of the subject, the course will be offered in Fernuniversität's continuing education program as well. Below, we briefly summarize the contents of each course unit.

First semester:

- Introduction: real-time computer control of technical processes, examples of safety-related real-time computer control systems, statement of the problems, safety and reliability, prevailing standards.

- Fundamental principles of safety-related real-time computing: hardware and software features of computing system features considered harmful, causes and effects of faults and failures, recognizability of faults, principles and methods to recognize faults, diversity.

- Concepts of safety-related real-time computing systems: exclusion, reduction, and influencing effects of faults and failures as measures to achieve safety, single/multi-channel and distributed system structures, special considerations for man-machine systems.

- Hardware of safety-related real-time computing systems: conventional, hard-wired electronic, and programmable electronic implementations of safety-related single and dual-channel systems, dual-channel signal representation, detectability of faults, families of fail-safe logic gates, electromagnetical compatibility.

- Software of safety-related real-time computing systems: system design, requirements engineering, fault avoidance and tolerance, forms and application of diversity, classical constructive and analytical methods to assure software quality and their assessment, application-oriented black-box testing of distributed real-time software by simulation of external environments and output verification.

- Case studies for safety-related real-time computing systems: an experimental, diverse multimicroprocessor system, its configuration, hardware and software, fail-safe comparison of intermediate results, empirical validation; a commercial dual-channel system with data-flow-independent failure recognition, safe state, and safety-oriented operating system.

- Quantitative assessment of safety-related real-time computing systems: basis and precondition for assessments, assessment of identical channels with respect to dangerous faults and failures, assessment of diverse channels with respect to dangerous faults and failures, assessment of software diversity, significance of input values.

Second semester:

- Graphical specification and design of real-time control software structures: the traditional paradigm of function blocks diagrams in process control, "canning" functionality into composable building blocks, complete function block libraries for various application areas in industrial automation, specification-oriented software design with function block diagrams, structuring industrial processes with sequential function charts.

- Safe real-time control employing programmable logic controllers: PLC architecture and operation principle, relation to synchronous multiprogramming and the Cy-Clone approach, fail-safe hardware components, measures to achieve software and operational safety, temporal predictability of PLC software execution behavior.

- Resource-adequate hardware implementation of function block diagrams: a set of fail-safe hardware building blocks, means to achieve exactly predictable and non-varying time behavior and safety-licensing of these components, mapping function block diagrams onto dedicated hardware with mechanically matching structure composed of these modules.

- A safety-licensable computing architecture: a fault-detecting dual-channel hardware architecture with fail-safe comparators and strictly enforced time behavior, clear physical separation of function block execution and realization of connecting data flow, architectural support of sequential function charts and rigorous verification of application software by diverse back-translation.

- Correct function blocks: a safe subset of the language Structured Text standardized in IEC 1131-3, using this language to implement function blocks, review of formal methods and their suitability for correctness proofs of various function block types, case studies on formally verifying function block implementations.

- Predictably behaving and safe real-time computer control with multitasking systems: minimizing mutual contention in asynchronous multitasking, real-time programming in inherently safe languages such as High-Integrity Pearl and a predictable subset of Real-Time Euclid, dependability of sequential program modules, a priori run time estimation techniques, schedulability analysis.

- Guidelines and last resort: strict application-oriented software design and verification rules based on the international standard IEC 880; cause-effect tables as a programming paradigm for protection systems and other applications with highest safety requirements relinquishing the need for generally difficult software verification.

7. Conclusion

The advantages of computers, namely, flexible adaptation to modifications of controlled processes just by re-programming instead of re-wiring and high information processing capabilities, are very desirable for implementing safety-related functions. As computers become increasingly complex, the technology is becoming more and more difficult to understand and to assess and, therefore, the engineers involved in the specification, design, implementation and maintenance of such systems lack a thorough understanding of the underlying principles. This is the main reason why hard-wired relay-based or discrete electronic logic is still prevailing for the implementation of safety-related automation functions and our course attempts to change this perception.

There is already a number of established methods and guidelines, such as [10], which have proven their usefulness for the development of high-integrity software employed for the control of safety-related technical processes and automation systems. Prior to its application, such software is still subjected to appropriate measures for its verification and validation. However, according to the present state of the art, these measures cannot guarantee the correctness of larger programs with mathematical rigor. Depending on national legislation and practice, the licensing authorities are still very reluctant or even refuse to approve safety-related systems, whose behavior is exclusively program-controlled. Our course uses educational vehicles to respond to this situation.

In summary, the course introduced in this paper addresses a pressing educational need. It does not provide solutions to all open questions of safety-related real-time computing, but a beginning is made which is practically feasible and applicable to broad class of safety-related process automation problems. Hence, we expect that the concepts presented here will find acceptance in the engineering community, and that engineers will acquire proficiency in applying them. This would ultimately lead to the replacement of discrete or relay logic by programmable electronic systems based on fail-safe hardware and executing safety-licensed software in charge of safety-critical functions in industrial processes.

References

[1] DIN 31 000 Teil 2, Allgemeine Leitsätze für das sicherheitsgerechte Gestalten technischer Erzeugnisse. Begriffe der Sicherheitstechnik. Grundbegriffe, Beuth-Verlag, Berlin, 1987

[2] L. Gowen, Mississippi State University, Private information, April 1996

[3] W. A. Halang et al., A Safety Licensable Computing Architecture, World Scientific, Singapore, 1993

[4] W. A. Halang, S.-K. Jung, A Programmable Logic Controller for Safety Critical Systems, High Integrity Systems, Vol. 1, No. 2, 1994, pp. 179-193

[5] W. A. Halang, B. J. Krämer and N. Völker, Formally Verified Building Blocks in Functional Logic Diagrams for Emergency Shutdown System Design, High Integrity Systems, Vol. 1, No. 3, 1995, pp. 277-286

[6] L. Hatton, Safer C: Developing Software for High-Integrity and Safety-Critical Systems, McGraw-Hill, New York, 1995

[7] H. Hecht et al., Review Guidelines on Software Languages for Use in Nuclear Power Plant Safety Systems, Report NUREG/CR-6463, Nuclear Regulatory Commission, Washington, DC, June 1996

[8] T. Hilburn, J. Zalewski, Real-Time Safety-Critical Systems: An Overview, Proc. 2nd IFAC Workshop Safety and Reliability in Emerging Control Technologies, Elsevier Science, Oxford, 1996

[9] C.P. Hoes, T. Herzog, System Safety in Education, Proc. 10th Int'l System Safety Conf., System Safety Society, New York, 1991, pp. 5.5-4-1/4-6

[10] IEC Pub 880, Software for Computers in Safety Systems of Nuclear Power Stations, International Electrotechnical Commission, Geneva, 1986

[11] IEC Pub 1131-3, Programmable Controllers, Part 3: Programming Languages, International Electrotechnical Commission, Geneva, 1992

[12] IEC Draft 1508, Functional Safety: Safety-Related Systems, International Electrotechnical Commission, Geneva, June 1995

[13] B.W. Johnson, A Course on the Design of Reliable Digital Systems, IEEE Trans. Education, Vol. 30, No. 1, February 1987, pp. 27-36

[14] A. Kornecki, J. Zalewski, A Real-Time Systems Track in the Master of Software Engineering Program. Real-Time Systems Education, J. Zalewski, ed., IEEE Computer Society Press, Los Alamitos, Calif., 1996 (this volume)

[15] J.C. Laprie, ed., Dependability: Basic Concepts and Terminology, Springer-Verlag, Wien, 1992

[16] N.G. Leveson, Software Safety, SEI Curriculum Module (Preliminary), Report SEI-CM-6-1.1, Software Engineering Institute, Pittsburgh, Penn., July 1987

[17] N.G. Leveson, Safeware: System Safety and Computers, Addison-Wesley, Reading, Mass., 1995

[18] J. McDermid, ed., Education and Training for Safety-Critical Systems Practitioners. Software in Safety-Related Systems, B. Wichmann, ed., John Wiley and Sons, Chichester, UK, 1992, pp. 179-207

[19] A. McKinlay, University of Southern California, Private information, July 1996

[20] D.L. Parnas, Software Documentation and Inspection: An Intensive Course for the Software Professionals. Course Outline, McMaster University, Hamilton, Ont., Canada, June 1996

[21] D.G. Raheja, Software Safety: Principles and Practice. Course Outline, University of California at Los Angeles, August 1995

[22] F. Redmill, ed., Dependability of Critical Computer Systems, Vol. 1, Elsevier Science, London, 1988

[23] J. Rushby, Critical System Properties: Survey and Taxonomy, Reliability Engineering and System Safety, Vol. 43, No. 2, 1994, pp. 189-219

[24] J. Zalewski, What Every Engineer Needs to Know about Rate-Monotonic Scheduling: A Tutorial. Advanced Multimicroprocessor Bus Architectures, J. Zalewski, ed., IEEE Computer Society Press, Los Alamitos, Calif., 1995

[25] J. Zalewski, A New Taxonomy for Critical System Properties, High-Assurance Computing Workshop, Arlington, VA, February 21-23, 1995

Appendix. Overview of Related Courses

A.1. University of Washington

One of the first courses in the area of Software Safety has been developed by Nancy Leveson, at the University of California, Irvine, currently at the University of Washington, Seattle. The description presented here is taken from the original document [16]. Current version mostly follows the book by the same author [17].

Objectives. The goal of the course is to equip software engineers with the extra knowledge and skills necessary to participate in a safety-critical software development project.

Prerequisites. There are no explicit prerequisites beyond a basic introduction to software engineering. Indepth coverage of such topics as software safety design techniques and risk assessment and measurement will require some prerequisite knowledge depending on how much background material the instructor wants to supply while teaching the course.

Course Outline

- What is Software Safety (Introduction; What is safety and safety engineering; Why is there a safety problem with software; Relationship of safety with other software qualities)
- Introduction to System Safety (Motivation; Hazard analysis; Hazard control)
- Management of Safety-Critical Software Projects (Importance in achieving safety; Responsibilities of software management; Duties of software safety group)
- Software Safety Modeling and Analysis (System hazard analysis; Software hazard analysis; Software safety requirements)
- Software Design Concepts to Enhance Safety (Why the need for runtime measures; Hazard prevention vs. hazard control; Hazard prevention; Hazard detection and treatment)
- Verification and Certification of Safety
- Assessment of Safety (Introduction to quantitative risk assessment; Software reliability and safety)
- Man/Machine Interface Considerations
- Miscellaneous Issues

A.2. University of California at L.A.

This course on Software Safety has been taught by Dev G. Raheja [21]. The information is excerpted from a promotional brochure. Most of the topics listed here are associated with more intensive workshops.

Objectives. The objective of this course is to guide software engineers and managers in preventing software hazards. It emphasizes sound software design principles for building inherent safety into complex systems.

Prerequisites. Participants are expexted to have some education or experience in software engineering and programming.

Course Outline

- Software Safety Principles
- Software Risk Management from Early Design
- Design Rules for Safety
- Hazard Analysis Process
- Hazard Analysis Techniques
- Robust Design for Safety
- Safety Concerns for Real-Time Systems
- Language Concerns
- Testing for Safety
- Quality Assurance for Safety-Critical Components
- Safety Standards
- Software Safety Program
- Conclusions.

A.3. University of Southern California, L.A.

This is taught by Arch McKinlay as a four-day course on Software System Safety Engineering and Management. It emphasizes lessons learned in software system safety. The description is based on a version run in May 1996 [19].

Objectives. Provide standards and "best practices" for managers and engineers, for both the acquirer and supplier. Provide full life-cycle development system approach to minimizing hazards, program cost control, and residual risk.

Prerequisites. None explicitly stated but from "Objectives" it's clear that an engineering degree and/or a management position is sufficient.

Course Outline

- Safety Risk (System safety program; Subsystem hazard analysis; Matching hazards to functions; Testing and monitoring safety-related code)
- Technical Risk (Languages and compilers; Development, test and integration environments)
- Development Risk (Product life-cycle; Statistical process control; Change control procedures; Documentation process)
- Risk Management (Focuses on issues listed above).

A.4. Mississippi State University

This course has been taught for the past four years, by Lon Gowen, as a graduate-level course in Software

Safety at Mississippi State. The material used for this course is a collection of papers from various journals, in particular, papers dealing with the following topics: specifying the requirements, specifying the design, coding, and testing safety-critical software systems [2].

Objective. To cover prior and current issues relating to the research and practice of software and systems safety.

Prerequisites. A prior course or understanding in the basics of software engineering is helpful but not required.

Course Outline

- Introduction (System-based life cycle; Relationship between system and software safety; Examples of accidents; Overview of safety-based ideas and techniques)
- Requirements Issues (Preliminary hazard analysis; Requirements langauges; A look at available standards)
- Design Issues (Levels of protection; Design-level hazard analysis; Fault-tree analysis; Event-tree analysis; FMECA; Fault tolerance)
- Coding Issues (Which programming languages? What is missing?)
- Testing Issues (Fault-tree testing; Event-tree testing; Non-safety-specific techniques)

A.5. British Computer Society, U.K.

In the early nineties, in the U.K., the Safety Critical Systems Group of the British Computer Society established an Education Working Party to design courses in software development for safety-critical systems. It was meant to establish a framework for a series of courses related to the British industry structure model. The working party produced a report, from which this information is extracted [18]. The whole syllabus was divided into seven parts (A–G), composed of modules.

Objectives. The intention is that the courses should serve a postgraduate, post-experience level. Typical entrants to the courses should have the necessary qualifications and experience to receive Chartered Engineer status, but would not necessarily have been registered as a Chartered Engineer. The working party believed that it is necessary for those attending the courses to have a certain degree of maturity and industrial experience in order that they will be receptive to, and can appropriately interpret, guidance on difficult judgemental issues such as when it is appropriate to use software in control of critical systems.

Prerequisites. The courses are to serve several different markets. First, they provide basic background information for people who will be in managerial positions of responsibility associated with safety-critical

systems. Second, they aim to provide a thorough technical grounding for those who should be involved in the development or certification of software-controlled safety-critical systems.

Course Outline

- Part A. Introduction
- Part B. Hazard and Risk Analysis (Hazard Analysis; Risk Analysis and Requirements)
- Part C. Techniques and Technology (General Software and Systems Engineering Issues; Architectural Issues; Basic Discrete Mathematics; Formal Specification; Formal Approaches: Principles and Program Verification; Testing; Validation; Fault Tolerance; Psychology – Human-Computer Interface; Implementation)
- Part D. Management (Principles and Techniques; Safety-Critical Systems Management)
- Part E. Evaluation (Basic Probability and Statistics; Software Reliability)
- Part F. Building Safe Systems (Integration of Techniques; Examples)
- Part G. Principles and Problems – Reprise

A.6. University of York, U.K.

This course is offered by the Department of Computer Science, at the University of York, in the U.K. (see: `http://dcpu1.cs.york.ac.uk:6666/CS/SC.html`). It is titled "Modular MSc in Safety Critical Systems Engineering" and clearly follows the recommendations listed in the previous section. It encompasses 15 modules, each taught approximately for one week. Current edition lasts for about one year (May 1996–97).

Objectives. The course is designed to develop a new generation of system designers and implementors for work in this demanding field by exposure to the latest science and technology. It emphasizes the issues of construction of safety critical software.

Prerequisites. Typical applicants will have achieved at least a second class degree in Computer Science or a related discipline with an appropriate mathematical basis. The part-time version of this course is specifically directed at experienced designers and programmers, and industrial experience is also useful for full-time applicants. However, applications will also be considered from those who do not fit this profile.

Course Outline

- Introduction to Safety
- Requirements Engineering
- Mathematics for Safety
- Formal Methods for Safety Critical Systems
- Timing Analysis
- Human Factors
- Development of Safe Software

- Dependable Systems Analysis
- Safety and Hazard Analysis
- Software Testing
- Software Architectures
- System Architectures and Device Interfaces
- Computer Systems Security
- Operation, Management and Maintenance
- Management of Safety Critical Projects
- Legal and Environmental Aspects of Safety.

A.7. Telecommunications Research Institute of Ontario, Canada

This course named "Software Documentation and Inspection" is based on a software cost reduction method, refined and enhanced by the Software Engineering Research Group at McMaster University. The course is being taught by David Parnas at the Telecommunications Research Institute of Ontario (TRIO). It is conducted as a three-day course on software inspection and documentation, combined with an optional one/two-day introduction to software design principles. This course presents a procedure for software inspection that is based on a sound mathematical model and can be carried out systematically by large groups. The information presented here has been compiled by the authors based on a version of the course presented at Ottawa, on July 15-19, 1996 [20].

Objectives. This course presents an approach to active design reviews that has the reviewers writing precise documentation about the program and explaining their documentation to an audience of other reviewers. Participants inspect a small, working program that they bring with them from their company

Prerequisites. A background in software engineering principles and some familiarity with logical and mathematical notation. To accommodate the diversity of backgrounds, participants can select either a core three-day, or optional four- or five-day sequence.

Course Outline

- Overview and Case Study: A Discussion of Previous Applications of the Method
- Tabular Expressions: Writing of Readable Predicates Using Two-dimensional Notations
- Describing Program Function: Writing Program Descriptions Using Predicates and Tables
- Presentation of "Palav"
- Participant Decomposition and Inspection of Palav
- Discussion of Inspection Results for Palav
- Presentation of Dijkstra's Dutch National Flag (DNF) Problem
- Discussion of the DNF

- Inspection of a Real Program
- Preparation of Inspection Reports
- Report on the Inspection Results.

A.8. University of Virginia

This is a course on the "Design of Reliable Digital Systems", thus, basically related to the reliability of hardware. However, it is important to be mentioned here, if one wants to provide a broader coverage. It has been developed by Barry W. Johnson, at the University of Virginia, Charlottesville. The material below is excerpted from [13]. The course lectures are interleaved with student presentations.

Objectives. The course has four primary goals. First, it is desired to introduce students to the terminology used in the fault tolerance community. Second, the students are to be exposed to modern techniques that are presently available for designing and analysing reliable and fault-tolerant digital systems. Third, the students should be provided with practical knowledge and experience in the design of reliable digital systems. The final goal is to expose the students to current research.

Prerequisites. The course is offered as an intermediate level graduate course available to all masters and doctoral students. The prerequisite is an understanding of basic digital logic design and computer organization.

Course Outline

- Introduction
- Basic Definitions
- Application Areas
- Examples of Each Application
- Causes of Faults
- Design Techniques
- Concepts of Redundancy
- Hardware Redundancy
- Detailed Example: Aircraft Flight Control System
- Information Redundancy
- Detailed Example: Error Correcting Memory
- Time Redundancy
- Detailed Example: Arithmetic Logic Unit
- Software Redundancy
- Detailed Example: Self-Test in Avionics
- Reliability Analysis
- Maintainability Analysis
- Availability Analysis
- Detailed Example: Reliability Analysis of an Avionics System
- Design Project.

Chapter 4
Teaching Formal Methods for Real-Time Systems

The Role of Integrated Specification Techniques in Teaching Complex System Modeling and Analysis

Robert B. France
CS&E Department
Florida Atlantic University
Boca Raton, FL 33431, USA
robert@cse.fau.edu

Jean-Michel Bruel
Laboratoire IRIT/SIERA
Université Paul Sabatier
31062 Toulouse, France
bruel@irit.irit.fr

Abstract

The development of complex systems often requires the use of a variety of software modeling and analysis techniques. For example, in a single project one may use a graphically-based object-oriented modeling technique to model the structure of a system and a formal method to specify and analyze the critical parts of the system. Unfortunately, multiparadigm approaches to development are often overlooked in academic software courses and texts.

In this paper we describe a software engineering course we developed that emphasizes a multiparadigm approach to software modeling. In the course the students are introduced to an object-oriented and a formal method, and are shown how the two methods can be effectively integrated through examples in lectures and group projects involving the use of the methods.

1. Introduction

Many academic software engineering texts and courses present real-time system development techniques through a variety of formal and less-formal software development techniques. The problem is that most academic materials treat the development methods as alternatives, and present their application in singular terms, that is, specification examples and case studies are often presented in terms of a single method. This leaves the students with a collection of 'single-method' approaches to specification and analysis. This is not necessarily a 'bad' thing. If students are made to understand the strengths and limitations of the various specification techniques then they are in a position to choose the most appropriate techniques for particular types of problems. A deficiency of the 'single-

method' approach is that it does not exploit another approach to specification problems: the integrated-method approach (or the multi-paradigm approach). The integrated-method approach takes the view that a single project may require the application of specification techniques from a variety of methods, for example, one may use a graphical object-oriented technique to model structure and a formal specification technique to specify the more critical aspects of behavior within a single project. We feel that students should be prepared to apply a variety of specification and analysis techniques, possibly from different methods, that are appropriately integrated.

The particular problem that we attempt to address in our formal methods and software engineering courses relates to the use of formal specification techniques (FSTs) and graphical, structured object- and function-based techniques, such as Fusion and Structured Analysis/Real-Time, in the development of complex systems. The 'single-method' view taken in most academic materials often leads students to the the view that FSTs and the more graphical, but less formal structured techniques are alternative approaches to system development. Students are often mistakenly led to believe that FSTs cannot be applied in the context of more 'traditional' development methods. Our research indicates that integrated FSTs and structured methods can be used in the context of practical development processes and that they are benefits to their application over use of single FSTs, and structured methods.

We have used integrated methods and supporting processes in two undergraduate software engineering project courses to date. In both classes, students were asked to develop requirements models of a Students Advising System using an integrated Structured Analysis (SA) and Z method we developed as part of our research. At the end of the projects students presented their results and discussed their experiences with the use of the integrated methods. The students experiences indicated that they observed the complementary roles that the informal and formal techniques can play in system development and realized the benefits in terms of a deeper understanding of the problem they were modeling [6].

One of the major complaints made by students in these two projects was the lack of tool support for the integrated method. We have since then developed a tool environment, called FuZE, that supports the application of an integrated Fusion and Z method. FuZE is intended to facilitate practical application of FSTs in the development of complex systems. The environment supports the building and rigorous analysis of models that are precisely expressed and rigorously analyzable.

The conceptual integration model on which FuZE is based is given in Figure 1.

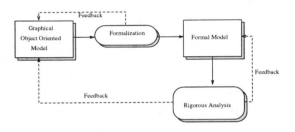

Figure 1. The integration process

In the model a graphical object-oriented model is 'formalized', the result being a more precise model of the behavior and/or structure captured by the graphical OO model. The formalization activity can uncover problems with the graphical OO model related to incomplete, imprecise, ambiguous, and inconsistent requirements and design information. The insights gained from formalization can be used to improve the graphical OO models, that is, make them more precise and informative. The effect of formalization on the graphical OO model is shown as feedback from the formalization activity to the OO model. Once a formal model is produced, rigorous analysis of behavior and structure is possible. Such analysis can yield further insights into requirements and designs that can be used to further improve both the formal and OO models.

In the software engineering graduate project course that will be offered in the Fall 1996 term, students will use FuZE with the Octopus [11] OO real-time system development method to build and analyze requirements and design models for a traffic management system. A major objective is to make students aware of how formal specification techniques can be used in conjunction with more graphical, but less formal, object-oriented analysis methods. In the following sections we describe the structure, and materials that will be used in the project part of the graduate course, CEN 6040 Computer-Aided Software Engineering.

2. Course Overview and Objectives

The Computer-Aided Software Engineering course will have two components: a lecture component and a laboratory component. The lecture component will focus on presenting to students materials on the principles, methods, and processes underlying the tools they will be using in the laboratory. In the early part of the course the laboratory sessions will reinforce the lecture components by providing students with case studies and exercises that complement materials on the development methods and notations covered in the lectures. Later, laboratory sessions will be used mainly for project related activities.

For the project, students will be divided into groups of 5 persons. They will be charged with developing requirements models, an architectural design, and implementable subsystem designs for a traffic controller. The students will use the FuZE tool, developed by the Integrated Methods Group at FAU, in their project with the Octopus real-time system design method. FuZE supports the building of Fusion object-oriented (OO) models and their translation to Z specifications. For analysis, the translation to Z is mostly mechanical. For design, the translation requires significant human interaction, but the tool provides good support for the more mundane tasks of formal specification, as well as support for rigorous analysis of creative results.

At the end of the course students should:

- understand the complementary roles that formal and less formal, highly-structured, graphical techniques can play in modeling and analyzing application behavior and structure,

- be familiar with, and understand the rationale behind processes required to make effective use of integrated formal and informal techniques in the object-oriented modeling and analysis of complex systems,

- have created and analyzed a problem with safety-critical and real-time properties, and

- have working knowledge of the FuZE CASE environment, and its underlying modeling and specification techniques.

3. Support materials for course

A World Wide Web (WWW) page on FuZE is currently being developed to support the use of FuZE on projects. Included in the page will be a tutorial for first time users, case studies on the application of FuZE (for a simple traffic control system, a student advising system, and a gas dispensing system), and a selection of papers on the tool and the underlying rules.

Students will also have one day of scheduled classes in the Software Engineering Laboratory (consists of Sun workstations). The scheduled Lab times will not be sufficient to complete the project; students are expected to use the open lab outside of class hours.

The following will be the text books for the course:

Required Texts:

- Object-Oriented Technology for Real-Time Systems: A Practical Approach Using OMT and Fusion; by M. Awad, J. Kuusela, and J. Ziegler; Prentice-Hall.

- An Introduction to Formal Specification and Z; by B. Potter, J. Sinclair, and D. Till; Prentice-Hall.

Recommended Texts:

- Object-Oriented Development: The Fusion Method; by D. Coleman et. al.; Prentice-Hall.

- Object-Oriented Modeling and Design; by J. Rumbaugh et. al.; Prentice-Hall.

- The Z Notation; by J. M. Spivey; Prentice-Hall.

The text books will be supplemented by lecture notes and a set of papers on FuZE and real-time system modeling.

Students are assumed to have the following skills and knowledge:

- Skills related to programming in the small (e.g., structured programming).

- Knowledge of key software engineering principles (e.g., separation of concerns, rigor, and incrementality), in particular, basic design principles (e.g., design for change).

- Knowledge of software development processes.

- Familiarity with object-oriented modeling methods.

- Have at least undergraduate level Discrete Maths.

4. Course Contents

Each lecture is one hour and twenty minutes. Lectures are held twice a week.

1. Introduction (Lecture C1; week 1)

   (a) Review of object-oriented software engineering principles and development processes.

   (b) Real-time system development: an overview.

2. Integrating formal and informal techniques (Lecture C2; week 1)

   (a) Introduction to formal specification techniques.

   (b) Rationalizing integrated techniques.

   (c) A development model for integrated techniques.

3. Integrated OO techniques and Z (Lectures C3-C16; weeks 2-14)

   (a) The development process.

   (b) A small example.

   (c) The Fusion analysis notation.

   (d) The Z notation.

   (e) Integrating Fusion analysis and Z.

   (f) Real-time extensions of Fusion design: The Octopus approach.

   (g) Integrating Z and real-time extensions of Fusion.

4. Using FuZE (Lab L1-L3; weeks 3-5)

   (a) Modeling in FuZE.

   (b) Rigorous analysis in FuZE.

   (c) Small case study.

5. The Problem (Lab L4; week 6)

   (a) Presentation of the Traffic Control System problem.

   (b) Refining the problem statement.

6. Project planning and execution. (Lab L5-L12; weeks 7-14)

7. Project reviews. (Lab L13; week 15)

8. Project analysis. (Lab L14; week 16)

Sections 1 to 3 will be covered in the lecture component of the course, and sections 4 to 8 will be covered in the lab component of the course. The lab component will commence after the Fusion notation is introduced in the lecture component (i.e., after 3(a) lectures). Early lab assignments will focus on reinforcing Fusion and Z modeling concepts introduced in the lectures, through the use of FuZE.

5. The Lecture Component

5.1. Introduction

The introductory part of the course gives students an overview of the principles they will be applying in the project. The materials presented in this section should provide the students with the context needed to understand and justify the use of the processes, methods, and tools used later in the course. The intent is to make clear to students how the development mechanisms they use support (and/or hinder!) real-time system development goals.

The nature of software engineering will be discussed, a review of significant software engineering principles (as discussed in [4]: Rigor and formality, separation of concerns (e.g., views, abstraction, modularity), generality, anticipation of changes, and incrementality), and a review of how object-oriented techniques support software engineering principles and concerns will be given.

Students will also be given an overview of the special concerns of real-time system development here.

5.2. Integrating formal and informal techniques

The objective of this part of the course is to motivate the use of integrated formal and informal techniques in software development, and to instill in the students an appreciation for the complementary roles formal and graphical informal techniques can play in software development.

During the early eighties research on systematic approaches to software development resulted in a number of graphically-based specification methods for real-time system, which we will collectively refer to as *structured specification methods* (SSMs) (e.g., see [8]). In most cases, these methods were extensions to existing *Structured Analysis/Design* (SA/SD) methods. The specifications produced by SSMs were often more concise and sometimes more precise than purely natural language specifications. The evolution of SA/SD-related research and practice has resulted more recently in the creation of *object-oriented methods* (OOMs) (e.g., see [5, 13]). Most popular graphical object-oriented modeling techniques support the creation of models that are concise, visually-appealing, and abstract. On the other hand, the lack of firm semantic bases for the modeling constructs used makes it difficult to rigorously reason about the structures and behavior modeled, and can make understanding the models more apparent than real. Most SSMs and OOMs are *informal* in the sense that their applications are likely to produce ambiguous specifications that are not amenable to rigorous semantic analyses. In this course, we refer to such techniques as *informal specification techniques* (ISTs).

The critical nature of some real-time software systems often necessitates the use of FSTs. Here, a FST consists of a precise language and mechanisms for deriving consequences from statements in the language. Despite the benefits FSTs can bring to development, there are some problems with their application to the development of non-trivial applications. Among the problems are the lack of adequate structuring mechanisms, making specification development a mostly monolithic task and the resulting specifications difficult to read, and the scarcity of tools that ease the creation and analysis of specifications.

The application of *Integrated FSTs and ISTs* (FISTs) can be beneficial in the following respects:

- *FISTs enable an evolutionary approach to the use of FSTs in industry.* An FIST enables the use of FSTs in the context of the ISTs. This allows specifiers to become familiar with FSTs while still taking advantage of their IST skills. FISTs allows an organization to preserve, and even enhance, its investment in ISTs while taking advantage of FST-related benefits.

- *FSTs and ISTs can complement each other.* The highly-structured and graphical nature of IST specifications makes them more presentable than the more detailed, often textual, formal specifications. Furthermore, the flexibility resulting from the use of intuitively-defined concepts and visual constructs makes ISTs suitable for the early, probing phases of software development, since they are more likely to result in abstract models that can be used to gain a high-level understanding of the problem or solution. The abstract models produced through the use of FSTs are often more difficult to understand. On the other hand, the lack of a firm semantic basis for ISTs inhibits their use in rigorous specification and analysis of behavior. FSTs are needed for such activities. FSTs can also enhance the applications of ISTs. Formalizing an informal specification often reveals ambiguities, inconsistencies, and gaps in the informal specification.

- *An FIST can be used as a basis for systematic transformation of abstract notions of behavior and structure to more precise expressions.* Requirements engineering is concerned with transforming vague statements of requirements into more precise statements of the problem. During this transformation a number of intermediate specifications, each varying in degree of rigor and detail, may be produced. FISTs allows one to impose structure on the transformation of vague requirements to formal specifications. FISTs can play a similar role in design, where design is viewed as the creation of a series of decreasingly abstract solution specifications.

In this course the students will use a formalization process called the *P-E-V* model to guide the application of the integrated techniques to the project problem. In the P-E-V model, development within a life-cycle phase is viewed as an activity consisting of a *probing (exploratory) phase*, an *elaboration phase*, and a *validation phase*.

In the probing (exploratory) phase, the modeler attempts to impose a structure on the problem or create a solution structure. Given the exploratory nature of this phase, the tool support should be flexible, that is, allow for the easy incorporation of changes, and should allow the modeler to view the problem or solution in an abstract, but insightful, manner. Graphical object-oriented methods (OOMs) such as Fusion and Octopus are well-suited to this phase since they mostly employ graphical constructs supported by rich structuring mechanisms, and provide visual abstract views of structure and behavior from a variety of perspectives. Formal specification techniques, on the other hand, are not well-suited to this phase because they may produce models of structure and behavior that are not as easy to understand and modify.

When the modeler is satisfied that an adequate structure has been developed, then he proceeds to the elaboration phase where details pertaining to elements in the structure and their relationships are more rigorously specified. In this phase, formality should be favored over informality because the objective is to create a specification that is analyzable and precise. During the elaboration phase, ambiguities, inconsistencies and incomplete information may be identified,

and attempts at resolving them may lead to modifications of the structure initially defined for the problem or solution. Development in this model is thus an iteration of probing and elaboration phases activities, as indicated by the double headed arrow between the two phases in Figure 2.

The validation activity is concerned with establishing the validity of the models. Animation and proof techniques can be used to support formal reviews here.

5.3. Integrated OO techniques and Z

In this section of the course the students will cover the integrated techniques and processes that will be used in the project. The integrated technique is based on Fusion, Z, and the Octopus [11] real-time extensions to Fusion.

The system development process that will be introduced (and used in the project) is based on the Octopus development method. The model, shown in Figure 2, consists of three major phases: Requirements Specification, Architectural Design, and Subsystem Development.

The Requirements Specification phase is concerned with modeling the desired behavior of the system in terms of the behaviors that are observable at the boundaries of the system. Concurrency is implicit at the requirements level, that is, each object is assumed to have its own processing resources. Fusion analysis models and Z specification will be used to to express the static and dynamic aspects of the required behavior. Constraints (i.e., non-functional requirements) will be expressed in English text, and, when appropriate, used to annotate the models.

In the Architectural Design phase subsystems and their interfaces will be identified and defined. Here, a subsystem consists of objects and their relationships. The Fusion object model produced in the requirements phase will be used as a base for identifying subsystems; classes in the model will be grouped together into subsystems, where a subsystem is intended to capture a particular domain (i.e., an area that has a relatively independent body of knowledge, terminology, and solution strategies). The structure of the architecture is modeled by Fusion analysis models, and the interfaces are defined using Fusion operation schemas.

Once the subsystems are identified each subsystem is analyzed, designed, and implemented. In the analysis phase the object model is extended with design objects, a high-level description of state dependent behavior for the subsystem is created, and the significance of events is determined. The state-dependent behavior of a subsystem is defined in terms of Harel's

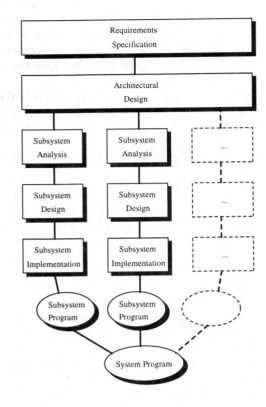

Figure 2. A Development Process for Real-Time Systems

statecharts [7], and is produced using the guidelines provided by the Octopus method. The analysis of the significance of events is also guided by the Octopus method.

The design phase of subsystem development introduces concurrency, priorities and time. The extensions to the Fusion Object Interaction Graphs made by Octopus will be used to model interactions between object instances in a model. The Octopus also provides guidelines for grouping objects into operating system level processes (instances that communicate synchronously are grouped into processes) and for handling shared objects (objects belonging to more than one group).

In each of the phases the P-E-V model will be used, that is, students will first express their ideas using the graphical notations and then attempt to formalize those parts that are deemed critical and/or requires some analysis (using Z). The students will not be required to formalize all aspects of their design.

In the lectures students will be introduced to Fusion, Z, and the particular Octopus notations that will be used in the project. In the Fusion part, analysis and design models will be covered. For analysis the Fusion object (static) and interface (dynamic) models will be emphasized, and for design the Fusion Object Interaction Graphs, statecharts (used in Octopus), and scenarios will be introduced. The material in this part will be covered in 4 lectures. In the laboratory section, the students will develop Fusion analysis and design models for a small library problem.

The Z part of this section will include a review of predicate logic and set theory, the Z type system, coverage of Z functions, relations, sequences, schemas and schema operations (inclusion, decoration, logical connectives, composition, piping), and an introduction to formal reasoning with Z. The material will be covered in 4 lectures. Students will develop Z specifications for the library problem in the lab component of this course using the Formalizer tool.

The materials in this part of the course will be covered in 12 lectures.

6. The Laboratory Component

6.1. Using FuZE

FuZE (Fusion/Z Environment) is an automated support environment for creating Fusion object-oriented analysis models and for transforming them into Z specifications [14]. FuZE is built on top of the Paradigm Plus object-oriented modeling CASE tool [12]. The extensions to the tool we have made thus far allow modelers to generate Z specifications from Fusion object models and from state transition diagrams. From Paradigm Plus, Z analysis tools, e.g., typecheckers and animators, can be called to analyze the generated specifications.

Paradigm Plus (Release 2.01) provides support for modeling based on OMT [13], Fusion [5], Booch [2] and others, and automatically generates C, C++, Smalltalk or Ada code from the models. A powerful script language allows custom reporting, checking, and code generation. We used the script language to build FuZE on top of Paradigm Plus. Figure 3 gives an overview of the process that allows one to formally analyze a Fusion model in FuZE. Beginning with an Object Diagram in Fusion, the formalization process generates a .out file of the corresponding Z specification. A Z tool, ZTC [10] is then launched by running a script, to type-check the specification and produce a printable file. A .tex file can also be generated by a script to allow the use of LaTeX to generate a Postscript

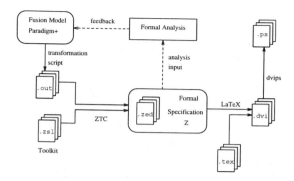

Figure 3. From a Fusion Object Model to a type-checked Z specification

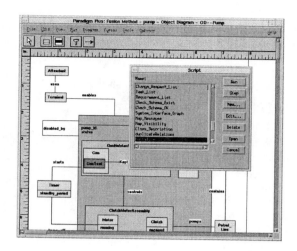

Figure 4. Selection of a transformation rule

version of the specification. The .zed file can also be analyzed by a Z animator such as ZANS (this tool has not been integrated into FuZE as yet).

It is not our aim to detail the rules in this paper (for more details see [1]).

Paradigm Plus can be customized by its powerful, full-featured script language. The script language supports methods checking, reports and code generation. The script language syntax is similar to the syntax of Basic-like languages. Familiarity with higher level languages makes writing scripts in Paradigm Plus easier.

To translate a Fusion model into a Z specification, one selects from a menu the option to run a script (see Figure 4). More details about the results of automatic translations in FuZE can be found in the draft FuZE technical report [3].

As illustrated by Figure 3, we use ZTC to type-check the specification. The Paradigm Plus script language allows one to access the operating system shell. We use this feature to invoke ZTC with the script output and the mathematical toolkit as its inputs. After the output result of the translation rules, ZTC is launched to type check the generated Z specification and to generate (if the specification is correct) the corresponding LaTeX output.

We also include in the output specification some comments used by the ZANS [9] animation tool that allows one to animate the specification by defining very simple operations that manipulate the objects in the model.

6.2. The project

The project problem is stated as follows:

On the island of St. May there is an intersection at the top of a hill that is notorious for its rush hour traffic snarls and pedestrian accidents. The junction, known as Casson Hill Point, occurs where a major road linking the east side to the west side (this is the only link) intersects with a road linking two residential areas. The Works department, after numerous complaints from residents in the area, have decided to install traffic and pedestrian lights at the junction. Each approach to the junction will have a pedestrian crossing (with pedestrian lights on each side), a sensor to detect the presence of vehicles on the approach, and turning lanes. The traffic system is required to be safe, reliable, maintainable, easy to extend, and effective.

One of the first tasks of the requirements analysis is to analyze the problem statement and make it more precise. This involves first identifying and distinguishing the functional and non-functional requirements. There is a single functional requirement: the system should control the flow of traffic. The non-functional requirements concern safety, reliability, maintainability, extensibility, and effectiveness. The functional requirement can be refined using the models supported by FuZE and Octopus. Refinement of the non-functional requirements is also needed so that their impact on the required behavior can be precisely determined. For example, the non-functional safety requirement can be refined as follows:

A safe system will not cause traffic to flow across a designated crossing point at the same time, and will allow a safe period to elapse between stopping a flow and allowing a crossing flow to proceed. More precisely, no two crossing flow roads should allow traffic flow within 2 seconds of each other.

The effectiveness requirement can be refined as follows:

Deadlock of the system should not occur, specifically, the system should not allow the four approaches to the intersection to be closed for more than 5 minutes when traffic has arrived during the first 4 minutes of the period. Also, no motorist or pedestrian should have to wait more than one minute to proceed. During rush hours (between 7 and 8am and between 4 and 5pm) the traffic on the east/west road is heavier; in these cases, motorists on the residential road may have to wait more than one minute, but no more than 2 minutes, before proceeding.

The result of the requirements refinement is a precise model of the functional requirements, expressed in terms of Fusion analysis models and Z, and statements detailing how the non-functional requirements constrain the functionality of the system. When these are produced, a review meeting is held. Before the meeting, the students will exchange their requirements documents. They will be given 7 days to carry out the review. In the next scheduled lab class (at the end of the 7 days) a review meeting will be held where the students discuss problems they uncovered. The lecturer will play the role of the customer in the review. After the review, the students address any problems uncovered and submit the changed requirements document to the lecturer. The students will be given 3 weeks to complete a first pass at requirements specification.

The design will be done in an incremental manner, where the students first focus on defining the core subsystem(s) and then (as time permits) extend the design to cover other aspects of the design. For example, the students may decide to ignore pedestrian control and turning signals in the first increment. It is expected that students will spend approximately 5 to 6 weeks on the design. At the end of each increment a review will be held. The review will be carried out as described previously. It is expected that students complete at least one increment during this course.

7. Conclusion

We realize that the course outlined as above is intensive. Some of the problems we expect to encounter are as follows:

- Students will be overwhelmed by the number of notations used.

- Students may spend more time on learning to use the tool than on developing solutions to the problem.

- For class sizes greater than ten, course management could be a nightmare.

To alleviate these problems we plan to keep class size below ten students (i.e., two groups), and provide facilities such as an online tutorial for the tool, a WWW page on using the tool, and an electronic bulletin board where students can post their questions and complaints to the lecturer and the research assistants that developed the tool. Furthermore, we plan to have a research assistant hold tutorials, one hour per week on the tool. During these tutorials, students will delve deeper into features of the tools introduced in the classroom, and the research assistant will address any project-related problems that the students may have.

Acknowledgments

This work was supported in part by NSF grant CCR-9410396. The authors wish to thank Maria Petrie for her participation in this project. We are also grateful to Bharat Chintapally and Gopal Raghavan for implementing the rules into FuZE. The authors would also like to thank the referees for their valuable comments.

References

[1] B. W. Bates, J.-M. Bruel, R. B. France, and M. M. Larrondo-Petrie. Formalizing Fusion Object-Oriented Analysis Models. In E. Najm and J.-B. Stephani, editors, *Proceedings of the First IFIP International Workshop on Formal Methods for Open Object-based Distributed Systems, Paris, France.* Chapman & Hall, London, U.K., 4–6 March 1996.

[2] G. Booch. *Object-Oriented Analysis and Design with Applications.* Second edition. Benjamin/Cummings, Menlo Park, CA, 1994.

[3] J.-M. Bruel, B. Chintapally, R. B. France, and G. K. Raghavan. FuZE–Draft of the User's Guide. FAU Technical Report TR-CSE-96-9, Department of Computer Science & Engineering, Florida Atlantic University, Boca Raton, USA, February 1996.

[4] M. J. C. Ghezzi and D. Mandrioli. *Fundamentals of Software Engineering*. Prentice Hall, Englewood Cliffs, NJ, 1991.

[5] D. Coleman, P. Arnold, S. Bodoff, C. Dollin, H. Gilchrist, F. Hayes, and P. Jeremaes. *Object-Oriented Development: the Fusion Method*. Prentice Hall, Englewood Cliffs, NJ, 1994.

[6] R. B. France and M. M. Larrondo-Petrie. Understanding the role of formal specification techniques in requirements engineering. In *Proceedings of 8th SEI Conference on Software Engineering Education*, pp. 207–222. Springer-Verlag, New York, 1995.

[7] D. Harel. Statecharts: A visual formalism for complex systems. *Science of Computer Programming*, 8(3), 1987.

[8] D. Hatley and I. Pirbhai. *Strategies for Real-Time System Specification*. Dorset House, New York, 1987.

[9] X. Jia. *An Approach to Animating Z Specifications*. Division of Software Engineering, School of Computer Science, Telecommunication, and Information Systems, DePaul University, Chicago, IL, USA, 1995.

[10] X. Jia. *ZTC: A Z Type Checker, User's Guide, version 2.01*. Division of Software Engineering, School of Computer Science, Telecommunication, and Information Systems, DePaul University, Chicago, IL, USA, May 1995. Available via anonymous ftp at ise.cs.depaul.edu.

[11] J. Z. M. Awad, J. Kuusela. *Object-Oriented Technology for Real-Time Systems: A Practical Approach Using OMT and Fusion*. Prentice Hall, Upper Saddle River, NJ, 1996.

[12] Protosoft, Inc. *Paradigm Plus – Release 2.0*. Protosoft Technical Support, Houston, Texas, USA, January 1994.

[13] J. Rumbaugh, M. R. Blaha, W. Premerlani, F. Eddy, and W. Lorensen. *Object-Oriented Modeling and Design*. Prentice Hall, Englewood Cliffs, NJ, 1991.

[14] J. M. Spivey. *The Z Notation: A Reference Manual*. Second edition. Prentice Hall, Englewood Cliffs, NJ, 1992.

Process Activities for Student Projects Involving the Formal Specification of Real-Time Software

Thomas B. Hilburn
Department of Computer Science
Embry-Riddle Aeronautical University
Daytona Beach, FL 32114
hilburn@db.erau.edu

Abstract

There is increasing interest in the use of formal specification languages for the specification of software requirements, especially for safety-critical systems and for software that has rigorous timing constraints and requires high reliability. Unfortunately, there has been little attention to the process used to develop such specifications. This paper discusses issues related to student projects for the formal specification of real-time systems; it advances the need for a specification process; and it defines the elements of such a process. The definition is based upon the current interest and activity in defining software processes, reports about formal specification activities in industry and government, and experiences in teaching and preparing graduate students to write formal specifications for real-time systems. The process definition includes a methodology for carrying out the specification (including a defined inspection process), organizational and language structure standards, guidelines and checklists, measures of size and effort, and process forms for gathering and retaining data.

1. Introduction

In recent years there has been a great deal of emphasis on the assessment and improvement of the software development process. The Capability Maturity Model (CMM) developed at the Software Engineering Institute is used by many organizations as a basis for the formulation and the maintenance of an effective development process [2, 15]. At Embry-Riddle Aeronautical University we offer an undergraduate program in Computer Science and a Master of Software Engineering (MSE) program that both concentrate on the development of effective processes for development of software [7, 13].

The literature is filled with horror stories about cost and schedule overruns in the development of software systems [14]. Many of these problems are attributed to errors in the specification of requirements [16]. Such errors, when undetected at an early point in the lifecycle, are extremely costly to remove in the latter stages of development. Hence, it is cost-effective to invest resources in an effective specification process.

There is increasing interest and activity in using formal methods in specifying a system's requirements. In particular, there have been a number of documented successes in the formal specification of safety critical software [6]. Because of the mathematical nature of formal specifications, they have advantages over less formal approaches: it is easy to represent abstractions; the specifications are well-defined, unambiguous and precise; and both the formal and informal verification of such specifications can provide greater assurance of the correct mapping of requirements into design.

The mathematical nature of formal specification techniques requires special training; hence, communication problems often arise between the analyst and the customer (or designer). Also, the mathematical structure of such specifications does not mean that they do not contain errors. As in any software artifact produced my humans, there is the potential for defects. Hence, the need for a defined process for writing specifications is possibly even more important when using formal methods. This paper (along with [9]) presents such a process and discusses its use in an academic setting.

2. Formal Specification Courses

The Computer Science Department at Embry-Riddle Aeronautical University offers an introductory course in formal methods that is taught at the senior/first year graduate level. The primary objective of the course is to provide students with the mathematical foundations and experiences necessary for study and research in software engineering. The course concentrates on discrete mathematics, logic, and the use of the Z language to specify software. After students gain some familiarity with the Z language, they are assigned small specification problems to work on individually. Then in the last three weeks of the course they are divided into teams and assigned a more involved specification problem. A recent project involved writing a Z specification for an Automated En-Route Air Traffic system (AERA) [8].

We also offer a course in formal methods for the specification of real-time systems. The course includes a study of temporal logic and reading current literature in the field. Although the course does not require a specification project, some students have worked on special projects that involve applying real-time formal methods to a specification problem. Most of the work, thus far, has involved using a combination of the Z specification language and Real Time Logic (RTL) [12]. The inclusion of RTL constructs for specifying timing requirements has proved to be an easy transition for students already familiar with Z. Fidge [3] introduces two pivotal schemas, History and OccurenceFn, that provide a simple, straightforward way to represent the state transitions for a real-time system and to specify timing constraints on system operations. Information and guidance on the use of these schemas is provided in [9].

In two recent problems the Z-RTL language was used for the specification of an electronic pager system and the specification of the AERA system. Both systems provided students with good experience in specifying real-time systems. Unfortunately, the literature on Z-RTL is limited and published examples of the application of Z-RTL are rather simple. This required students (in consultation with the instructor) to devise a process for applying the formal method. In addition, it was necessary to develop additional Z-RTL constructs. One construct of particular interest was the use of Z piping [1, 12] to incorporate "start" and "stop" events into the specification of a system operation. Another construct that was devised involved the use of Z schema types [1] to specify a timing requirement for a class of objects.

Without a defined process the problem of converting a natural language statement of requirements into a formal specification can be a daunting challenge. This is even more of a problem if the requirements involve timing constraints and the student has little or no real-time specification experience. The problem starts with a determination of exactly what are the timing requirements: some requirements involved explicit timing constraints (e.g., "The collision alarm must be issued within one second of detection of the separation violation"), while in other cases the timing requirement is not so obvious (e.g., "When an aircraft enters the sector its flight plan will be moved from the pending list to the active list."). In order to provide adequate guidance and support for student projects that involve writing a formal specification for a real-time system, the author has written a document that defines a specification development process [9]. The document is based on experience gained in supervising student projects and the Embry-Riddle focus in process education. The concepts and ideas for this process were gathered from a number of sources [1, 3, 5, 10, 11, 17]. The process document and this paper extend the ideas presented in [8].

3. Process Document Objectives

The process document [9] defines a process for developing a formal specification for the requirements for a software product. It is designed to be used by graduate students in the Master of Software Engineering (MSE) program at Embry-Riddle Aeronautical University. The process was developed with the following objectives:

- provide information and guidance about formal specification of software

- improve the quality of formal specifications

- produce data about effort, size and quality that can be used to assess and improve the process

- provide students with experiences that involve using a defined process

4. Standards

The process document begins with a delineation of a set of standards to be used in development of a formal specification. The following sections briefly describe each standard.

4.1. The Specification Language

Typically the choice of a specification language will be made by (or in consultation with) the faculty supervisor of a formal specification project. Thus far, the Z specification language has been used in all formal specification projects in the MSE program. Some projects that involve real-time requirements have used elements of Real Time Logic (RTL) [12]. The process standard uses a Z-RTL hybrid developed by Fidge [3] and includes definition and discussion of the History and OccurenceFn schemas. The language standard addresses issues related to symbols, identifiers, schema format and schema types.

4.2. The Specification Document

The process provides direction for the organization and style of the specification. This includes guidance about documentation, what type of narrative information to include, and how to order the Z and RTL elements of the specification.

4.3. Process Forms

A critical part of the process definition is to establish standards on how to record information about project planing, progress, and completion. Such standards provide a framework for organizing and tracking the specification work. They also can be used to improve the quality of the specification and are essential in assessing the effectiveness of the process. Table 1 gives a description of the forms that are used in recording specification project data.

5. The Specification Process

The actual process for developing the specification is divided into the following six phases:

- Training
- Team Formation
- Customer Interface
- Specification
- Inspection
- Postmortem

The process document [9] describes the specification activities in each phase and assigns responsibility for their completion.

6. The Inspection Process

In those specification projects at Embry-Riddle that involve multiple teams of students working on the same problem, inspection teams are formed to inspect the work of each team. After the teams complete their initial version of the specification, the instructor selects portions of each team's specification for inspection. The process document includes a definition of an inspection process. Elements of this process are discussed in the following sections.

6.1. Inspection Objectives

The following are the stated objectives of the inspection process:

- identify defects in the specification
- identify improvements that can be made in the specification
- affirm those parts of the specification that properly satisfy the software requirements.
- ensure that the development team understands and agrees with the technical work in the specification
- achieve technical work that is of uniform quality and satisfies those standards that are in place

6.2. Inspection Guidelines and Checklist

The process includes the following guidelines and questions that can be used in designing a inspection checklist:

- concentrate the inspection on assessing the following four qualities of the specification:
  - organization and format
  - syntax and logic errors
  - completeness of requirements specification
  - readability and understandability
- hold at least one inspection preparation meeting to discuss roles, review inspection objectives and to study/modify the inspection checklist
- the inspection meeting should last no more than two hours
- only members of the inspection team are allowed to participate; observers must remain silent

Table 1: Process Forms

Form	Purpose	Responsibility
Project Schedule	A schedule for project activities.	The project team leader is responsible for developing and tracking the schedule.
Time Log	An individual log used to record the time spent in each project activity.	Each team member maintains their own time log.
Z Specification Defect Log	A log used to record the defects found in a formal inspection.	The Inspection Team scribe is responsible for completing this log.
Inspection Team Comment Form	A form used by individual inspection team members to record comments, suggestions, and recommendations.	One form is filled out by each member of an inspection team.
Specification Inspection Report Form	A report form used to summarize the results of the formal inspection of the specification.	The inspection team scribe is responsible for preparing the inspection report.
Schema Log	A log for recording the size and effort for each schema.	The project team leader is responsible for maintaining this log.
Planning/Summary Form	A summary form use to record the estimated and actual size and effort, and inspection data for the entire specification project.	The project team leader is responsible for collecting time, schema, and defect logs and summarizing on this form.

- identify problem areas, but do not attempt to solve every problem noted

- when inspecting the predicate part of a schema translate each assertion into an English language statement and informally verify that it is a valid requirement

- develop a checklist of things to be used in reviewing in the specification document. The following is an example:

  - Does the specification document follow the format and organization specified in the process standards?

  - Is there sufficient narrative to support the understanding of the Z specification?

  - Are basic data types and global constants declared properly? Are they adequate?

  - Does each schema satisfy the following:

    * use the correct symbols, notation and format?

    * use only variables that are declared within the current schema or in properly referenced schemas?

    * use first order logic correctly in the specification of assertions?

    * include only those predicates that are consistent with the system requirements?

  - Do the "state" schemas specify all of the system invariants?

  - Is the system state initialized correctly?

  - Do the "operation" schemas specify all of the required system functions? Do the assertions correctly specify the required functionality?

  - Is there a appropriate separation between functional requirements and timing requirements: functional requirements in operational schemas and timing requirements in separate schemas that use occurrence functions?

  - Are all real-time events of the system expressed in terms of the occurrence of system operations or the occurrence of a system attribute becoming true (or becoming false).

  - Are the exception handling schemas sufficient to cover all externally generated exceptions?

  - Is there adequate and proper use of schema modularity and reference?

  - Are there adequate axiomatic and generic schemas? Are they employed correctly?

6.3. Inspection Activities

Table 2 details the activities (and responsibilities for the inspection process).

Table 2: Inspection Process

Phase	Activity	Responsibility
Planning	Make a plan, estimate time, assign roles, schedule activities.	The inspection leader is responsible for planning.
Preparation	Provide orientation and training for inspection team. Prepare inspection checklist and assign inspection tasks. Schedule meeting time and place, and publish an agenda.	The faculty supervisor is responsible for orientation and training; and the inspection leader is responsible for setting up the meeting, assigning inspection tasks, and preparing the inspection checklist.
Inspection Meeting	Meet and inspect the formal specification document.	The inspection leader is responsible for moderating the inspection meeting. The inspection scribe is responsible for recording defects, suggestions and recommendations.
Postmortem	Prepare inspection report and deliver to specification team.	The inspection scribe is responsible for preparing the inspection report. The chief analyst is responsible for using the inspection report to prepare the final specification document.

Thus far, the most effective part of the process, when used in a team-project setting, has been concerned with inspection activities. There have been several observable side-effects of using an inspection as part of a formal specification process:

- students get additional practice in reading Z specifications

- it reinforces the importance of formal methods: if not before, then while inspecting, students realize the value of precise, unambiguous and verifiable requirements

- students get to see and study an alternate solution to the problem they worked on

- students receive peer evaluation of their work and see the rather dramatic results that such assessment can produce

- they get practice in technical communication (oral and written) by articulating inspection results

7. Summary and Conclusions

In this paper I have presented some ideas about defining a process for the formal specification of software and about using the process in a teaching environment. The development of a high quality mathematical model for software requirements, especially for real-time systems, can be a challenging and risky undertaking. A defined process provides a framework for analysts to organize and track their work. The data collected during application of the process can provide valuable information for assessing and improving the quality of a specification and the process used to develop it. This is an even more critical issue when students, new to software engineering and formal methods, are involved in the development of a formal specification. The direction and guidance provided by a defined process can be the difference between a meaningful educational exercise and a disorganized and unproductive nightmare. Although the process document [9] is still in the draft stage and has not been "class" tested in its entirety, it is hoped that it will provide assistance and incentive to those that would like to combine process activities with formal methods.

References

[1] A. Z. Diller, *Introduction to Formal Methods, 2nd Edition*, John Wiley and Sons, New York, 1994.

[2] R. Dion, "Process Improvement and the Corporate Balance Sheet", *IEEE Software*, Vol. 10, No. 4, July 1993, pp. 28-35.

[3] C. J. Fidge, "Specification and Verification of Real-Time Behavior Using Z and RTL", *Proc. of*

2nd International Symposium on Formal Techniques in Real-Time and Fault- Tolerant Systems, January 1992, Springer-Verlag, New York, 1992, pp. 393-409.

[4] M. E. Fagan, "Design and Code Inspections to Reduce Errors in Program Development", *IBM Systems Journal*, Vol. 15, No. 3, 1976, pp. 186-211.

[5] R. G. Ebenau and S. H. Strauss, *Software Inspection Process*, McGraw-Hill, New York, 1994.

[6] S. Gerhart, D. Craigen and T. Ralston, "Experience with Formal Methods in Critical Systems", *IEEE Software*, Vol. 11, No. 1, January 1994, pp. 21-28.

[7] T. B. Hilburn, I. Hirmanpour and A. Kornecki, "The Integration of Software Engineering into a Computer Science Curriculum", *Proc. of the Eighth SEI Conference on Software Engineering Education*, March 1995, Springer-Verlag, New York, 1995, pp. 87-97.

[8] T. B. Hilburn, "Inspections of Formal Specifications", *SIGCSE Bulletin*, Vol. 28, No. 1, February 1996, pp. 150-154 .

[9] T. B. Hilburn, *A Process for Formal Specification*, Embry-Riddle Aeronautical University, Daytona Beach, FL, 1996.

[10] W. S. Humphrey, *Managing the Software Process*, Addison-Wesley, Reading, Mass., 1989.

[11] W. S. Humphrey, *A Discipline for Software Engineering*, Addison-Wesley, Reading, Mass., 1995.

[12] F. Jahanian and A. Mok, "Safety of Timing Properties in Real-Time Systems", *IEEE Transactions on Software Engineering*, Vol. SE-12, No. 9, September 1986, pp. 890-904.

[13] S. Khajenoori, "Process-Oriented Software Education", *IEEE Software*, Vol. 11, No. 6, November 1994, pp. 99-101.

[14] P. Neumann, "System Development Woes", *Communications of the ACM*, Vol. 36, No. 10, October 1993, p. 146.

[15] M. Paulk, "Capability Maturity Model, Version 1.1", *IEEE Software*, Vol. 10, No. 4, July 1993, pp. 18-27.

[16] R. S. Pressman, *Software Engineering: A Practitioner's Approach, 3rd Edition*, McGraw-Hill, New York, 1992.

[17] N. R. Reizer and J. G. Gallagher, *Process Handbook, Report No. CMU-MSE-TALUS-PHBK-3.0*, Software Engineering Institute, Carnegie Mellon University, Pittsburgh, PA, 1994.

Design of Distributed Systems Using Petri Nets: a Graduate Computer Science Course

Boleslaw Mikolajczak
Computer and Information Science Department
University of Massachusetts Dartmouth
Dartmouth, MA 02747, USA
bolek@cis.umassd.edu

Abstract

This paper shares educational experiences in teaching design of distributed computing systems using Petri nets with application to engineering software for embedded systems. We put special emphasis on understanding of fundamental concepts and their applications to specification and design of distributed software systems using Colored Petri nets. The paper contains a description of lecture contents, a formulation of two project assignments, and topics of research papers, explored over a period of several years, on applications of Petri nets in software engineering. Timed and stochastic Petri nets are used to model real-time events and to evaluate computer systems' performance. The material is based partly on two graduate courses: CIS 525, Topics on Parallel Computations, and CIS 578, Performance Evaluation of Computer Systems, taught by the author during last several years at the University of Massachusetts Dartmouth. In both courses, Colored Petri nets play a significant and unifying role in systems' design.

1. Introduction

Parallel and Distributed Computing is an important component of a contemporary computer science curriculum including software engineering and real-time embedded systems curricula. In undergraduate computer science curriculum, usually there exists a time slot for a parallel or distributed programming course. In addition, we developed at the University of Massachusetts Dartmouth several graduate courses that emphasize different aspects of parallel and distributed computing, such as: Neural Networks, Parallel Computer Architectures, Parallel Algorithms, Software System Design in Ada, and Real-Time Systems. One of them, CIS 525, Topics on Parallel Computations, is devoted exclusively to Petri nets and their applications in parallel or distributed software development. The second graduate course CIS 578, Performance Evaluation of Computer Systems deals with applications of timed and stochastic Petri nets to performance evaluation of single- and multi-processor computer systems. Approximately half of this course is based on queuing networks approach. The second part is based on Petri nets. Comparison of both approaches is also studied at the end of the course. With public availability of powerful software tools such as the CASE package Design/CPN from MetaSoftware Corp. [1] and other such tools, especially for performance evaluation, these courses attract more students.

Previously Petri nets were used in computer science education mostly to represent graphically concepts in courses like operating systems [3]. According to author's best knowledge this is the first published course description in which Colored Petri nets are explicitly used in software specification and design as a unifying factor in software modeling, specification, validation, and performance evaluation [11].

2. Course Syllabus

The first course explores advanced topics in the area of parallel and distributed computations. The following are the main issues discussed in the course: modeling of parallel systems using non-hierarchical and hierarchical Petri nets, such as: Condition/Event nets, Place/Transition nets, Colored Petri nets, and Hierarchical nets. Applications of Petri nets in various areas of computer science are also presented. As a textbook we use two volumes of Jensen's book [4] with

126

frequent references to Reisig's books [8,9]. Application-oriented research papers are also studied. This course has been in place for six years. Three *main objectives* of the course are:

- to discuss structural and behavioral properties of systems using Petri nets as a mathematical model
- to specify and design parallel and distributed software applications using Petri nets
- to provide professional experience with Petri nets using tools such as Design/CPN and various Petri net-based performance evaluation tools.

A detailed course syllabus for a fourteen-week long semester is presented below as a set of educational units, split in two parts: theoretical part and modeling part with projects.

2.1. Theoretical part

Introduction to Condition-Event Nets

Condition-Event (C/E) nets are discussed. Examples of the four seasons problem, producer-consumer problem with bounded and unbounded buffer, modeling of non-sequential programs, and representation of logical expressions. Examples of system modeling, such as access rights of several processors to memory with Exclusive WRITE and Concurrent READ. Modeling of organization of the public library with several refinements is also presented.

Applications of Condition/Event and Place/Transition Nets

Examples of systems' modeling using C/E and place-transition (P/T) nets, such as gas pump system with deadlock, concrete production process, several versions of the five philosophers problem, sender/receiver system, instruction execution cycle in a modern processor, instruction pipelining in a processor. Fault-tolerant systems and their synthesis using Petri nets are discussed, Representation by means of Colored Petri nets of p-process and q-process system with several types of resources. Synthesis of a digital system using Petri nets with hardware/software co-design.

Dynamic Properties of Condition/Event Nets

Contact-free C/E nets. What does it mean to have the contact situation? An algorithm of designing contact-free C/E net from an arbitrary C/E net. Design of a a dual net and a subnet. Computing a *case graph* of C/E nets. Serialization of concurrent events. *Matrix representation* of C/E nets and P/T nets. Complete design example of a of a digital system with two independent wagons. Reachability graph and hardware/software implementation of C/E nets and P/T nets.

Concurrency in Condition/Event Nets

Processes of C/E nets. Relation of concurrency and linear relationship in C/E nets. concepts, such as slices, cuts, and linear segments of a concurrent system. Behavioral subclasses of the C/E nets and systems, such as sequential vs. concurrent, deterministic vs. non-deterministic, conflict vs. conflict-free. Several structural conflicts, such as conflict set, confusion, increasing confusion, decreasing confusion. Confusion as a composition of concurrency and conflict.

Synchronization in Petri Nets

Synchronic distance of events in C/E nets. Algorithm to compute the synchronic distance using distance of events and variance. Computing *synchronic distance* for concurrent, sequential, and cyclic systems. Processes and their compositions, elementary processes. Ambiguity of the synchronic distance concept from concurrency point of view.

Systems Modeling Using Colored Petri Nets and Design/CPN Software Package

Tokens as indicators of a local state and as not objects that need to be conserved. Representing resources by the net states rather than by conserved objects. Goal of modeling is not to generate a simulacrum of a system, but to abstract from it the behavioral properties that are of interest and then to create a model that also has those properties. It is of no importance how much or how little the model resembles the system structurally; only the behavioral similarity is significant. Characteristics of the Design/CPN software package: place inscriptions, event inscriptions, arc inscriptions, bindings, and transition guards. Examples of hierarchical modeling of *the five philosophers problem* and of the *producer/consumer problem* with *bounded/unbounded buffer* using Design/CPN.

Static Analysis of Systems-Place Invariants of Colored Petri Nets

Equation/matrix representations of Colored Petri nets. *Well-formedness* and *soundness* of matrix representation of Colored Petri nets. Methods of matrix reduction similar to the *Gaussian elimination* technique. *Reachability trees* for Colored Petri nets: backgrounds, *dining philosophers* problem. Examples of Colored Petri nets with reduction and invariant computations: distributed database system, public phone system, and hierarchical version of the five philosophers' system.

Occurrence Graphs of Colored Petri Nets

Occurrence graph(OG): occurrence element, occurrence set, firing strategies; fairness and scheduling algorithms. Computer demonstration of the p/q-processes problem with several different resources. Experimental presentation of the deadlock and liveness in concurrent systems. Example of modeling a distributed database system using Design/CPN: analysis of the model, computing place invariants, proving deadlock and liveness properties of the system using place invariants.

Simulator of Colored Petri Nets as a Debugger of Parallel Programs

By an occurrence set we understand a set composed of occurrence elements. An *occurrence element* is a pair composed of transition and binding. We use occurrence sets as a method of adjudicating conflicts, i.e. a help to the simulator to execute the net more efficiently, to provide a medium through which the observer can control the details of execution so as to study a net in more detail or to debug it more efficiently. The execution algorithm of the simulator follows the following major three steps:

A. Construct a list of all enabled transitions.

B. Scan the list of enabled transitions and select from that list a set of transitions and bindings that are not in conflict and hence can fire concurrently.

C. Fire transitions as specified by the occurrence elements in the occurrence set.

Additional topics include the following problems: what can be proved by formal analysis of the Colored Petri nets and what can be achieved by simulation? Meaning of nondeterminism in parallel computing: *don't know* nondeterminism, *don't care* nondeterminism, and *conflict* nondeterminism. Major functions of a *parallel debugger* should satisfy the following requirements: detecting and avoiding deadlocks, detecting and controlling conflicts (nondeterminism), fairness of conflict resolution. Proving system properties of readers/writers problem using place invariants. Prediction of all global states of the concurrent system, and reachability between arbitrary two global system states.

Semantics of Timed Petri Nets

A superclass of real-time systems is called a responsive system. A system is said to be *responsive* if it is a real-time system, fault-tolerant system, parallel and/or distributed system. To include responsive systems into considerations one has to be able to model time. A general idea of representing time in Petri nets can be expressed by two simple principles:

- each token has a *timestamp* attached to represent the "local" time of the token
- tokens are carrying information including time.

A transition is *enabled* to fire if there is at least one token in each of its input places and at least one value of the set produced by application of the time condition to the tokens' timestamps is not less than the maximum of such timestamps. There are two possible time semantics: *WTS=Weak Time Semantics*; if transition fires, it does so within the time set specified by the time condition (the transition is not forced to fire); i.e. if transition ever fires then its firing time must belong to its time set. The second time semantics is: *STS=Strong Time Semantics*. If a transition gets enabled by some tuple of tokens at some enabling time t_1 then it must fire at some time $t > t_1$ of its associated time set. When the set S of possible firing times is unbounded then the two semantics coincide; then attention is focused on minimal time that is needed to perform action. There are two practical techniques to represent time in Petri nets:

- *attaching time to transitions*: a transition must fire provided that it is not disabled in the meantime; let us assume that t is the enabling time of a transition, i.e. time when the last token arrived to input places, then the firing window of this transition is: $[t+t_{min}, t+t_{max}]$, where $\Delta = t_{max} - t_{min}$ is the firing duration time.
- *attaching time to places*: each input place p_i of a transition has a waiting time Δ_i.

Other topics discussed include: an algorithm transforming timed Petri nets with places into timed Petri nets with transitions, timed Petri nets with duration and delay assigned to transitions. To illustrate different concepts of time in Petri nets, several examples of *timed* Petri nets are discussed, such as modeling of the apples reselling process and modeling of a chemical reaction with three compounds using the timed Petri nets. For Timed in Colored Petri nets we also discuss the following technical issues: how simulation of Petri nets with time proceeds using Design/CPN software package? What are main factors having influence on size of the timestamps: current model of time, colors of the Petri net variables, reference variables, and input files.

2.2. Examples and Modeling Part

Several illustrating sufficiently complex examples are discussed in this part of the course.

Example 1. Modeling and simulation of the Boston-Cape Cod ferry system using Design/CPN timing facilities with performance evaluation of the whole system. Several weaknesses of the time definitions in Petri nets are also indicated in this part of the course:

- notations that suffer from the lack of formally defined semantics; two models of time do not cover all practical cases; for instance if the firing time interval of a transition must depend on the arrival time of a token in only one input place, then this situation could not be represented in any of the previous models
- violation of fundamentals of Petri nets, i.e. *principle of locality* of the decision on the transition firing; i.e. token decisions are local; however time is global for a specific transition
- there are particular timing conditions forcing the firing of a transition and hidden mechanism of arrival times for places.

Example 2. Time conditions are attached to transitions (see Fig.1). P1-place representing customer's request to buy the perishable item; P2-place representing the availability of a perishable item (apples); P3-place representing availability of other resources (sugar, preservatives) to make a jam; T1-transition representing an action of 'selling of the item to the customer'; this transition may fire if apples are ripe but not rotten; the firing time of this transition is:

$$I_1 = [time(P2) + t_{1min}, time(P2) + t_{1max}]$$

T2-transition representing an action of 'trashing of a rotten item'; the firing time of this transition is:

$$I_2 = [time(P2) + t_{2min}, +\infty]$$

T3-transition representing an action of 'making a jam'; the firing time of this transition is:

$$I_3 = [time(P2) + t_{3min}, time(P2) + t_{3max}]$$

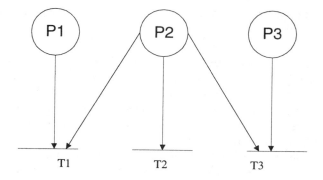

Fig.1. Timed Petri net from Example 2.

From these definitions of times we conclude that an item is good to be sold and also available for making a jam between t_{3min} and t_{1max}. Similarly, apples are completely rotten after t_{2min}.

Example 3. In this example we model an Ada code using timed Petri nets. Let us assume that an action can be delayed at most for a specified time but, before the time expires, the action must take place. For instance the Ada **select** statement does this:

```
select
        accept E
        OR
        delay D
end
```

Place P1 represents Ada task A executing the **select** statement; place P2 represents task B to call entry E up to D time units; T1-transition represents **delay** statement and can execute during the following timespan $[time(P1)+D, \infty]$; transition T2 represents **accept** statement and can execute during the following timespan $[time(P1), time(P1)+D]$.

Example 4. In this example we model the chemical reactions of several compounds. Place P1 represents chemical compound created as a result of a reaction represented by transition T1; place P2 represents chemical compound created as a result of reaction represented by transition T2; transition T3 represents a reaction in which both P1 and P2 compounds participate; Θ_1, Θ_2 - are times required to make compounds 1 and 2 stable before being ready to be used in consecutive chemical processes; τ_1, τ_2 -after this time the compounds will decompose and the reaction cannot take place anymore. Transition T3 can therefore fire during the following time interval $[\Theta, \tau]$, where

$$\tau = \min\{\tau_1 + time(P1), \tau_2 + time(P2)\}$$
$$\Theta = \max\{\Theta_1 + time(P1), \Theta_2 + time(P2)\}$$

If $\Theta > \tau$, then the transition cannot fire.

Example 5. Petri nets are considered inappropriate to be used to solve optimization problems. In this example we show that applying Timed Petri nets one can make an optimal decision to travel in minimal time with minimal cost between two cities A and D with the following choices available:

- there exist two intermediate cities B and C (in this order) through which you have to travel: to reach D from A
- one has two options to travel from city A to city B; the first one is a direct connection between A and B that takes 15 minutes and costs 1600 units; the second one uses additional intermediate city A'. Traveling from A to A' costs nothing and takes 10 minutes. Traveling from A' to B costs 150 units and takes 15 minutes
- traveling from B to C costs 310 and takes 45 minutes (there is no other option in this case)
- traveling from C to D can be done in two different ways: the first one is to travel directly from C to D; this option costs 3200 units and it takes 80 minutes. The second option uses the intermediate city C'. To travel form C to C' costs 190 units and it takes 30 minutes; to travel from C' to D costs 1260 units and it takes 100 minutes.

A problem is to find a method of transportation which will transfer you from A to D in minimal time and with minimal cost. One can solve this problem by constructing first a timed Petri net and then exploring all possibilities of the state space.

Modeling of Flexible Manufacturing Systems by Hierarchical Colored Petri Nets

Hierarchical Petri net-based models have several positive features: hiding of details in a consistent way, separation into well-defined reusable components, support of both top-down and bottom-up development strategies, and strong graphical expressive capabilities. Hierarchical models have to possess the following qualities: executability, modeling language must support the notion of behavior for its components in a precise and consistent way, modeling language must make it possible to observe the execution of large, and complex system models at different levels of detail. Inadequacies of single level system models are: missing overview, too many details at one time, the structure of the system is not mirrored adequately.

Other topics discussed in this part include: *Hierarchical Colored Petri nets* and their constructs: static page instances, prime pages; semantics of *hierarchical substitution* of places, ADTs and recursive application of hierarchical substitution; semantics of hierarchical substitution of transitions, dynamic *page instances*: semantics of *hierarchical invocation* of transitions, global *fusion of places*. Example of factory assembly line modeled with hierarchical Colored Petri nets is discussed in this part. A concept of folding is applicable when one has identical objects, but it is less suited for asymmetrical

arrangements. Examples of other hierarchical modeling languages, such as SADT and IDEF (by Marca and McGowan [5]); Yourdon's data flow diagrams [10], and Harel's statecharts [2] are mentioned here and compared with the hierarchical Petri net approach.

Modeling of a Phone System Using Hierarchical Colored Petri Nets

Modeling assumptions made for this example: we consider the *phone system* as perceived by the user, no time-outs are allowed, no special services are considered. Analysis of subnets: *Establishing Connection, Breaking Connection by the Recipient, Breaking Connection by the Sender* is also presented. Proving system properties using place invariants: what happens when user calls himself, what happens when someone calls a number which has already Established Connection, what happens when Established Connection is broken by the Recipient. We present the computer simulation of the phone system using Design/CPN.

Modeling of Cache Coherency Protocols in Multiprocessor Systems

Architectures of multiprocessors with private caches and an interconnection network are discussed. Top-down description and modeling of the Archibald's cache coherency protocol is presented. Description of synchronization in the Archibald's protocol is modeled by a Petri net. Derivation of invariants from Petri net. Behavioral properties of the cache coherency protocol, such as correctness, fairness, bounds for hardware resources, are elaborated in details.

3. Software Design Projects and Research Papers

Two software design projects form major parts of the course. Their short description is presented below.

3.1. Petri Nets and Embedded Systems Modeling-a Lift System

In an embedded system the interfaces between computers and their environments are not trivial. The environments include various technical components or may be even more human-oriented as for example the office support systems. In order to understand the role of computers in such systems it is essential to have a precise comprehension of the behavior of their environment. A formal model is required, not only of the involved computers' behavior, but also of the environment's behavior. For proof of correctness of software components it is useful if the software and the system environment both are depicted by making use of the same description language.

Lift control system is a typical example of an embedded system. The difficulty of designing such a system does not result from the complexity of the involved programs but from the interaction between the program and the lift cabin, the motor and the buttons pressed by customers. Below we present the *project specification*: develop a lift model by distinguishing the object system, the control system, and the signaling channels that link both systems. The object system includes the motor, the cabin, the customer's button, the floor doors, etc. The control system is to process signals to and from the components of the object system. These signals are transmitted via the signaling channels. Four assumptions are in place:

- the scheduling of concurrent requests is not included
- upon serving a customer, no intermediate stops are possible
- two categories of tokens are used: "black" tokens indicating presence or absence of binary activity and "number" tokens indicating a number of a wanted floor
- some events are inscribed by additional constraints for their occurrence.

To better understand the system behavior let us follow a typical course of the lift. A customer may press a button and indicate the wanted floor. This results in an individual token, n, being allocated on the *"wanted floor"* place. If the *"door closed"* signal is present, then the information about the wanted floor, n, should be copied to other place (or places) which also represents "wanted floor". Predict also events with the following inscriptions: "$x<n$", "$x=n$", "$x>n$", where x represents encoding of the currently visited floor. The outcome of these comparisons makes the motor start either clockwise or counterclockwise. Between each two neighboring floors, signal finger of the moving lift triggers a signal to a control unit. In this moment we defer the conditions to trigger this signal. The signal causes an update of the *"current floor"* token in a corresponding place. In case the current floor coincides with the wanted floor, special place *"wanted floor"* is updated too, and a stop signal is sent to the motor place. So the motor slows down and sends a *"motor stopped"* signal to the control system. Based on this signal, and on the number of the current floor in the *"current floor"* place, the number of the door to be opened is given to *"door number to be opened"* place. So the corresponding door will be opened; it will be closed after a while, and a *"door closed"* signal is available, to serve the next customer.

By construction of the lift object system it should be guaranteed that the lift triggers exactly one signal when moving in between two floors. This constraint may be modeled by an additional place which forces that signal can be given to the *"next floor signal"* place only after starting the motor (clockwise or anticlockwise) or in case the moving lift has not yet reached the wanted floor. This follows from the overall dynamic structure of the object lift system: whenever the cabin passes one of the signal fingers installed in the wall of the elevator well, a *"next floor"* signal is triggered. One signal finger is installed between each two neighboring floors. It is clear that a signal can be triggered only as long as the motor is running. The signals are used in the corresponding control component to control the actual position of the lift. These tracing steps are assumed much quicker than the cabin needs to trigger the next signal. One has to take into account situation when the customer wants the current floor. In this case *"motor stopped signal"* should be generated, causing the opening of the corresponding door.

Using place invariants show that in your lift system:

- never more than one door is open
- motor is running only in case when all doors are closed.

A task in this project was to formulate a final solution using several intermediate refinements. Final refinement must be consistent with the above-presented behavior. Students were asked to prepare their project using Design/CPN software package.

3.2. Public Phone System

This project was also realized using Design/CPN software package as an extension of a demonstration example provided by the MetaSoftware Corp. The following computations, models, and simulations were required as parts of the project:

- a Hierarchical Colored Petri net describing on one page a telephone system from user point of view; several additions to the existing model were required to be implemented: the following special service numbers should be handled from each other phone number: OPERATOR, DIRECTORY SERVICE, POLICE, EMERGENCY
- an English language specification corresponding to the modified Hierarchical Colored Petri net
- a matrix representation for the modified Hierarchical Colored Petri net with initial marking
- place invariants and a proof of the following six static properties of the phone system: place ENGAGED is implicitly complementary to the place INACTIVE, what happens when a phone is calling itself, RINGING phones are exactly those for which a CALL is waiting, a phone is connected or

REPLACED iff it is contained in a CONNECTION, phone has NO TONE iff it is contained in a REQUEST, and phone is LONG iff it is contained in a CALL
- computer simulation of the existing Hierarchical Colored Petri net and the modified Hierarchical Colored Petri net
- implementation of a multi-area telephone system and formulation of its specification.

Application of hierarchical structures such as: substitutions and fusion sets in the phone system was also required.

3.3. Research Papers on Applications of Petri Nets

As an integral part of the course students are asked to choose an application of their interest and apply Petri nets to solve a software design problem. Results of their study are presented in a form of a written report and oral presentation to the class. A list of topics that students explored during several years is as follows: Environment for Object-Oriented Conceptual Programming based on PROT Nets, Petri net representation of sentences in natural languages, a Predicate-Transition net model for parallel interpretation of logic programs and proof procedures; answer extraction in Petri net model of logic programs, programming a closely coupled multiprocessor system with high-level Petri nets, Communication Sequential Processes (CSP) as a Condition/Event system, detection of Ada static deadlocks using Petri net invariants, stepwise construction of non-sequential software systems using a net-based specification language, performance evaluation of asynchronous concurrent systems using Petri nets, Petri net tools for the specification and analysis of discrete controllers, control flow analysis of distributed computing system using structured Petri nets, combining queuing networks and Generalized Stochastic Petri Net models for analysis of some software blocking phenomena, stochastic high-level Petri nets and their applications, timed Petri nets in modeling and evaluation of multiprocessor systems, realization of fault-tolerant systems by proper coding of a Petri net: a design using PLAs and Petri nets, PROTEAN: A high-level Petri net tool for the specification and verification of communication protocols, and modeling and analysis of communication protocols using numerical Petri nets.

These research topics were selected from IEEE Transactions on Software Engineering, IEEE Transactions on Computers, and from Proceedings of the Annual Conference on Applications and Theory of Petri Nets and Bi-annual Conference on Petri Nets and Performance Models (PNPM).

4. Performance Evaluation of Client-Server Systems

Both a system designer and a customer are interested in system's performance. This is especially important for real-time systems. Teaching real-time systems one can be interested in performance evaluation. In principle one can choose an approach from the following list of applicable techniques:
- *measurement* - this is the most accurate approach; it is only possible only after complete system's implementation; this approach is expensive; as typical measures of quality the following two parameters are used: elapsed times and the service demand on idle systems
- *simulation* - discrete-event simulation is possible at a design stage; this technique is however expensive from time point of view to get statistically significant results
- *analytic modeling* - using this technique many different designs may be evaluated; it is possible to include the product-form queuing network models; (semi)-Markov models and Markov reward models can be included in analytical models.

In our teaching strategy we selected the client-server system as an example suitable from real-time and Petri net perspectives. We defined the client-server system as a distributed system of one or more servers and many clients. Examples of such systems are: a set of workstations which access a file server over a local area network (for instance the token ring protocol) [6].

4.1. Analysis of Client-Server Systems

It appears that analysis of client-server systems from performance point of view is quite complicated. The following two factors contribute to the difficulty of the analytical approach to performance evaluation of the client-server systems:
- various dependencies that can occur in the request arrival process at the server (in a LAN, request A from station i can receive service later than another request B from station j ($j<>i$), even though A is generated before B; this phenomenon is called the *overtake condition* and it appears due to randomness of the process by which stations can gain access to the network and the fact that request A can be generated when there are messages waiting to be transmitted at station i while request B is generated when the queue of station j is empty - i.e. queuing requests at the server are not necessarily in the same order as clients generated these requests).

- arrival process at the server depends on client workstations' behavior and the arrival processes at client workstations depend on the server's behavior.

It is instructive at this point to observe that the product-form analysis method and other methods known in literature [12] are inappropriate because of interdependencies of arrival processes and the overtake condition. To avoid these problems an approach we studied is based on:

- *continuous-time Markov models* which capture dependencies in the request arrival process
- *stochastic Petri nets* which can be treated as means of specification and automated generation/solution of large Markov models.

However, it has to be mentioned that Markov models have limitations in a form of time parameters which have to be exponentially distributed. This limitation can be overcome by a method of stages. Another problem with Markov models is the size of the state space. To eliminate this problem we use the *superclient aggregation method* in which all clients which are not physically connected to the server are represented by a single client, called a superclient.

To model client-server systems we apply a class of generalized stochastic Petri nets [7] called *stochastic reward nets*. We make the following assumptions concerning this model:

- distributed computing system consists of N homogenous workstations
- each machine has to get an access write to the communication medium to transmit request/reply message
- workstation does not generate a new request until it has received the reply to the previous one; the main reason for this assumption is potential dependency of new client requests based on server's response; however, local processing of a client is still permitted
- each time the server captures the access right to the network it transmits at most one reply message; it is straightforward to extend this case to a sequence of messages from server or to the case when the response is shared
- requests are serviced in a FIFO manner; a station transmits when the channel is idle; if it is busy the station listens until the channel is idle and then transmits immediately; if the transmitted message is involved in a collision then the station waits a random amount of time and listens to the channel again
- a service of a file server system can be divided into several suboperations, such as disk access and disk read/write operation; service is considered as a single generic operation parametrized by the service rate, understood as the mean number of services accomplished by the server in a unit time in absence of contention
- workload depends on number of workstations, service request rates, and the network traffic
- global distributed computing systems are characterized by workload, network architecture, and access protocols
- client-server model can be considered as a general framework of a file server, database server, or a compute server.

We point to two major differences of this approach comparing with other known models of the token ring: message interdependencies introduced by the clients-server structure and the approximate analytic-numeric method rather than simulation used to solve the models.

Stochastic Petri nets (SPNs) have the following major capabilities: represent asynchronous and concurrent events, reachability set and the reachability graph can be easily computed by execution of the *SPN*, introduce the multiplicity of arcs. *SPN*s have exponentially distributed firing time for each transition. In continuous time Markov chains (CTMC) each edge has assigned a weight equal to the firing rate of the associated *SPN*. The *GSPN*s allow both transitions with zero firing time and inhibitor arcs.

A transition which has inhibitor arcs may fire only if each of its ordinary input places contains at least as many tokens as the multiplicity of the input arcs and each of its inhibitor input places contains fewer tokens than the multiplicity of the inhibitor arc. The tokens in the ordinary input places are removed as this transition fires; the tokens in the inhibitor input places remain unchanged.

Stochastic Reward Nets (SRN), being an extension of Generalized Stochastic Nets (GSNs) introduce association of reward rates with the markings of a SPN and allow generation of the Markov Reward Models (MRM). This permits a combined evaluation of performance and fault-tolerance. The *variable multiplicity arc* permits the removal of a marking dependent number of tokens from a place to an output place. The *general marking dependency* permits the rate or probability of a transition to be a function of the number of tokens of any place in the net including its input place. The *enabling/disabling functions* allow the firing of a transition based on the global structure of the net.

4.2 The Token Ring Network-Based Client-Server System

One has to make several general assumptions when dealing with the token ring client-server system [12]:

- network tokens are different than Petri net tokens
- the time until a client generates a request is an exponentially distributed random variable with mean value $1/\lambda$ and the time to transmit this request is also exponentially distributed with mean value $1/m$
- the walk time (called also the polling time), i.e. the time for the network token to move from one station to the next, is assumed to be exponentially distributed with mean value $1/g$
- the time required for the server to process a request is assumed to be exponentially distributed with mean value $1/h$
- the time required to transmit a reply message is assumed to be exponentially distributed with mean value $1/b$
- there are N homogenous clients and one server.

To compare experimental results of client-server systems' performance with results achieved through modeling we used stochastic Petri nets to model performance of client-server architecture. This approach allows to validate accuracy of performance results achieved from stochastic Petri nets in case when experimental results are not available, i.e. for a new architecture. Typical errors in estimation of performance parameters (systems' response time) were in the range of 10%. This seems to be very promising results taking into account savings in experimentation costs and highly aggregated nature of stochastic Petri net models applied. Attempts to study more detailed models usually end up in too long simulation times or too long execution times of related Markov chains (assuming simulations on a single processor). This last observation indicates that good modeling skills in designing accurate aggregate stochastic Petri net models are very important to assure efficiency of solving such models on current machines. It also suggests importance of parallel simulations of Petri net models to achieve higher accuracy.

4. Conclusions

Colored Petri nets can be treated in teaching real-time systems as a unifying model-based framework to design complex software systems, to study statically their structural properties, to investigate their dynamic properties, and to evaluate performance of designed systems. These activities can be completed before an implementation stage of the system. This feature makes this approach very comprehensive and economical. In our two courses we applied such approach in a comprehensive and unifying manner. This makes the design of responsive systems very systematic and decreases the learning time because the model used in all stages of the design is the same. Availability of the computerized Petri net-based simulators both for modeling and performance evaluation allows to assign to students more significant term projects [13].

References

[1] *Design/CPN, Reference Manual and Tutorial.* MetaSoftware Corp., Cambridge, Massachusetts, 1992.

[2] D.Harel, *Statecharts:* A Visual Formalism for Complex Systems. in: *Science of Computer Programming*, 8; 231-274, North-Holland, 1987.

[3] J.M.Jeffrey, *Using Petri Nets to Introduce Operating System Concepts*, SIGCSE Symposium, ACM Press, 1991.

[4] K.Jensen. *Colored Petri Nets, Basic Concepts, Analysis Methods and Practical Use*, vol. 1 and 2, in series: EATCS Monographs on Theoretical Computer Science, vol.27, Springer Verlag, Berlin, New York, 1992 and 1994.

[5] D.A.Marca, C.L.McGowan. *SADT*, McGraw-Hill, New York, 1988.

[6] E.D.Lazowska, J.Zahorjan. File Access Performance of Diskless Workstations, *ACM Transactions on Computer Systems*, 4(3);238-268, August 1986.

[7] A.Marsan, G.Balbo, G.Conte, G.Chiola. Generalized Stochastic Petri Nets: A Definition of the Net Level and Its Implications, *IEEE Transactions on Software Engineering*, 19(2); 89-107, February 1993.

[8] W.Reisig. *Petri Nets, An Introduction*, in series: EATCS Monographs on Theoretical Computer Science, vol. 4, Springer Verlag, Berlin, New York, 1985.

[9] W.Reisig. *A Primer in Petri Net Design*, Springer-Verlag, Berlin, New York, 1992.

[10] J.A.Rolia, K.C.Sevcik. The Method of Layers, *IEEE Transactions on Software Engineering*, 21(8); 689-700, August 1995.

[11] E.Yourdon, *Managing the System Life Cycle*, Yourdon Press, 1982.

[12] O.C.Ibe, Hoon Choi, K.S.Trivedi. Performance Evaluation of Client-Server Systems, *IEEE Transactions on Parallel and Distributed Systems*, 4(11); 1217-1229, November 1993.

[13] M.Juergens, *Performance Evaluation of Client-Server systems with Stochastic Petri*, MS Thesis, Computer and Information Science Department, University of Massachusetts Dartmouth, pp.130, May 1996.

Chapter 5
Real~Time Systems in Systems and Control Engineering

Systems Engineering Education at Linköping University

Ch. Krysander, A. Törne
Dept. of Computer and Information Science
Linköping University, S-581 83 Linköping, Sweden
{ckr, andto}@ida.liu.se

Abstract

This paper describes ongoing work at Linköping University, Sweden, to improve the engineering education in the systems engineering area, with special focus on systems with embedded real-time software. Three approaches are described: development of courses with software engineering in focus, courses with real-time software design contents and courses with (aircraft) systems engineering focus. The issue discussed is that a curriculum in real-time systems cannot be developed isolated from system engineering aspects. In particular, the industry, and the aircraft industry in particular, advocates a view which means that real-time systems are components of larger systems and must be developed and designed concurrently with mechanics, hydraulics and electronics. Therefore, real-time system design should be viewed as a basic component of a systems engineering curriculum for all kinds of engineering education and not only as a specialization of a computer engineering or computer science programme.

1 Introduction

Linköping is situated in the middle of one of four population centres in Sweden. The technological industry in the area is substantial. The largest are the Swedish aircraft manufacturer - Saab, cellular telephones - Ericsson Radio, telecom equipment - Ericsson Telecom, household appliances - Whirlpool, and turbines for electric power plants - ABB Stal. The university has a long tradition of good relations with the regional industries, and engineering education at Linköping in particular has been influenced by this.

Education in engineering and related subjects at the Institute of Technology at Linköping University comprises about 6000 students, of which 4000 are undergraduate in Master of Engineering programmes, 500 are graduate students and the rest are in Bachelor and/or Scientific programs. The four main Master of Engineering programmes are Applied Physics and Electrical Engineering, Mechanical Engineering, Computer Science and Engineering, and Industrial Engineering and Management. The last one mixes a traditional engineering education with economics and related subjects. There are also two new, and presently minor, programmes - in Engineering Biology[1] and in Information Technology[2]. The scientific programmes contain most notably a Master of Science education in Computer Science.

The masters programmes are nominally 4-4,5 years and the students take their exam at roughly the age of 24-26. The Swedish Master of Engineering education is a well established concept (100-year tradition) and the level of standards is recognized throughout Swedish industry. As such, it is important that the education is dynamic and changes when major shifts occur in the technologies used or when new technologies emerge. The difficulty in this is of course to identify important shifts and filter out waves which settle after some years. In this respect, Linköping University was the first Swedish university to implement special programmes in Computer Science and Engineering in the seventies, together with Industrial Engineering and Management in the eighties. Most of the other Swedish universities soon followed,

---

1. For more information on this programme contact Prof. P-E. Danielsson, ped@isy.liu.se
2. For more information on this programme contact Prof. I. Ingemarsson, i2@isy.liu.se

and the programmes have been a success from an industrial viewpoint. Currently new programmes in Engineering Biology and in Information Technology are launched. The latter is essentially a computer engineering education, but uses what is called "problem based learning" [1], with the goal to give a holistic view on engineering to the students.

Systems engineering in the broad sense has been the focus all since the university started its Institute of Technology in the sixties. An early decision was to specialise in computer technology and applications within traditional engineering areas. Therefore it is natural that the institute contains one large department of Electrical Engineering and the largest department of Computer and Information Science in Sweden.

2 Engineering Embedded Real-Time Systems

In the late eighties and beginning of the nineties the need for more system oriented courses in the curriculum became evident. The industrial systems had become complex and large, with subsystems built in different technologies - the aircraft industry is a good example. In particular, the contents of embedded software in the systems increased and became essential to product functionality and competitiveness.

The traditional contents in the non-computer engineering tracks did not cover this aspect - mechanical engineers and electrical engineers had little or no insight when they graduated in systems engineering or development of embedded hardware/software for their area of specialization. The situation was only marginally better for computer engineers. In this paper, we describe three different approaches taken to improve the situation.

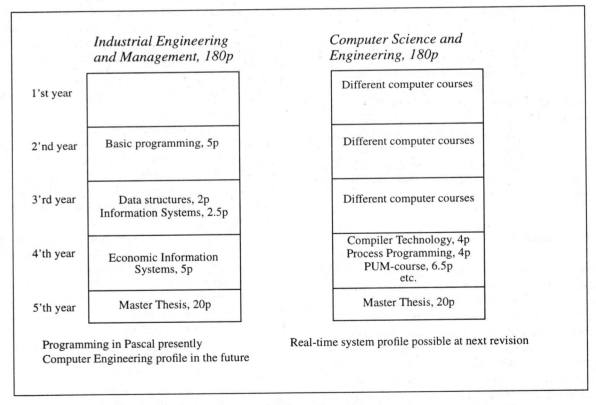

Figure 1.   A selection of courses relevant to systems engineering in two of the Master of Engineering programmes (40p <=> 1 year studies)

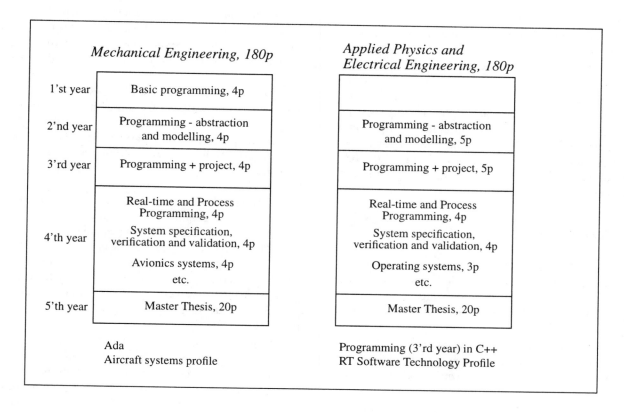

Figure 2.   A selection of courses relevant to systems engineering in two more of the Master of Engineering programmes (40p <=> 1 year studies)

The first approach was to start specific, larger project courses in the Computer Science and Engineering programme, covering areas like Software Engineering and Human Computer Interaction. In this paper, we describe the PUM-course (PUM is an acronym for Software Development Methodology - in Swedish), which is a popular project course in the third or fourth year for computer engineering and computer science master students.

The second approach was instigated by industry. A discussion group between Saab Military Aircraft and the university was started in 1993. The focus of this discussion was systems engineering, where systems not only meant hardware/software systems, but integrated systems including hydraulics, electromechanics, mechanics, computers and software. The discussion covered both research issues and undergraduate education issues. The result for the undergraduate education is now emerging - new courses in systems engineering, both related to traditional engineering and to embedded software. At the same time an industrial interest in research and undergraduate education in human-system interaction emerged, which is connected to this approach.

The improvement of the traditional education in computer operating systems and real-time systems is the third approach taken. There are two relevant views on systems engineering from a software perspective - one is the heterogeneous system view presented above and the other is the embedded software system view. The assumption of the latter is that the requirements on the embedded software system can be captured statically by what is known as "the requirements specification". This is, however, an oversimplification, at least for industries such as the aerospace industry, which are advocating the more heterogeneous systems view. The courses given for computer engineering and in particular the non-computer focused programmes have to be influenced by this.

Figures 1 and 2 shows schematically the current situation for the largest four Master of Engineering tracks. For the non-computer engineering tracks the background in programming before the fourth year is given.

In the fourth year some relevant courses for real-time systems and systems engineering are given. The course in "System specification, verification and validation" will be given for the first time in 1997.

The three approaches presented above have to be integrated in order to provide the students with the needed systems engineering competence. In the next sections we discuss this and also give an epilogue with some comments on the development. This presentation focuses on the Master of Engineering programmes, since they normally are fore-runners to the other programmes at the institute.

3   The PUM-course

The PUM-course (Methodology of Program Development and Programming Development Project) is a comparably large course, corresponding roughly to two months work for each student. The course has two main parts:

- one lecture part, which presents program development from an industrial viewpoint - different processes like specification, inspection and testing, different methods for program development.
- a project part, where the students are grouped in groups of about seven people, that will perform a practical, programming project under realistic circumstances.

The course has well developed course materials for each phase of the project and there is a library of 120 different subprocess descriptions available.

In an independent software quality course the student projects in the PUM-course are analysed following IEEE Std. 730 [2] and by using capability maturity models (CMM) [3].

4   Real-Time Courses

Typically real-time systems related material is presented in operating systems and process programming courses. The prerequisites are normally basic programming courses and a course in data structures.

In the Computer Science and Engineering programme there are courses in process programming, Ada, operating systems and compiler technology that relates to real-time systems. These courses are also, to a large extent or at least in a modified form, available in the other (non-computer) Master of Engineering programmes. In the other programmes there is also a specific course,

"Real-Time and Process Programming" which essentially brings the embedded system view into focus. In this course, specific issues are presented, like scheduling and resource management, from a real-time system perspective.

This situation is going to be changed in the future, in favor of real-time systems. Currently the non-computer programmes are revising their curriculum and have increased the contents of programming and software courses. The Mechanical Engineering programme is implementing a complete switch to Ada (from Pascal) from the basic programming course in the first year to the fourth year courses. The Industrial Engineering and Management programme will also cover the combination of computer engineering and economics in the future. The Applied Physics and Electrical Engineering programme is implementing a specific software profile with the intention to cover real-time software technology in particular. A corresponding revision of the Computer Science and Engineering programme can be anticipated.

Much of this change has its origin in the view expressed by industry in discussion groups and the industrial representatives in the steering boards for the different programmes. The revision work is also influenced by the expressed opinion of graduated students, when they are contacted a few years after graduation in surveys made by the student organization and the university in cooperation.

5   System Engineering Courses

During the last two years two new profiles have been implemented in the Mechanical Engineering programme - aircraft building and aircraft systems. This has its particular background in that Linköping is the center of the Swedish aerospace industry.

In the latter - aircraft systems - several new courses for the fourth year are planned. Each one of them brings up the system issue from different perspectives:

- Human-System Interaction - including, for example, pilot-aircraft and driver-car scenarios
- Avionic Systems - i.e., navigational-, orientational-, aircraft monitoring and other subsystems
- Hydraulic and Mechanical Aircraft Systems - in particular integrated with computer control systems and embedded software
- System Specification, Verification and Validation - with the specific intention not to be software specific.

6 The Integration of PUM, Real-Time and Systems Engineering Courses

It is obvious that all of these three approaches are connected and that there exists a possibility for improvements in the courses to give a better fit to the need - for example, from a real-time systems perspective.

The PUM-course could contain more real-time or embedded software system projects. The different project courses in the systems engineering area could benefit from a cooperation with both real-time courses and software engineering courses like the PUM-course. The real-time system courses could definitely use an input from the system engineering courses.

From our perspective the question should not be asked - "How does a programme for Real-Time Systems Engineering look like?". The specific focus on real-time software will make the programme too narrow to be attractive to industry. This would mean that such a programme will never be the main direction of engineering education. On the other hand, a real-time profile as a specialization, within for example a traditional computer engineering education, is not only possible but actually required.

Another main point in our discussion about systems engineering and real-time systems is that it is important to consider the non-computer engineering programmes. Important not only because these programmes produce the main cadre of engineers, but it is also this category that needs good understanding of the implications of software technology embedded into traditional engineering systems. This means that real-time systems curricula should have two approaches - one as a specialization of computer engineering programmes and one as a complement or a specialization in non-computer programmes. It is important to realize that these two approaches put different requirements on the courses.

7 Epilogue

Linköping University has a long tradition in cooperation across department borders and among different undergraduate programmes. This is of great benefit in integrating different views on the issues presented above. Even if computer engineering is a programme in its own right, it has been recognized by other disciplines that this kind of competence should be regarded as basic, alongside with mathematics and physics. This means that computer engineering is recognized as a "contributing technology" in any engineering field. This insight has made it possible to create cooperation over department borders and create a vision of the engineering education in an interdisciplinary way.

Acknowledgement

We are grateful for the support and cooperation of many in this ongoing revision work - people from fluid power technology, production technology, industrial ergonomics, quality engineering, automatic control, vehicular systems and of course our colleagues at the Dept. of Computer and Information Science. Our part in the revision work is small compared to the total work put into it by all these people.

References

[1] D. Boud, G. Feletti, editors: "The Challange of Problem Based Learning", Kogan Page Limited, London, 1991.

[2] ANSI/IEEE Std 730 Standard for Software Quality Assurance Plans (revision of IEEE Std 730-84 and redesignation of IEEE Std 730.1-89), IEEE Computer Society, January 22, 1990.

[3] M. Paulk et al., "Capability Maturity Model for Software, Version 1.1", Report CMU/SEI-93-TR-24 ESC-TR 93-177, Software Engineering Institute, Pittsburgh, PA, 1993.

Real-Time Systems Education: Emphasis on the System Level

Thomas J. Marlowe *   Alexander D. Stoyenko
Michael G. Hinchey   Sanjoy Baruah
Ami Silberman   Rich Scherl
Phillip A. Laplante
Real-Time Computing Laboratory
Department of Computer and Information Science
New Jersey Institute of Technology
University Heights, Newark NJ 07012, U.S.A.
`alex@rtlab12.njit.edu`

Abstract

In this position paper, we argue the importance of systems (languages, operating systems, architectures) as a component in real-time systems education. We begin by considering the facets of real-time systems and discussing the current state of real-time systems education. We then present two recommendations, for attention to systems issues and to complex systems, respectively. We close by discussing approaches to real-time systems education used in our practice.

1. Introduction

The discipline of Computer Science has been divided by Tucker [19] into Theory (mathematics), Design (engineering), and Experiment (science). While this breadth-first division is valuable in understanding the origins, history and intellectual outlook of the discipline, it is perhaps not as useful in characterizing major facets of courses, or emphases of faculty, programs, and departments.

We believe that for these purposes, and in considering application development, a more useful view is to consider Computer Science to include as major facets Architecture, Software Engineering, Theory, and Systems. The term "Systems", as a subfield of Computer Science, generally refers to the design and implementation of the support environment for applications, principally the software support environment (such as operating systems, languages and compilers, database managers, and tools), but also its interactions with application code, and certain aspects of architecture –

---

*Marlowe is also with the Department of Mathematics and Computer Science, Seton Hall University, South Orange, NJ 07079 USA.

such as memory hierarchies – directly affecting these software levels.

Development and implementation of an application, whether real-time or not, must for correctness and efficiency take into account guidelines provided by software engineering and theory, must necessarily operate on a platform of architecture and systems software, and should interact with tools and analyses in testing, debugging and maintenance.

Real-time systems certainly require even more thorough consideration of all four facets, since:

- The *architecture* of a real-time application comprises not only computer hardware, but also networking, sensors and actuators, and other resources.

- The need to reason about time complicates all phases of *software engineering*, that is, requirements elicitation, constraint specification, and verification. Moreover, for both specification and code, these phases have been well-codified in design methodologies, and are often required to use formal methods.

- Various *theory* constructs, including scheduling disciplines, resource allocation, formal models such as Petri nets, and proof techniques are important elements of real-time system design.

- The *systems* programming level, including the operating system, the network and scheduler managers, the programming language, the compiler or interpreter, the development environment and tools, has a major impact on design, development, evolution, and maintenance.

2. Real-Time Systems Education Today

There are many issues of pedagogy and content in real-time systems education. Systems analysis and systems engineering are held to be essential for developing large distributed applications. Course content should involve conceptual learning, case-based analysis, and hands-on experience. All of these are important, although only dealt with tangentially in this article, but all are affected, we feel, by the emphases given to the facets mentioned above.

In courses at other institutions of which we are aware, three of these facets are heavily represented in real-time systems education. Namely:

- The basic/machine model of a real-time system relies on a virtual *architecture*/machine model, and there is typically substantial discussion both of special-purpose real-time components, and of the means of using off-the-shelf computer and non-computer components.

- Most programs have a significant *software engineering* component, and the better or more recently modified programs even have a separate course in formal methods.

- Real-time systems courses and programs inevitably devote the largest portion of time to *theory*, from the theory and use of rate-monotonic analysis/scheduling and other scheduling disciplines, through graph models such as Petri nets, to (in better programs) techniques for proof of safety and liveness properties.

Systems may be given a nod with discussion of real-time operating systems (such as Real-Time POSIX, RT-Unix [3], Real-Time Mach [10], YARTOS [5], and the like), but even this is often subsumed in the discussion of scheduling theory or real-time kernels. Even if this lack of emphasis could have been considered justified in the past, there are several trends in real-time systems that argue that this lack of coverage is no longer defensible, for the following reasons:

- With the increasing use of commercial-off-the-shelf (COTS) components (throughout hardware, environment, and application), it will no longer be possible to write applications completely in a dedicated real-time language, nor to encode them completely in hardware, nor to make a priori assumptions about the operating system, the scheduler, or other components of the environment. In particular, it is no longer possible to assume that a real-time application will necessarily be operating in isolation on dedicated hardware, with an application-specific language, operating system, and environment.

- Conversely, the need to make real-time modules portable/reusable, and the need to make real-time applications evolvable, will require development and then specialization of general-purpose modules, and development of compilers/linkers and/or operating systems to perform the specialization.

- There is a growing number of large complex applications, as in multimedia or modern military/naval applications, for which modern development environments *aware of real-time considerations* and development tools will be a necessity.

- Further, these large applications cannot conceivably be written entirely in assembler, nor hand-optimized, nor, we argue, left unoptimized or alternatively optimized in ignorance of real-time considerations.

- With the growing emphasis on formal verification, and on formal methods in particular, there will be a need for static analysis tools to extract information about applications, whether written as an executable specification or in a standard programming language, and for automatic or semi-automatic transformers for code analysis and improvement.

3. Including Computer Systems in Real-Time Systems

These trends strongly suggest implications for courses and programs in real-time systems education. First, while single courses or course sequences cannot cover any topic in depth, they should at a minimum contain a component considering language, compiler, environment, and tool issues, and stress the importance of a systems viewpoint in developing and implementing real-time applications. Second, more extensive programs, whether a certificate, track, or concentration, should require appropriate systems pre- or co-requisites, and should include a course which examines the interaction of systems and real-time issues.

Third, and most importantly, instruction in the other three components (Architecture, Software Engineering, and Theory), as well as other optional areas such as Artificial Intelligence or Databases, should be informed by systems considerations. In discussing Architecture, more attention must be paid to the interaction with operating systems, the need for the compiler to know architectural details, and systems issues in using COTS hardware for real-time applications.

For Software Engineering, part of the emphasis has to be on tool-based development, and on encoding requirements and specifications for use by analyzers, and by environment and compiler tools; some attention should also be paid to matching the language to the application, where in some cases this may involve a use of an assertion language [2], or an embedding language [11], visible to the compiler and tools, in addition to the language used for application coding. In addition, more attention must be paid to reuse, to fault tolerance, and to other systems properties, and tools to support requirements in these areas should also be discussed. Finally, the coverage of Theory should include theoretical issues related to systems, including but not limited to: (1) issues in developing and using tools for real-time environments, (2) issues arising from use of non-special-purpose, COTS components, (3) static analysis as related to graph models, compilers, schedulability analyzers, and formal methods, (4) support for reuse and evolutionary systems, and (5) use of transformations and proof of safety for real-time systems.

Fourth, the future of real-time systems education will also be affected by increasing heterogeneity in large real-time applications. Particularly in safety-critical or high-security applications, it is impossible to treat timeliness in isolation, without considering other non-functional criteria such as fault-tolerance, security, safety, as well as classical criteria such as performance and resource use. In addition to these heterogeneous constraints and objectives, an increasing number of real-time applications are large in scope and number of components, increasingly long-lived, and executed on distributed heterogeneous platforms. Thus, realistic approaches to teaching real-time systems should include consideration of these *complex systems* [9, 17], and the need for techniques and approaches to handle these additional properties and criteria is another powerful argument for a systems orientation in a real-time systems course.

4. One Approach to a Systems-Based Real-Time Systems Course

One reasonable organization represents a bottom-up approach moving from the less abstract hardware to the more abstract systems. For example, in [6], the material is presented in the following order.

1. Basic real-time concepts.
2. Hardware and programming languages.
3. Software engineering; software specification and design.
4. Real-time kernels.

5. Real-time memory management; intertask communication and synchronization.
6. Reliability, fault-tolerance, and testing.
7. Queuing systems; multiprocessing systems.
8. Systems integration.
9. Real-time applications.

Our experience has shown that these topics (not necessarily presented in this precise order) reflect a holistic, systems approach that integrates theory and practice. The effect of compiler code generation and improvement on performance is emphasized, through studies of systems built in different programming languages. This systems approach provides numerous opportunities to inject theory when talking about reliability (probability), testing (formal methods), design (formal methods and discrete mathematics), queuing systems (scheduling theory and continuous mathematics), and so on. In short, theory and traditional "real-time" topics can and should be used to support a curriculum designed to teach student how to build systems. In contrast, in other approaches, systems issues may be covered only through a smattering of contrived applications used to justify dearly-held theoretical viewpoints and research programs.

At least one of the authors [6], uses case studies and real-world examples to illustrate the application of theoretical concepts in actual, practical applications. For example, the halting problem is applied to the process of debugging systems that "hang-up" and an analogue of the Heisenberg Uncertainty Principle is used when discussing systems integration to illuminate the effect of probing real systems with "debug" code. This approach has been presented in many settings, including introductory graduate courses and continuing professional education workshops.

5. Our Experience at NJIT

We have attempted to provide adequate real-time systems education at the Department of Computer & Information Science, through the Real-Time Computing Lab (RTCL), at NJIT. Building on our early experimental efforts [12, 13, 16], a basic Real-Time Systems course has been taught once a year for the past five years, mostly to M.S. and Ph.D. students, where about half the former are part-timers from industry. The course spends probably 60% of its time on Systems, 25% on Software Engineering and 15% on Theory. Architectural issues, to the extent they are treated, are covered largely in the systems component. Approximately half the material is based on the textbook [4] and the other half comes from an extensive body of published literature, from both inside and outside the Lab. Moreover, there is an advanced weekly seminar (year-round) which covers all aspects of Real-Time Systems.

In addition to written exams and oral presentations in these courses, there is a significant experimentation component, using the CRL [18] platform [14, 15, 20, 22] and the DESTINATION (mostly Resource Allocation [1, 7, 8]) platform, and other RTCL projects (such as [21]). Working on our own platforms allows us finer-grained control over language, compiler, and operating system, in order more readily to formulate and investigate in isolation issues such as granularity of timing constraints, or assignment algorithms; however, it becomes more difficult to share our approaches and results with others, although we hope to address this problem in the near future.

Student projects are monitored not only by faculty, but also by other students involved in RTCL research. Many have led to Master's degree projects, and in several cases, even Master's degree theses, which are optional at NJIT. Typical projects have included translating and compiling standard applications into CRL, developing a workload generator, developing cost-function modules for DESTINATION (e.g., for real time or security), and writing and validating various aspects of our compiler and run-time environment. The resulting code often needs some modification, but most of it is still in use. Most student projects work fairly well, although open-ended projects, whether selected by faculty or initiated by students, tend not to succeed so well, with students either discouraged early on, or trying to complete their projects well after the semester is over.

Most of the students, other than full-time members of the lab, are part-time students already employed in computer-related positions. Student and employer reaction appears largely positive; employers seem ready to believe that, at least for graduate students already in their employ, systems expertise they get translates fairly easily from one system to another.

The RTCL itself, founded in Fall 1990, now consists of six on-campus and three visiting faculty, and 15 Ph.D. students. Lab faculty are responsible not just for real-time courses, but also for courses in operating systems, programming languages and formal methods, and compilers. The lab has recently graduated its first Ph.D. student, and expects to graduate two more in the next year. The strong systems orientation of research on our two platforms has been a significant plus in placing these and other students in summer internships. The combination of computer systems (particularly compiler) and real-time systems background was also a strong factor in the several academic and industrial offers to our first Ph.D. graduate.

6. Conclusion

As we have described, the suite of computer systems components — languages, compilers, operating and run-time systems, and tools, and related architectural features — will inevitably have an ever greater importance in design and implementation of real-time systems, particularly large, complex, heterogeneous real-time applications. Moreover, in our experience, employers, both academic and industrial, place a high value on systems experience, especially if integrated with another area such as real-time systems.

This growing importance strongly suggests that real-time systems courses and programs should either require or provide exposure to computer systems, and should provide greater visibility to the interaction of real-time applications with systems components. We have pointed out a number of connections, and described how these are addressed in two programs in which the authors are involved.

Acknowledgments

We wish to acknowledge fruitful discussions with members of the Real-Time Computing Lab at NJIT, in particular Mohamed F. Younis and Grace Tsai, in which a number of our positions were articulated and refined. We also wish to acknowledge the assistance of other members of the RTCL, and the intellectual and financial support of various government agencies and corporate sponsors, in developing the systems and tools mentioned above. In particular, we wish to thank the U.S. ONR (Grants N00014-92-J-1367 and N00014-93-1-1047) the U.S. NSF (Grant CCR-9402827), the U.S. NSWC (Grants N60921-94-C-0106, N60921-94-M-1250, N60921-93-M-3095 and N60921-93-M-1912) and the AT&T UEDP Program (Grant 91-134).

References

[1] C. C. Amaro et al., "Economics of Resource Allocation," *1994 Complex Systems Engineering and Assessment Technology Workshop*, Beltsville, Maryland, U.S.A., July 1994.

[2] T. M. Chung, H. G. Dietz, "Language Constructs and Transformation for Hard Real-Time Systems." *Proc. ACM SIGPLAN Workshop on Languages, Compilers, and Tools for Real-Time Systems*, La Jolla, Calif., June 1995, pp. 45–53.

[3] B. Fuhrt, "The Reality of a Real-Time UNIX Operating System", in *Real-Time Computing*, W. A.

Halang, A. D. Stoyenko, editors, Springer-Verlag, Berlin, 1992, pp. 503–507.

[4] W. Halang, A. D. Stoyenko, *Constructing Predictable Real-Time Systems*. Kluwer Academic Publishers, Boston, 1991.

[5] K. Jeffay, D.L. Stone, D. Poirier, "YARTOS: Kernel support for efficient, predictable real-time systems," Proc. Joint Eighth IEEE Workshop on Real-Time Operating Systems and Software and IFAC/IFIP Workshop on Real-Time Programming, Real-Time Systems Newsletter, Vol. 7, No. 4, Fall 1991, pp. 8–13.

[6] P. A. Laplante, *Real-Time Systems Design and Analysis: An Engineer's Handbook*, Second Edition, IEEE Press/IEEE CS Press, New York and Los Alamitos, Calif., 1996.

[7] M.S. Harelick et al., "A Constraint Function Classification for Complex Systems Development, "*Proc. 1st IEEE Int'l Conf. Engineering of Complex Computer Systems (ICECCS'95)*, November 1995, pp. 286–289.

[8] T. J. Marlowe et al., "Multiple-Goal Objective Functions for Optimization of Task Assignment in Complex Computer Systems," *Control Engineering Practice,* Vol. 4, No. 2, 1996, pp. 251–256.

[9] M. G. Hinchey, editor, *Newsletter of the IEEE Technical Committee on Complexity in Computing* (previously TSC on Engineering of Complex Computer Systems); Universal Resource Locator http://www.rtl.njit.edu/TC-CIC/.

[10] T. Nakajima et al., "Integrated Management of Priority Inversion in Real-Time Mach," Proc. 1993 Real-Time Systems Symposium, IEEE Computer Society Press, Los Alamitos, Calif., 1993, pp. 120–130.

[11] A. Silberman, "RTM — Design and Implementation", Ph. D. Thesis, University of Illinois at Urbana-Champaign, 1996.

[12] A. D. Stoyenko, "Predictable Real-Time Systems: A Challenge for Computer Science and Engineering Curricula," Report CIS-91-17, New Jersey Institute of Technology, July 1991.

[13] A.D. Stoyenko, L. R. Welch, "Towards A Platform for Teaching and Research in Predictable Real-Time Systems," *IEEE 1991 Real-Time Systems Symposium*, San Antonio, Texas, U.S.A., December 1991.

[14] A. D. Stoyenko, T. J. Marlowe, "Polynomial-Time Transformations and Schedulability Analysis of Parallel Real-Time Programs with Restricted Resource Contention." *Journal of Real-Time Systems*, Vol. 4, No. 4, November 1992, pp. 307–329.

[15] A. D. Stoyenko, T. J. Marlowe, W. Halang, M. F. Younis, "Enabling Efficient Schedulability Analysis through Conditional Linking and Program Transformations." *Control Engineering Practice*, Vol. 1, No. 1, January 1993, pp. 85–105.

[16] A. D. Stoyenko et al., "A Platform for Complex Real-Time Applications," *1993 Complex Systems Engineering and Assessment Technology Workshop*, Beltsville, Maryland, U.S.A., July 1993.

[17] A. D. Stoyenko, P. A. Laplante, R. Harrison, T. J. Marlowe, "Engineering of Complex Systems: A Case for Dual Use and Defense Technology Conversion," *IEEE Spectrum,* Vol. 31, No. 11, December 1994, pp. 32–39.

[18] A. D. Stoyenko, T. J. Marlowe, M. F. Younis, "A Language for Complex Real-Time Systems." *The Computer Journal*, Vol. 38, No. 4, November 1995, pp. 319–338.

[19] A. B. Tucker (editor), "Computing Curricula 1991." *Report of the ACM/IEEE-CS Joint Curriculum Task Force*, Final Draft, IEEE, Washington, DC, 17 December 1990.

[20] M. F. Younis, T. J. Marlowe, A. D. Stoyenko, "Compiler Transformations for Speculative Execution in a Real-Time System." *Proc. 15th Real-Time Systems Symposium*, IEEE Computer Society Press, Los Alamitos, Calif., 1994, pp. 109–117.

[21] M. F. Younis et al., "Performance Enhancement of Various Real-Time Image Processing Techniques Via Speculative Execution", *Proc. IS&T/SPIE Symposium on Electronic Imaging: Science and Technology*, San Jose, Calif., January 1996, pp. 55–64.

[22] M. F. Younis et al., "Improving the Performance of Fault Tolerance in Real-Time Systems Using Speculative Execution." *Proc. 1st IEEE Int'l Conf. Engineering of Complex Computer Systems (ICECCS'95)*, November 1995, pp. 349–356.

Laboratory for Distributed Real-Time Control

Zdeněk Hanzálek
Department of Control Engineering, Karlovo nám. 13
Czech Technical University in Prague
121 35 Prague 2, Czech Republic
hanzalek@rtime.felk.cvut.cz

Abstract

This paper presents an experimental laboratory setup aimed at creating a flexible manufacturing system for use in teaching real-time control. The machine models (robots, conveyors, etc.) are self-contained elements with their own intelligence, communicating with a master computer. A supervisor program running on the master computer is implemented by a real-time operating system, enabling the dynamic creation of processes. The supervisor program is fully parameterized, with parameters specifying manufacturing subtasks of all machines and synchronization among them. This makes the control system modular and flexible. A manufacturing task is specified by Petri nets that are automatically decomposed into a set of unique P-invariant generators. The choice of concurrent processes corresponding to P-invariants is done semi-automatically to reflect the physical tenor of the manufacturing system.

1 Introduction

Five and half years of full-time study at the Czech Technical University is divided into three periods. The basic stage, which gives students theoretical principles of electrical engineering (namely, mathematics and physics). This stage is completed with the first state examination and its average duration is about 4 semesters.

The second period of study ends with the Bachelor's degree. A set of obligatory subjects provides basic ground for student's knowledge in a specific discipline, such as control engineering. Beside subjects oriented towards theory of control and towards electronic systems, there is a set of courses dealing with the use of computers in control engineering. These courses are supported by laboratories such as Logic Systems, Computers for Control and Operating Systems for Control. Optional courses from all-departmental offerings complete the curriculum structure with subjects from other areas. Graduates of bachelor study submit

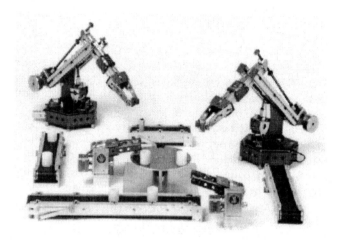

Figure 1: A flexible manufacturing system

their project work and receive the title of Bachelor, after examinations.

The third and last part of full-time study at the Department of Control Engineering is to obtain the title of Enginner. In this period, students choose among many elective courses of their specialization (e.g. Control Systems, AI, Robotics, Mechatronics, Biocybernetics). Laboratories of Distributed Control, Modern Control Engineering (microcontrolers, PICs, PLCs, XLINXs) and Design of Control Systems (Intouch, Control Panel, etc.) are supporting the courses related to real-time control. At the end of the engineering period, students submit their diploma thesis and take a final state examination covering three main subjects: Theory of Control, Computers, and Electronic Systems.

Students coming to our labs are already familiar with programming (Pascal, C, low-level languages), so they can fully concentrate on conceptual aspects of systematic design. They are taught the basic principles of real-time control (real-time requirements, inter-

147

rupt system, synchronous/asynchronous events handling, etc.), using simple physical models (decoding incremental sensor signals, generating waveforms, etc.) in the laboratory of Computers for Control. In the two next laboratories, *Operating Systems for Control* and *Distributed Control Systems*, we use a flexible manufacturing system, whose elements are described briefly in this article.

The material related to real time is organized in a modular fashion, which allows its use in a variety of courses offered by the Department. Below, one such module is described, based on Petri nets formalism. This is followed by a presentation of an experimental setup and a summary.

2 Real-Time and Concurrency

To understand the concept of real-time requirements, students are taught the basic principles, first. In the real-time applications, a computer is connected directly to the physical equipment and is dedicated to controlling that equipment. Consequently, the system must meet response requirements that are mandated by the equipment itself, rather than those being dictated by the computer. The requirement to meet externally imposed deadlines is at the heart of what is termed a real-time system. The definition of a real-time system states that it has to respond to externally generated events within a specified and finite interval. Consequently, the software must be designed to meet these response time requirements [3].

A characteristic of a computer supervising a distributed system is that many activities within it proceed in parallel. For example, some parameters must be sampled and controlled at a very fast rate, whereas other parameters need only be sampled once per second. Logically, those two operations proceed in parallel, while of course the CPU executes them in an interleaved fashion. Similarly, controlling several I/O devices at once usually results in some parts of the control software waiting for the devices to complete an operation while other devices, having finished their operations, are being serviced.

Whether recognized or not, this parallelism, or concurrency, adds a major complication to the software. To avoid all kinds of problems, programmers must take care of mutually exclusive access to shared resources, signaling one task by another task or by an interrupt handler, and sending messages from one task or an interrupt handler to another task.

A multitasking operating system (OS) usually provides the facilities necessary to solve that kind of problems [1], [11], [12], [13]. It does it via system calls for creating and deleting tasks, suspending and resuming

their execution, and so on. The system automatically takes care of task scheduling. Although tasks may logically proceed in parallel, the CPU is physically capable of running only one task at a time; therefore the scheduler interleaves their execution.

3 Petri Net Formalism

The use of Petri nets has been shown to be very promising for modelling and analysing real-time systems as well as many other concurrent systems [2]. Debugging costs are a major difficulty for real-time distributed systems. Therefore, it is valuable to perform as many checks as possible on specifications before implementation. For that reason, it is of interest to present the students with an abstract model capable to express parallelism and to derive formal proofs. Petri net (PN) is an excellent formalism of this kind for its ability to validate behavioural properties [8], [10], [14].

The state-transition dynamics in a manufacturing system are modelled as a controlled Petri net (CtlPN), which is an extension of standard Petri nets with external control inputs as additional enabling conditions on transitions [4].

Definition 1: Let a Petri net as a four-tuple $< P, T, Pre, Post >$ is such that
P is a finite and non-empty set of places
T is a finite and non-empty set of transitions
Pre is an input function (precondition)
$Post$ is an output function (postcondition).
1. A Matrix $C = (c_{ij})$ where $(1 \leq i \leq n, 1 \leq j \leq m)$ is called the incidence matrix of PN iff

$$C = Post - Pre \qquad (1)$$

2. A vector $f : (1, ..., n) \in Z^+$ is called a P-invariant of the given PN, iff

$$C^T \times f = 0 \qquad (2)$$

3. A vector $s : (1, ..., m) \in Z^+$ is called a T-invariant of the given PN, iff

$$C \times s = 0 \qquad (3)$$

Definition 2: An invariant f of $C^T \times f = 0$ is called standardized iff f can not be written in the form $f = x_i + x_j$, where x_i, x_j are invariants and $x_i \neq 0$, $x_j \neq 0$

More generally the decomposition and the composition of a given invariant f can be described by

$$f = \sum_{i=1}^{g} \lambda_i x^i \qquad (4)$$

with factors λ_i and generators x^i.

Level	$\lambda_i \in$	Generators x^i	Set $\{x^i\}$
1	Q	$x^i \in Z^n$	$\{x^i\}$ Base
2	Z	$x^i \in Z^n$	$\{x^i\}$ Base
3	Q^+	$x^i \geq 0$	$\{x^i\}$ Unique
4	Z^+	$x^i \geq 0$	$\{x^i\}$ Unique
5	$\{0,1\}$	$x^i \in \{0,1\}^n$	$\{x^i\}$ Unique

Table 1: Generator computational levels

Methods calculating invariants are published by Martinez and Silva [7] and others. Kruckenberg and Jaxy [6] considered several algorithms calculating generators and divided the computations into five levels as shown in the Table 1.

We will focus only on the third level, where each invariant is a positive linear combination of generators. It is evident that in the case of event graphs $\lambda_i \in Z^+$ and $x_i \in \{0,1\}^n$ already for the third level. The generators from this level will be called simply generators in the rest of this article. In [9], it is proved that the set of generators is finite and unique.

Kruckenberg and Jaxy give an algorithm calculating generators, based on the Kannan and Bachem [5] algorithm to calculate Hermite normal form and on the theory of polyhedral cones. This algorithm serving as a base for a task decomposition was implemented in Matlab and is available from the author upon request.

Having generators of P-invariants, it is evident which transitions have to be fired in sequence. The problem now is to choose the set of generators covering all places representing actions. The selection could be done automatically seeking for an optimal solution (e.g., minimal number of generators). But this choice is very artificial and does not reflect the physical tenor of the manufacturing system. It is better to choose the generators manually so that they represent separate machines of the manufacturing system.

To make use of this theory, students are given a manufacturing problem. Using PN simulator they first draw a Petri net model of the problem. In this environment, they simulate the behaviour of the system and extract the incidence matrix C and an initial marking vector M_0. Using Matlab, they obtain the generators of P-invariants and choose those corresponding to separate machines and serving as input data for the supervisor program described in the next section. Having the generators of P-invariants and the initial marking vector M_0, students prove that there is no deadlock in the system. In this subclass of PN called event graph, it is sufficient to prove that there is at least one token in each P-invariant. That corresponds to a simple matrix operation in Matlab.

4   Experimental Setup

The model of a technological process developed at the Department of Control Engineering, CTU Prague, is presented in Figure 1. This model consists of several kinds of machines: robots, conveyor-belts, storing plates and simple manipulators. A number of technological processes can be realized using various configurations of the machines.

Local control systems were realized by universal boards based on a microcomputer (Intel 8051) working in a multiprocessor mode. The boards are interconnected by a common link (modified serial interface RS232) with a PC acting as a master (see Figure 2).

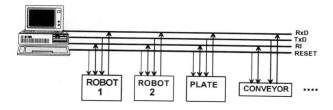

Figure 2: An experimental environment structure

The operating system kernel allows to create dynamically several concurrent processes. Figure 3 shows a block diagram of a fully parameterized program acting as a manufacturing system supervisor.

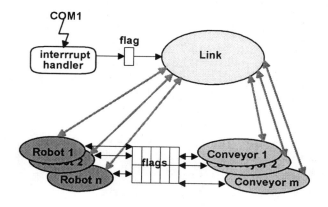

Figure 3: The supervisor structure

The program reads all the required information from a file containing specifications of separate tasks corresponding to the chosen generators. Synchronization among the generators (tasks) is done simply by flags. The tasks are connected to machines by a common link (Figure 2) performing communication in both directions (PC → machine, machine → PC). The shared link is accessed by a special process (named Link) pending for a flag from the interrupt handler on a serial port COM1 and performing demultiplex of messages coming from the machines.

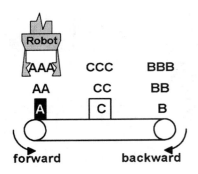

Figure 4: A sample problem

Place	Robot Activity
P_1	move to AAA
P_2	wait
P_3	move to A, close, move to AAA
P_4	wait
P_5	move to AA, open, move to AAA
P_6	move to BBB
P_7	wait
P_8	move to BB, close, move to BBB move to CCC, C, open, move to CCC

Place	Conveyor Activity
P_9	forward to A
P_{10}	wait
P_{11}	forward to A
P_{12}	wait
P_{13}	backward to B
P_{14}	wait

Place	Flag Meaning
$P_{15}...P_{20}$	wait

Table 2: The actions corresponding to places in Fig. 5

Figure 4 shows a simple manufacturing system consisting of two machines and two objects: a conveyor running forward/backward, a robot in different posi-

tions, white object in position C and black object in position A. The function of a system performing an object composition in position A and a decomposition in position B is depicted in Figure 5 and Table 2.

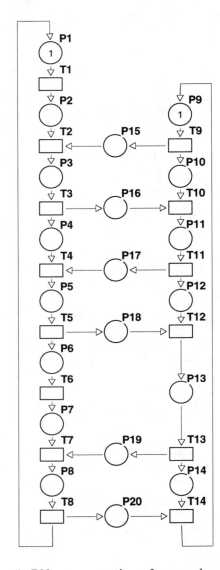

Figure 5: PN representation of a sample problem

In order to represent all the states of the system, it is necessary to guarantee that the input places to the synchronization transitions have no action meaning (e.g., P_2, P_{15} to T_2). The PN in Figure 5 can be decomposed into two P-invariants corresponding to the machines (robot $P_1, P_2, P_3, P_4, P_5, P_6, P_7, P_8$ and conveyor $P_9, P_{10}, P_{11}, P_{12}, P_{13}, P_{14}$). The two P-invariants and separate synchronization points among them ($P_{15}, P_{16}, P_{17}, P_{18}, P_{19}, P_{20}$) are given in the file as parameters to the program acting as the supervisor. The program first creates three tasks (Robot1, Conveyor1 and Link) and six flags, and then starts the object composition and decomposition.

Handling asynchronous events with a real-time kernel is more difficult in the design phase (task decomposition is an NP-complete problem) than using a control system based on input ports polling in each sampling period. On the other hand this approach is more structural and allows more efficient programming.

The success of this procedure relies on the fact that students already have a theoretical background gained in courses on Linear Algebra and Theory of Systems. This allows them to deal with the use of the set of P-invariant generators that is unique for a given Petri net representing the manufacturing problem.

5 Summary

The system described above is used in two laboratory courses at the Department of Control Engineering. In the course *Operating Systems for Control*, students are given libraries that allow them to communicate with the manufacturing system and tune their own programs running under the multitasking OS and managing a specified manufacturing task on a fixed topology. In the course *Distributed Control Systems*, students specify various manufacturing tasks by Petri nets and decompose the problem into separate processes using algorithms that search for the set of P-invariant generators. Choosing a subset of P-invariant generators they create an input data file and run fully parameterized supervisor to control the distributed system.

The lab was realized on various software platforms (VRTX, Linux, and others). Separate implementations are used as physical models to test new components and control systems appearing on the market. New boards communicating via industrial fieldbus technologies such as CAN and Profibus, are under development. Thanks to the system modularity, it is easy to split the development into separate phases (mechanics, actuators and sensors, electronics, microcontroler programming, communication, supervisor level, PN token player, etc.) and realize them incrementally as projects done by the students.

Acknowledgments

I wish to thank anonymous reviewers, who provided comments and suggestions that improved this paper. This research has been conducted at the Department of Control Engineering as part of the research project New Control System Structures for Production Machines and has been supported by grant GACR No.102/95/0926.

References

[1] J.H.Anderson, S.Ramammurthy, K.Jeffay, "Real-Time Computing with Lock-Free Shared Objects", *Proc. Real-Time Systems Symposium*, IEEE Computer Society Press, Los Alamitos, Calif., 1995, pp. 28-38.

[2] C. Ghezzi et al., "A Unified High-Level Petri Net Formalism For Time-Critical Systems ", *IEEE Trans. Software Engineering*, 1991, pp. 160-172.

[3] Z. Hanzálek, "Real-time Neural Controller Implemented on Parallel Architecture", *in: A. Crespo (ed.): Proc. Artificial Intelligence in Real-Time Control*, Elsevier Science, Amsterdam, 1995, pp. 313-316.

[4] A. Ichikawa, K. Hiraishi, "Analysis and Control of Discrete Event Systems Represented by Petri Nets", *Discrete Event Systems: Models and Applications*, Springer-Verlag, Berlin, 1988.

[5] R. Kannan, A. Bachem, "Polynomial Algorithms for Computing the Smith and Hermite Normal Forms of an Integer Matrix", *SIAM J. Comput.*, Vol. 8, No. 4, 1979, pp. 499-507.

[6] F. Kruckeberg, M. Jaxy, "Mathematical Methods for Calculating Invariants in Petri Nets", *in: G. Rozenberg (ed.): Advances in Petri Nets*, LNCS 266, Springer-Verlag, Berlin, 1987, pp. 104-131.

[7] J. Martinez, M. Silva, "A Simple and Fast Algorithm to Obtain All Invariants of a Generalized Petri Nets", *in: C. Girault, W. Reisig (eds.): Application and Theory of Petri Nets*, Informatik Fachberichte 52, Springer-Verlag, Berlin, 1982, pp. 301-310.

[8] T.Murata, "Petri Nets: Properties, Analysis and Applications", *Proceedings of the IEEE*, Vol. 6, No. 1, 1990, pp. 39-50.

[9] K.H. Pascoletti, "Diophantische Systeme und Losungsmethoden zur Bestimmung aller Invarianten in Petri-Netzen", *Berichte der GMD*, No. 160, Bonn, 1986.

[10] J.L. Peterson, "Petri Net Theory and Modeling of Systems", Prentice Hall, Englewood Cliffs, NJ, 1981.

[11] J.A.Stankovic, K.Ramamritham, "The Spring Kernel: A New Paradigm for Real-Time Systems", *IEEE Software*, Vol. 8, No. 3, 1991, pp. 62-72.

[12] W.Tarng, T.H.Lin, "Fault-Tolerant Task Assignment in Distributed Real-Time Computing Systems", *Readings in Real-Time Systems, J. H. Lee, C.M. Krishna, eds.*, IEEE Computing Society Press, Los Alamitos, Calif., 1993, pp. 98-110.

[13] H.Tokuda, T.Nakajima, P.Rao, "Real-Time Mach: Towards a Predictable Real-Time Systems", *Proc. Usenix Mach Workshop*, 1990, pp. 1-10.

[14] R. Valette, "Analysis of Petri Nets by Stepwise Refinement", *J. Comput. Syst. Sci*, Vol. 18, 1979, pp. 35-46.

Using Matlab Real-Time Workshop in Teaching Control Design Techniques

C.Pous, A. Oller, J. Vehí, J.L. de la Rosa
Systems Engineering and Automatic Control Group
Industrial Engineering Department. University of Girona
E-17071 Girona (Catalonia)
carles@ei.udg.es

Abstract

This paper shows an application of how to use the Matlab-Simulink Real-Time Workshop environment for helping in some Control Lab Course. The main goal is to use a CACSD (Computer Aided Control System Design) environment in order to automate the implementation of a Real-Time controller. That is to say, once the controller is obtained and validated by simulation, it is implemented in the real process, a mobile robot, by means of the Matlab Real-Time Workshop. The main benefit of this method is that students can see immediately the effect of their controller when it is applied to the real plant without losing themselves in C programming.

1. Introduction

Control System Engineering projects can be divided into three steps : *analysis*, *design* and *implementation*. There are several powerful software packages to help in system analysis and control systems design steps. But, in general, there are no simple tools to generate executable code for real-time control. Therefore it is not easy to make changes or adjust parameters in the *analysis* and *design* steps, and then go through the implementation (Figure 1).

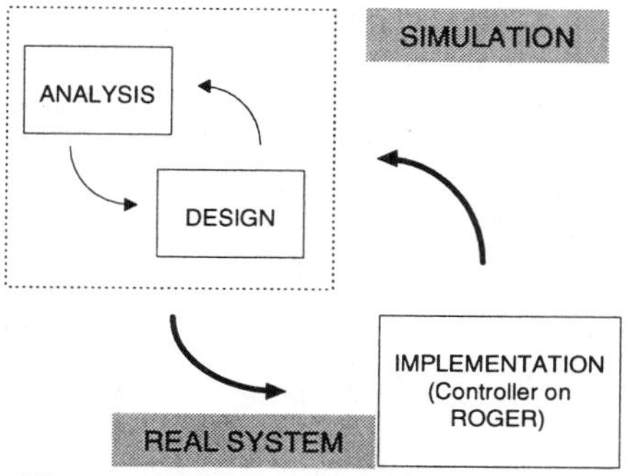

The idea is to provide a way to facilitate the *implementation* phase. Then, if a change in the design is needed, it can be downloaded to the implementation step almost in a straightforward manner. Matlab Real-Time Workshop makes possible to integrate the three steps in one software application.

This approach is applied to the new subjects of our specialisation in Industrial Engineering studies, and particularly to Computer Control and Industrial Robotics. The dependencies between particular subjects are presented in Figure 2.

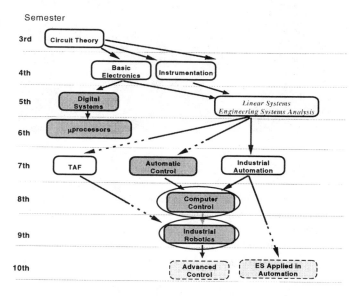

Figure 2. Subject dependencies in Industrial Engineering.

Figure 2 shows that students receive some knowledge of Electronics and Engineering Systems Analysis before taking specialisation courses. The course sequence is slightly different for Computer Control than for Industrial Robotics and other related subjects. Computer Control,

Figure 1. Development cycle.

for example, deals with principles how to generate code and how to link the generated code with libraries, using C. Industrial Robotics, on the other hand, doesn't require knowledge of C programming, and pays more attention to the results than to the implementation process itself.

This paper shows how the above mentioned approach is applied in teaching based on controlling a mobile robot. The robot's goal is to track an object and maintain a certain fixed distance to the target [1][2].

2. Hardware Configuration

The controlled process is a lab mobile robot called ROGER (acronym in Catalan of Operational Generic Robot for Research Experiments) that uses two rubber bands as a traction system (Figure 3).

Figure 3. The Lab Robot.

There are two electrical DC motors that produce the movement of the rubbers. The motors are controlled by means of a signal from an analog i/o board. The robot controller takes two co-ordinates (x cam, y cam) from the camera that are used by the control algorithm to derive the signal controlling both motors that move and steer the robot.

The real-time controller is based on a PC architecture with a video acquisition board, real-time image processor and an analog input-output board connected to the ROGER motors. A brief description of these components follows :

- *Video acquisition board.* It is a PIP Video Digitizer, plug-in card that allows an IBM PC microcomputer to perform frame grabbing operations on a video signal from an external video camera. Run-time libraries are

also provided to facilitate writing access routines between the PIP and the operating system.

- *Real -Time image processor.* A dedicated processor is used for real-time image processing using PIP output signal. Specified filter operations are allowed in real-time mode [3] after configuration.

- *Data acquisition board* : DAS-20 Keithley Metrabyte data acquisition card is used for the analog output [6]. Two signals needed to control the speed of the motors are provided with high linearity. To use real data in simulations, a set of Simulink Driver Blocks was developed (Figure 4) allowing direct access to the DAS-20 board for both input and output operations.

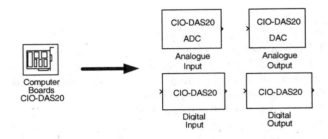

Figure 4. Simulink I/O Driver Blocks.

The range of input voltages applied to the motors allows for speed of 0m/s to 1m/s (meter/second) per each motor. The camera takes pictures from 0.5m to 4m (meters) distance, with a scope angle of 60° (degrees) and resolution of 512x512 pixels in colour. The target is detected by the vision system using segmentation of a specified colour (for instance blue, red, or other) at any given saturation. The position (x_cam, y_cam) of the target is the geometrical centre of the coloured image.

The hardware diagram of the whole system is shown in Figure 5.

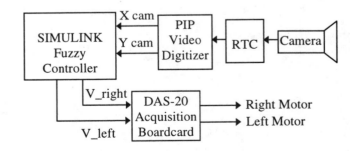

Figure 5. Hardware diagram of the system.

3. The Simulation Environment

Real-Time Matlab Workshop [5] is used in order to generate C code and executable files automatically from Simulink graphic models. It offers the following possibilities:

- Generate code only.
- Generate a Nonreal-Time executable.
- Generate a Real-Time executable.

This environment is very friendly and very simple to use. Once the executable file has been generated, the code is ready for use in the real application.

The model of the system is provided as a Simulink block. It has X-Y relative camera co-ordinates as outputs and voltage to be applied to left and right motors as inputs. The implementation of the controller must allow the robot to track the target. Different trajectories are simulated and the results of the simulation are shown on an X-Y graph or in a Simulink animation block. Some variables can be saved in a MAT-file for further analysis. Figure 6 shows the schematic of the simulation, where ROGER6 is a simulation model version of the real ROGER [4].

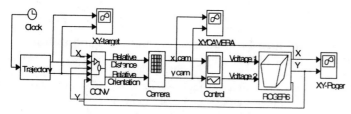

Figure 6. Schematic of the simulation.

This environment serves the purpose of providing students with a robot model in order to analyse the system and apply different types of controllers (PID, Fuzzy, etc.), and observe the response that they produce depending on the environmental conditions.

4. The Experiment

Here, a sample of control experiments realised by students in courses on Computer Control and Industrial Robotics is showed as example. The basic experiment consists of analysing, designing and implementing a fuzzy controller to make ROGER follow a certain given trajectory.

Some students have built a model of the robot in a modelling course. However, the Simulink robot model ROGER6 is provided to all students to let them have a fair start.

4.1 Controller Design

The structure of a Fuzzy Logic Controller (FLC) consists of a fuzzifier, an inference engine, a knowledge base (data base and rule base), and a defuzzifier which transforms fuzzy sets into real numbers to provide control signals.

Considering the angle between the target and the perpendicular to the camera (θ), and the distance from the target to the camera (d), as input variables (Figure 7), will be enough to define the fuzzy sets of the input variables.

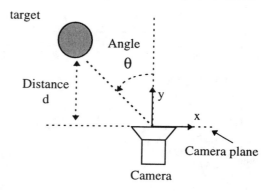

Figure 7. Variables used for space division.

Due to the camera placement, the image obtained is deformed. This image is divided into seven zones in the x direction and six zones in the y direction. The x variable gives an idea of how large the angle between the target and the perpendicular to the camera plane is, while the y variable gives information about how far the target from the robot is (distance in meters). The camera will see the zones in which y direction has been divided, that is narrower when farther. This effect is not as important in the x variable (Figure 8).

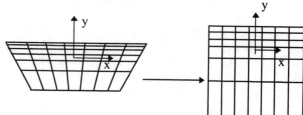

Figure 8. Space division for fuzzy sets definition.

The definitions of x_cam variable fuzzy sets, PL (Positive Large), PM (Positive Medium), PS (Positive Small), ZE (Zero), NS (Negative Small), NM (Negative Medium), NL (Negative Large), and six sets for y_cam variable, PL, PM, PS, ZE, NS, NL are presented in (Figure 9).

155

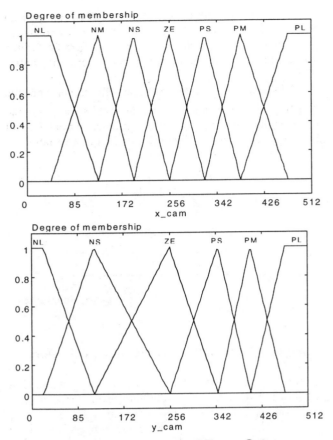

Figure 9. Definitions of Fuzzy Sets.

The assigned values for the output variables (voltage applied to left-hand and right-hand motors) provide design parameters. After calibration for satisfactory performance, six fuzzy sets are defined for both output voltages as follows: NL (-1), NS (-0.5), ZE(0), PS (0.33), PM (0.8), PL (1).

Analysing the input variables division, a set of 42 possible zones (7 zones x 6 zones) is obtained. Therefore it seems that 42 rules to control the process would be needed. But it is enough to control the robot with 12 rules, six for angle control, related with x variable, five for distance control, related with y variable and one for the zero position, where no action is needed. For instance, If x is large, a maximum signal on the corresponding motor will be applied to make the robot to turn in the proper direction. If y is large, a maximum signal to both motors will be applied to make the robot to advance. If x and y are in the zero zone, no action will be taken.

Fuzzy control rules have been derived based on the author's judgement instead of a mathematical model, learning algorithms or a fuzzy model of the process. The final 12 rules with the corresponding control action taken are shown in Figure 10. According to Sugeno's survey[7], singleton functions are used for consequent terms to simplify the process of reasoning. The inference process

which follows the weighted average method, calculates the centre of gravity of the aggregated consequent fuzzy sets.

1. IF	x_cam IS NL	THEN v_l=NS AND v_r=PL
2. IF	x_cam IS NM	THEN v_l=NS AND v_r=PS
3. IF	x_cam IS NS	THEN v_l=ZE AND v_r=PS
4. IF	x_cam IS ZE AND y_cam IS ZE	THEN v_l=ZE AND v_r=ZE
5. IF	x_cam IS PS	THEN v_l=PS AND v_r=ZE
6. IF	x_cam IS PM	THEN v_l=PS AND v_r=NS
7. IF	x_cam IS PL	THEN v_l=PL AND v_r=NS
8. IF	y_cam IS NL	THEN v_l=NL AND v_r=NL
9. IF	y_cam IS NS	THEN v_l=NS AND v_r=NS
10.IF	y_cam IS PS	THEN v_l=PS AND v_r=PS
11.IF	y_cam IS PM	THEN v_l=PM AND v_r=PM
12.IF	y_cam IS PL	THEN v_l=PL AND v_r=PL

Figure 10. Fuzzy Control Rules.

This FLC structure is implemented in Matlab/Simulink as presented in Figure 11.

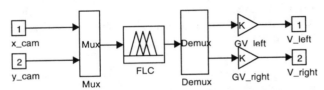

Figure 11. Matlab/Simulink implementation of an FLC.

The block that appears in Figure 6 as Control, should be substituted by the scheme of Figure 11.

4.2 Simulation Results

Figure 12 shows the proposed trajectory (set-point), and the result obtained by simulation is presented in Figure 13.

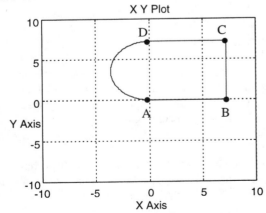

Figure 12. Proposed Trajectory.

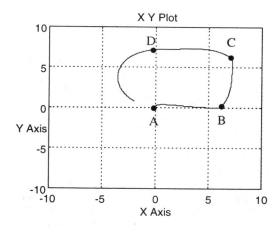

Figure 13. Simulated Trajectory.

Comparing Figure 12 and Figure 13, one can see that the trajectory followed by the robot in the simulation is similar enough to the set-point. The gap in the simulation result is because, at the beginning, the robot must wait until the distance to the target is the minimum specified (about 2 meter).

Analysing the motors' velocities (Figure 14), it is possible to distinguish when the robot follows a straight-line, a curve or changes direction. In section A-B from Figure 14, both motors have the same velocity, which means that the robot is following a straight trajectory. In section B-C, one of the motors (dotted line) begins to run before the other one does (continuous line). This forces the robot to turn. Similar analysis can be done with the remaining sections. Sections of following the trajectory are marked with letters A-D, Figure 13.

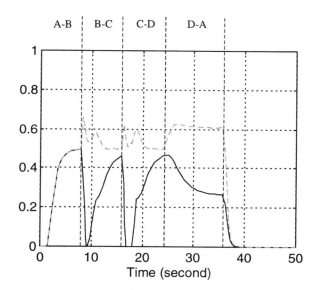

Figure 14. Motors signals.

4.3 Implementation

After the analysis and design of the controller, implementation procedure is performed as explained below :

- When the simulation results become as good as expected, a C program is generated using the *'Generate Code'* tool of the Real-Time Workshop. This code is *only* associated with the Control Block by means of inputs and outputs.

- An executable file is obtained after linking the appropriate modules (object modules and libraries) needed for the I/O operation of the vision system (camera, video digitizer cards, etc.) and control signals (digital acquisition boards connected to the motors).

- Finally, control parameters are tuned by intuitive procedures depending on the nature of the control system. This way, simulation results can be validated on real application with a few changes in the controller.

The controller validation is done by observing the movement of the robot. It is very spectacular, and by adding elements of competition (which group is able to design and implement a controller that follows better the target) it is a way to stimulate student work.

5. Conclusions and Future Work

Implementing a controller, by means of an integrated CACSD (Computer-Aided Control System Design) environment and a real system, is something that can be done straight away after the design process. So, for the Industrial Robotics students, all the effort can be focused on the control performance without wasting time on developing the program code. But at same time, it offers an easy way to program in C and link the libraries for Computer Control students.

A comparison between practical and theoretical results can be done, paying attention to the controller as well as to the system model. Students can observe that applying the same controller both in a model and in the real system can lead to results that are quite different. This can be caused by several factors, such as differences between the model and the real system (non-linearities, noise, etc.), errors in reproducing the target trajectory, the texture of the ground, light conditions, and so on.

Real-Time Workshop is useful in teaching modelling techniques. Due to the simplicity of implementing the controllers, it is easy to update the model from the real measured data. It is possible to obtain information about the real process in a fast way. Also some implementation aspects, such as sampling time selection can be easily explored.

Due to the simplicity provided by the Matlab/Simulink environment in simulation and controller implementation, other possibilities of its use are being investigated. In particular, other devices and PC peripherals are being added, for example a DSP board.

It is because of this simplicity that Real-Time Workshop has been selected for code generation instead of other real-time environments. We are aware that this environment is not the best one for real-time code generation, but it offers the possibility of simulating and implementing the controller in the same environment, which is a great advantage for the students.

Acknowledgements

Thanks are due to the Computer Vision Group of the University of Girona for their help with the robot implementation and image processing.

This Research is supported by CICYT project TAP96-1114-C03-03, *Plataformas integradas de CAD de supervisión y metodologías*, of the Spanish Government.

References

[1] J. Amat, J. Aranda, A. Casals, "Tracking capabilities in computer vision for industrial applications". *Optical Engineering*, Vol. 32, No 11: 2796- 2804, November 1993

[2] J. Amat, J. Aranda, A. Casals, "A tracking system for dynamic control of convoys", *Robotics and Autonomous Systems*, 11: 269-277, 1993.

[3] J. Batlle et al., "ROGER : Robot Operacional Genèric d'Experimentación en Recerca", Competition of Intelligent Autonomous Vehicles IAV'95, "2nd IFAC Conference on Intelligent Autonomous Vehicles, Otaniemi, Espoo, Finland, June 12, 1995.

[4] J.L. de la Rosa, J. Batlle, J.A. Ramon, J Meléndez, J. Colomer, J. Vehí , "A Comparison of Fuzzy, Neural and Qualitative Control Techniques Applied to a Mobile Robot" Symposium on Qualitative System Modelling, Qualitative Fault Diagnosis and Fuzzy Logic, Budapest, Hungary, April 1996.

[5] Real-Time Workshop Reference. Mathworks Inc., Natick, USA, May 1994.

[6] User Guide of DAS-20 Data Acquisition Board. Keithley Instruments Inc. Data Acquisition Division, Taunton, USA, February 1991.

[7] M. Sugeno, "An Introductory Survey of Fuzzy Control", Inform, Sci., Vol. 36, No. 1-2, July-August 1985, pp. 59-83.

Author Index

About the Editor

Janusz Zalewski is currently an associate professor at the Department of Electrical and Computer Engineering, University of Central Florida, Orlando, Florida. Most recently he was with Embry-Riddle Aeronautical University in Daytona Beach, Florida. Before taking a university position, he worked at various nuclear research institutions, including the Superconducting Super Collider (SSC), Dallas, Texas, and Lawrence Livermore National Laboratory, Livermore, California. His research interests include real-time multiprocessor systems, safety-related computer systems, and computer science/engineering education. He edited or co-edited three books: "Hardware and Software for Real-Time Process Control" (North-Holland, 1989), "Advanced Multimicroprocessor Bus Architectures" (IEEE Computer Society Press, 1995), and "Safety and Reliability in Emerging Control Technologies" (Pergamon, 1996). He serves on the editorial board of the IEEE Parallel and Distributed Technology and Control Engineering Practice (a journal of IFAC, International Federation of Automatic Control).

Zalewski received an MSc in electronic engineering and a Ph.D. in computer science from Warsaw University of Technology, Poland, in 1973 and 1979, respectively. He is a member of IEEE Computer Society, IFAC, and has been nominated for a chairman of IFIP Working Group 5.4 "Industrial Software Quality and Certification."

IEEE Computer Society Press Publications

The world-renowned Computer Society Press publishes, promotes, and distributes a wide variety of authoritative computer science and engineering texts. These books are available in two formats: 100 percent original material by authors preeminent in their field who focus on relevant topics and cutting-edge research, and reprint collections consisting of carefully selected groups of previously published papers with accompanying original introductory and explanatory text.

Submission of proposals: For guidelines and information on CS Press books, send e-mail to cs.books@computer.org or write to the Acquisitions Editor, IEEE Computer Society Press, P.O. Box 3014, 10662 Los Vaqueros Circle, Los Alamitos, CA 90720-1314. Telephone +1 714-821-8380. FAX +1 714-761-1784.

IEEE Computer Society Press Proceedings

The Computer Society Press also produces and actively promotes the proceedings of more than 130 acclaimed international conferences each year in multimedia formats that include hard and softcover books, CD-ROMs, videos, and on-line publications.

For information on CS Press proceedings, send e-mail to cs.books@computer.org or write to Proceedings, IEEE Computer Society Press, P.O. Box 3014, 10662 Los Vaqueros Circle, Los Alamitos, CA 90720-1314. Telephone +1 714-821-8380. FAX +1 714-761-1784.

Additional information regarding the Computer Society, conferences and proceedings, CD-ROMs, videos, and books can also be accessed from our web site at www.computer.org.